THROUGH
CORRIDORS
OF
POWER

David Pion-Berlin

THROUGH CORRIDORS OF POWER

Institutions and Civil-Military Relations in Argentina

The Pennsylvania State University Press
University Park, Pennsylvania

Library of Congress Cataloging-in-Publication Data

Pion-Berlin, David.
    Through corridors of power : institutions and civil-military
relations in Argentina / David Pion-Berlin.
        p.   cm.
    Includes bibliographical references and index.
    ISBN 0-271-01705-8 (cloth : alk. paper)
    ISBN 0-271-01706-6 (pbk. : alk. paper)
    1. Argentina—Politics and government—1983–   2. Civil-military
relations—Argentina.   3. Argentina—Military policy.   I. Title.
F2849.2.P565   1997
322'.5'098209048—dc21   96-48046
                                                                            CIP

To My Parents
Jim and Beverly Pion

Contents

List of Tables and Figures   ix

Preface   xi

List of Abbreviations   xvii

1. Introduction   1

2. Institutions, Policy, and Civil-Military Relations   13

3. The Changing Political Landscape in Argentina   45

4. Settling Scores: Human Rights Gains and Setbacks Under Alfonsín   75

5. Trimming the Fat: Military Budget-Cutting Successes Under Democratic Rule   107

6. Forgoing Change: The Failure of Defense Reform Under Democratic Rule   141

7. Argentina's Neighbors: Institutions and Policy in Uruguay and Chile   179

8. Conclusion   213

Selected Bibliography   223

Index   235

List of Tables and Figures

Table 5.1   Military expenditures (MILEX) and economic growth
            during the Argentine *Proceso*, 1976–1983   112
Table 5.2   Country size and military force levels in comparison,
            1984   114
Table 5.3   Military expenditures (MILEX) under Alfonsín,
            1984–1989   118
Table 5.4   Military expenditures (MILEX) under Menem,
            1989–1993   125
Table 6.1   Military expertise among Argentina's defense ministers,
            1983–1996   162
Table 7.1   The militarization of the Uruguayan National Defense
            Ministry   184

Fig. 2.1   Policy outcomes and institutional design   39
Fig. 4.1   Explaining human rights policy outcomes: the role of
            institutional authority and autonomy   105
Fig. 5.1   Explaining budget policy outcomes: the role of
            institutional authority and autonomy   139
Fig. 6.1   Explaining defense reform failure: the role of
            institutional authority and autonomy   177

Preface

Argentina has often been thought of despairingly. It is a nation of great expectations and potential, but also one of unfulfilled hope and missed opportunities. It is a place that seemed to have so much going for it during the first half of the twentieth century, only to see it squandered during the second half. Development specialists have despaired over Argentina's inability to take advantage of its enormous size, fertile land, abundant resources, and skilled work force to place itself on the path to modernization. And political scientists have bemoaned its self-destructive conflict, violence, and repression that have denied the country any long-term stability.

Few countries of Latin America—or any region for that matter—were so plagued for so long by persistent, uncontrolled, and unresolved confrontations between social classes, pressure groups, movements, governments and their opposition. Whether it be students, unionized labor, political parties, guerrillas, or the armed forces, organized interests of one kind or another observed no limits to their conduct, resorting to whatever means they had at their disposal. From 1948 to 1977, Argentina ranked (among 125 countries) 22 in political riots, 19 in protest demonstrations and armed attacks, 7 in politically motivated strikes, and 2 in assassinations.[1] Between 1970 and 1975, left-wing guerrilla groups roamed through city and countryside, staging abductions of businessmen, robbing banks, and making daring, deadly, though ultimately futile assaults on police and military installations. Their terror induced a far greater counterterror, as the armed forces seized and held control of the state between 1976 and 1983, visiting upon society (combatants and noncombatants alike) unprecedented hostilities and acts of cruelty that left tens of thousands of victims in their wake.

1. Charles L. Taylor and David Jodice, *World Handbook of Political and Social Indicators*, 3d ed., vol. 2, *Political Protest and Government Change* (New Haven: Yale University Press, 1983), pp. 22, 30, 33, 39, 44.

All of this conflict and violence took their toll on regimes, especially democratic ones. From 1955 to 1976, power changed hands seven times between democratic and military regimes. No elected leader was able to serve out his full term of office, each one falling prey to a military-led coup. Democracy, its leaders, and its institutions always lived precariously in Argentina. To its citizens and to those outsiders who came to observe the nation during its periods of political competitiveness, it seemed as if the system were teetering on the edge, about to fall into the abyss.

It was in this context that I took my first research trip to Argentina in 1984 just eight months after the election of President Raúl R. Alfonsín. The skeptic in me didn't give his democracy much chance of succeeding. How could it, with so much history of political upheaval behind it? I met with former members of the military regime who, rather than showing remorse for what they had done, seemed intent on justifying their disastrous political and economic policies. And I met with civilians who, while hopeful the military would stay out of politics, still worried about what the future held in store for their country.

A decade later something had changed. The mere passage of time itself was noteworthy since the democracy had survived intact. In the interim, power had been transferred peacefully between one elected president and another—a first since 1928. The society that like most others in the region had suffered greatly during the deep economic depression of the 1980s resisted calls for military intervention in order to somehow set the economy straight. Whereas only a few years before trouble over their shrinking budgets and the ongoing human rights trials had caused some army officers to rebel against their senior commanders, their actions never triggered any full-scale coup attempts. Although still burdened with unresolved problems, this new Argentina seemed more settled than the old.

I was in Buenos Aires for the fourth time, busily conducting interviews and digging up documents for this book. While there, I spoke to a distinguished gathering of defense specialists to convey my thoughts about civil-military affairs. My audience seemed genuinely interested in what I had to say yet perturbed that I had focused on the conflictual elements of the relation. For them conflict was a thing of the past. The armed forces were now compliant with democratic authority, they said. These experts were more concerned with and eager to talk about unifying themes, such as defense modernization, regional security, or Argentina's role in international peacekeeping missions.

Undoubtedly, the views of this audience reflected some wishful thinking or avoidance as much as sober reflection about Argentina's political realities. But then again, there may be something to their newfound air of optimism. My own research was uncovering evidence that suggested to me not that civilian control over the armed forces had been achieved, or that conflict had been eliminated, but rather that contact between soldiers and politicians had been routinized. Disputes over policy persisted but were now resolved within the confines of democratic institutions. The unbridled confrontations of the past had given way to more restrained interactions governed by organizational rules of conduct. There was, it seemed to me, a new stability to the Argentine civil-military relation. If this were true, it would represent substantial progress in and of itself.

Probing this idea required that I take a much closer look at the operation of government than civil-military specialists are normally accustomed to doing. There is a "military centric" thrust to much of the literature that confines itself to analyses of the institution of the armed forces—its history, structure, interests, strategies, and links to society—to the exclusion of the governing civilian side of the equation. In this study I try to tilt the balance the other way by viewing civil-military relations through the prism of democratic government and its policymaking machinery. This book, then, is devoted to an examination of politicians and soldiers seeking to advance their own interests by moving through official channels. It is an account of how their policy gains and setbacks may have much to do with the organizational features of government they encounter along the way. While the focus is on Argentina, comparisons are made with two other Southern Cone states, Uruguay and Chile.

A number of organizations made my investigative journeys easier and more productive. Travel to Argentina in 1993 and 1994 was made possible by grants from the American Philosophical Society, the Institute for Global Cooperation and Conflict, and the University of California at Riverside (UCR). Field work in Chile and Uruguay was fully supported with a Fulbright Scholar Award under the 1994/1995 American Republics Research Program. While in the Southern Cone, I had the good fortune to be hosted by several distinguished research centers. I associated briefly with the Argentine Centro de Estudios de Estado y Sociedad (CEDES), which provided me with comfortable work surroundings. The Chilean Centro de Estudios del Desarrollo (CED) and the Uruguayan Centro Latinoamericano de Economía Humana (CLAEH) furnished me with the same kind of environment, in addition to being quite helpful in arranging interviews.

Ultimately, it was the individuals I met and befriended along the way who made the real difference. It was they who by sharing with me their vast knowledge about their own homelands were able to ground my understandings in context. It was they who by introducing me to their own places of work and to their own associates were able to widen my network of contacts. A special debt of gratitude goes out to Ernesto López. As a friend, co-author, and leading authority on civil-military affairs, he generously and repeatedly gave of himself and his time to help me make sense of the enigmatic Argentina. My long association and many conversations with José Manuel Ugarte were also invaluable. He introduced me to former members of the Radical Party government and to members of Congress, and arranged easy access to all the relevant legislation I ever needed. Among the many other people in Argentina who aided my research endeavors in various ways I must mention Luis Tibiletti, Rut Diamint, Thomas Scheetz, Eduardo Estevez, Eduardo Stafforini, José Luis Manzano, and the late Carlos Nino. Aaron Cytrynblum was kind enough to allow me to peruse the newspaper archives at *Clarín* and then *Página Doce*. The countless individuals who agreed to be interviewed cannot be mentioned here by name, but their willingness to put up with my incessant questioning was greatly appreciated.

Before my departure to Chile, Gisela von Muhlenbrock placed her numerous contacts with former justice ministry officials at my disposal, and I am grateful to her for that. While in Chile, my work could not have proceeded as smoothly as it did without the invaluable help of Hugo Frühling. And the assistance I received from the archivists at the Chilean weekly *Hoy* was always friendly and prompt. In Uruguay, Gerardo Caetano, Romeo Pérez Anton, and the entire staff at CLAEH made my trip a more enjoyable and productive one. Cynthia Farrell de Johnson of the United States embassy in Montevideo placed me in touch with some key air force officers. And Juan Rial graciously responded to all my queries. Back in the United States I spent a few weeks in the summer of 1994 at the Hispanic Division of the U.S. Library of Congress. Special thanks goes out to its head of reference, Everette E. Larson, who showed me some computer shortcuts to the documents I was looking for. The Law Division of the Library of Congress was also helpful, as was the Foreign and International Section of the Los Angeles County Law Library.

Writing a book requires a considerable amount of unstructured time away from the classroom and from administrative assignments. I am grateful to the Department of Political Science at the UCR for providing that time by granting me a sabbatical leave in the fall of 1993 and to Carlos G. Vélez-Ibáñez, Dean of the College of Humanities, Arts, and Social Sciences, for approving a paid leave for me the following fall as well. The writing benefited immensely from the detailed comments of J. Samuel Fitch and Deborah Norden, both of whom read through the entire manuscript. Karen Remmer, Brian Loveman, Claude Welch Jr., Wendy Hunter, Paul Buchanan, Alison Brysk, and Craig Arceneaux reviewed specific chapters, and all had useful suggestions for revision. The production of the book went smoothly thanks to Sandy Thatcher and his staff at Penn State University Press. I thank them all, knowing full well that any errors of commission or omission in the writing are mine alone.

Finally, there are families to thank. In Buenos Aires my distant cousins made me feel part of their extended family. Julio and Regina Hubscher welcomed me into their home, giving me a place to rest my weary bones after a long day of interviews. They also provided me with good company and conversation, as did Roberto and Rut Hubscher. Back in Claremont my wife Lisa stood by me throughout the long period of research and writing. She was a source of constant encouragement, even while enduring my long absences from home. And our children, Jeremy and Emma, have helped me in more intangible ways than they could ever imagine.

List of Abbreviations

CALEN	Centro de Altos Estudios Nacionales (Center of Higher National Studies)
CELS	Centro de Estudios Legales y Sociales (Center of Legal and Social Studies)
CGT	Confederación General de Trabajadores (General Confederation of Labor)
COMIL	Comité Militar (Military Committee)
CONADEP	Comisión Nacional Argentina sobre la Desaparición de Personas (Argentine National Commission on the Disappeared)
CONASE	Consejo Nacional de Seguridad (National Security Council)
CTOAS	Comandante del Teatro de Operaciones Atlántico del Sur (Commander of the South Atlantic Theater of Operations)
DGFM	Dirección General de Fabricaciones Militares (General Directorate of Military Manufacturing)
DOD	Department of Defense
EMC	Estado Mayor Conjunto (Military Joint Staff)
ERP	Ejército Revolucionario del Pueblo (Revolutionary People's Army)
ESMA	Escuela Mecánica de la Armada (Navy Mechanics School)
IMES	Instituto Militar de Estudios Superiores (Military Institute of Superior Studies)
MOD	Ministry of Defense
MOE	Ministry of Economics
NCJ	National Council of Justice
NSC	National Security Council
NSD	national security doctrines
OMB	Office of Management and Budget
OPP	Oficina de Planificación y Presupuesto (Office of Planning and Budget)
OSD	Office of the Secretary of Defense
PRN	Proceso de Reorganización Nacional (National Process of Reorganization)
SECDEF	Secretary of Defense
UCD	Unión del Centro Democrático (Union of the Democratic Center)
UCR	Unión Cívica Radical (Radical Civic Union Party)

CHAPTER 1

Introduction

This is a book about Argentine politicians, institutions, and soldiers during the democratic period of 1983 to 1995. It accounts for why it is that political leaders who crafted policies that directly affected military interests, and who attempted to guide those policies through governmental agencies, either succeeded or failed at what they set out to do.[1] Unlike other studies that place the emphasis on the military as a dominating political force capable of thwarting civilian initiatives, this study shifts the focus to democratic institutions that, depending on their makeup, either enable *or* constrain the military's reach.

In the field of Latin American civil-military affairs, democratic institutions of state are often overlooked as political forces in their own right. Thought to be too vulnerable to be of any consequence, they are either treated as a kind of spectator arena that beholds the collision of conflicting

---

1. Civilian control is not the central topic of inquiry for this book. Supremacy over the armed forces remains viable, but it is still an aspiration, not an achieved end. Hence, I have chosen to focus on more tangible, knowable, and measurable objects of study: the successes or failures of military policy. Should politicians repeatedly get their way over military objections, it may indicate a movement toward civilian control. But the jury still remains out on the fate of civil-military affairs in the Southern Cone.

interests within them or relegated to the sidelines as the "real" civil-military contest unfolds elsewhere.[2] In this book they are brought front and center. Politicians and soldiers trade policy victories and defeats within their confines. Governmental agencies intervene between the expression of individual or group preference at one end and the delivery of actual programs at the other. Central decision makers are free to propose and armies are (within limits) free to oppose. But it is argued here that proposition and opposition are only as effective as institutional arrangements permit them to be. Those arrangements constrain the free will of actors by mediating or arbitrating conflicts, limiting options, molding policy, and defining prospects. In short, the translation from power to policy is an indirect one that occurs through the medium of institutions.

Historically, it has not always been this way. During periods of great instability and upheaval, armies of the region often held democratic governments in contempt. Resorting to threats, intimidation, and coercion against elected leaders, they would ignite a harmful chain reaction: the governments they attacked would be weakened, losing authority and credibility; the public would grow cynical, no longer believing in their elected officials and institutions; a political vacuum would then be created that antidemocratic forces would fill. The demise of the constitutional regime followed soon after.

The military coups that replaced democratic regimes with despotic ones were Latin America's worst recurring nightmare. With a monopoly on the means of coercion, the armed forces could dispense with democratic niceties and bring down governments with one devastating blow. But coups occur for specific reasons and only when conditions permit. Armies cannot overturn elected leaders at will: they must be sufficiently motivated to act; the balance of political, social, and economic forces must be decisively arrayed on their side; and they must seize the opportunity if and when it presents itself. At times these conditions hold, at other times they do not. There is, in other words, nothing *inherently* omnipotent about the region's armed forces nor is there anything *innately* fragile about its democratic institutions. If there were, we would be hard-pressed to account for long and uninterrupted periods of competitive rule in places like Uruguay and Chile. We would also be unable to explain the sustained revival of democracy in a nation like Argentina.

Since the democratic rebuilding effort began in Argentina in December 1983, governing institutions have held up well. The public, which has suffered economically, has disapproved of particular political figures and the

2. Consult Chapter 2 for references on this point.

policies they have made. But their disapproval has not resulted in cries for regime change; they have continued to support the democratic option against all others. And soldiers have complained—sometimes bitterly—about certain programs that would adversely affect their interests. But regardless of the policy consequences, most Argentine men of arms have complied with democratic arrangements most of the time because they must. Circumstances in the postauthoritarian era have not allowed them to ignore, circumvent, or threaten the prevailing order without serious costs to themselves and their profession. Thus, while military-relevant policies remain the subjects of debate, the continued survival of the regime and its institutions does not. Turning democracy from a question to a "given" is itself a great accomplishment for a nation that has seen its political system torn asunder too often in the past.

This is not to say that the military has relinquished all political influence. Far from it. But while the military remains a force to be reckoned with, the reckoning usually occurs within the democratic state, not outside of it. It is within the realm of courts, ministries, and legislative halls that key aspects of the civil-military relation unfurl. Substantively, that relation pivots around oftentimes controversial policies that are devised, deliberated, and acted upon inside government. It is for these reasons that this book takes an especially close look at how state institutions mediate between politicians and soldiers competing for influence.

The democratic state is a multiheaded creature. Not all of its institutional components look alike, nor do they necessarily operate in harmony with one another. They each have their own defining structures, norms, and rules of procedure. They vary, in other words, by organizational design, and each design is uniquely biased; it mobilizes some and demobilizes others by affecting the degree, direction, and impact of the influence they bring to bear upon each policy.[3] In a clash of interests, who will prevail in the policy struggle? Will political leaders have their way over soldiers or not? It depends upon the institutional environment through which a policy passes en route from conception to delivery. In order to know how easy or difficult a time a politician may have in winning passage of a desired program that the military opposes, we have to identify the characteristics of the agencies that have policy jurisdiction. From this follows the central hypothesis of the study: that as institutional designs change, so too does the civil-military balance of power.

3. I borrow this terminology from E. E. Schattschneider, *The Semi-Sovereign People: A Realist's View of Democracy in America* (New York: Holt, Rinehart, and Winston, 1960), pp. 30, 71.

This is not a shift of gravitational proportions: the core relationship between the democratic government and its defense forces remains unaltered. But it is an important change that tilts the policy advantage to one side or the other, depending on the issue and organizational context. Should the advantage fall more often to civilian leaders who prove capable of pushing through contested policies, it may enhance their authority, their credibility with the public, and in the longer term their chances to achieve civilian control. Even so, civilian failure is compatible with democratic stability so long as it does not occur too often, and so long as all parties concerned—especially soldiers—continue to respect the institutional rules of the game. This, then, is an analysis not just about who wins and loses but *how* they win or lose.

Certain institutional features of the democratic state warrant particularly close attention. One feature to be addressed in greater detail in the following chapter is that of autonomy. An agency may restrict points of entry for outsiders and reduce the occasions upon which government officials may be subject to duress from those who oppose their programs. In this case the institution is highly autonomous. By contrast, those institutions with fewer bureaucratic or procedural obstructions may be more permeable to outside influence. Accordingly, central decision makers who devise programs objectionable to the armed forces, and who must submit those programs to agencies with low levels of autonomy, will find the going a lot tougher.

Then there is the matter of authority. The chief executive, who is also commander in chief, prefers to have a maximal amount of authority concentrated in his own hands when dealing with the armed forces. Institutional norms must allow for it. If they do, then the president's singular policy preferences can more easily prevail, as he need not contend with the rules of other state agencies or with the divergent viewpoints of other governmental officials. What happens, then, when authority over military issues is dispersed across numerous institutions?[4] As the number of significant, civilian "players" in the policy process multiply, so too do the structures, rules, priorities, interests, and biases, making it more difficult for the president's program

---

4. Argentina is a highly presidential system as are most political systems in South America. The chief executive has considerable clout during the initial formulation of policy. During the processing phase of policy, however, the stamp of presidential preference can often fade from view. Measures must pass through institutions with their multiplicity of structures, rules, norms, actors, and opinions. Depending upon institutional arrangements and procedures, some policies can find the journey to completion exceedingly difficult. The wider the array of interests and points of view to contend with, the more difficult it will be for central decision makers to preserve their original designs intact.

to remain intact. The armed forces could very well take advantage of these differences, playing one branch of government against another.

The dispersion of authority, it will be shown, accounts for the derailment of certain policies in Argentina. And yet it is symptomatic of stable, democratic life: power is divided, and institutions often collide with one another. In other words, some policies will flounder not because democratic mechanisms succumb to willful military pressure, but because they work so well.

In pointing out a normality to policymaking and civil-military affairs, this book is, to be sure, considerably more sanguine about the state of democratic affairs in Argentina than is the conventional wisdom. Skeptics may bristle at the notion found here that most soldiers and politicians play by the rules of the game in a country once notorious in its disregard for democratic conventions. But the views expressed here do not constitute a form of idealism or wishful thinking; they are based on a hard-nosed appraisal of the evidence. And the evidence will suggest not only that democratic procedures have been observed with greater frequency but that those very procedures have helped to define the prospects for policy success and failure in the realm of civil-military affairs.

In fact, the institutional approach offered up here helps to answer some important policy questions that would otherwise remain unexplained. First, let us back up and consider the events leading up to the period covered in this book. In 1982 the worst tyranny to ever afflict the Argentine nation suddenly collapsed under the weight of its own brutality, malfeasance, and incompetence. The political and economic failures of the military regime known as the *Proceso de Reorganización Nacional* or *"Proceso,"* combined with the cataclysmic effects of the Malvinas War, undermined the military's historic role as political power broker. The regime had engaged in unrepentant corruption, presided over a ruined economy, turned a limited counterinsurgency operation into a wholesale slaughter of fifteen to twenty thousand innocent civilians, and went down to defeat at the hands of the British in a war they themselves had precipitated.[5] A loss of faith in programmatic objectives and the reemergence of personal and ideological cleavages within the ranks of the military contributed significantly to the regime's hasty demise.

---

5. Accounts of the *Proceso's* failures can be found in Peter Waldmann and Ernesto Valdéz, eds., *El poder militar en la Argentina: 1976–1981* (Buenos Aires: Editorial Galerna, 1983); Jorge Schvarzer, *Martínez de Hoz: La lógica política de la política económica*, Centro de Investigaciones Sociales Sobre el Estado y la Administración (CISEA), Ensayos y Tesis 4 (Buenos Aires: CISEA, 1983); William C. Smith, *Authoritarianism and the Crisis of the Argentine Political Economy* (Stanford: Stanford University Press, 1989), pp. 224–66.

The armed forces left political office vanquished, demoralized, and in dis-array, although with time they made a modest recovery. Torn by conflict and self-doubt, they made only half-hearted and unsuccessful attempts to control events during the transition to democratic rule. The balance of power had shifted decisively in favor of the incoming Alfonsín administration, which assumed office in December 1983 with an impressive electoral mandate and irreproachable moral authority. In an interregnum such as this one, charac-terized by an authoritarian collapse and civilian renewal, incumbents may find they have a freer hand in shaping national policy, less burdened as they are by the old order whose interests can no longer be adequately safe-guarded.[6]

And yet neither the authoritarian legacy, the terms of the transition, nor the resultant balance of civil-military power will resolve the policy dilemmas posed by the Argentine case. None of these historical "givens" could account for what was to come, as the civil-military relation would transcend its ori-gins, the political equation shifting across issues and circumstance. The events that would follow had an unpredictable quality to them.

What is puzzling is that within any given administration, over a narrow span of time, policy successes were remarkably uneven. On two issues civilian leaders appeared to be invincible, able to dispense with programs over and above military resistance. This was evident when it came time for rewriting the nation's defense law and budgeting fewer funds for the military. The armed forces registered strong complaints regarding provisions in the defense law that for the first time in their history would prohibit them from facing down security threats of an *internal* nature. And they repeatedly cautioned political leaders against further budget cuts, arguing that these would severely impair their capacity to adequately defend the nation. Yet all of these pro-tests were to no avail, as civilians essentially got the programs they wanted.

In the realm of human rights the record was mixed. At first the democratic administration made significant headway, despite military objections, by bringing to justice military leaders of the *Proceso* charged with human rights

6. On transition through collapse, see Constantine Danopoulos, "From Military to Civilian Rule in Contemporary Greece," *Armed Forces and Society* 10 (1984): 229–50; and David Pion-Berlin, "The Fall of Military Rule in Argentina: 1976–1983," *Journal of Interamerican Studies and World Affairs* 27 (1985): 55–76. The effects of the Argentine transition on the balance of power between the armed forces and the new democratic leadership has been well documented. See Andrés Fon-tana, "Fuerzas armadas, partidos políticos, y transición a la democracia en Argentina, 1981–1982," Kellogg Institute Working Paper 28, July 1984, pp. 29–32, and by the same author, "La política militar del gobierno constitucional Argentino," *CEDES*, July 1987, p. 6.

transgressions. Thereafter it stumbled and finally fell prey to a military uprising that made a reconsideration of policy imperative.

On other issues civilians seemed exceptionally weak. They were unable to overhaul the military's educational system or reform the nation's defenses. The failure to restructure defense forces was particularly noteworthy, since not all members of the armed forces found the idea of reform to be objectionable.

These facts are revealing for the following reasons. First, they indicate that historical antecedents do not provide satisfactory clues. If the transition via collapse had initially so weakened the armed services, then the dilution of their powers, one might expect, would have precipitated across-the-board policy gains for political leaders. Yet it did not. Moreover, the military's ability to resuscitate itself may have scored it a policy victory or two, but it did not advance its overall institutional agenda. Like the politicians themselves, the armed forces compiled a record that was strikingly erratic. Their occasional triumphs had no multiplier effect: gains in one arena did not generate gains in other arenas. Why then, when the scales of power turned in their favor, could neither politicians nor soldiers take advantage by triumphing consistently?

Second, contestation does not solve the policy puzzle since there were times when, despite its protests, the military came up empty-handed, other times when protest paid off, and still other occasions when policies languished despite the lack of concerted military resistance. For example, a rebellion led by a group of middle-rank army officers in April 1987 did lead to reversals in the president's human rights policy. But try as they may, the rebels could not exploit this momentary threat by winning major concessions on other issues vital to them such as military promotions, assignments, and the budget. Why do pressures work on certain issues and not others?

And third, the change in government from the Radical Party administration of Raúl Alfonsín (1983–89) to the Peronist Party administration of Carlos Menem (1989–95) cannot account for the observed outcomes. The budgetary accomplishments of *both* leaders were as impressive as the defeats they *shared* when it came to defense reform. This pattern of policy inconsistency cuts across these two governments and ties victories and defeats not to the ideological and personal differences between the two leaders (which were sizable) but to the issues at hand. Why do policy outcomes seem to be relatively insensitive to changes in political leadership?

If there is a common denominator to all of this, it is the various institutional arrangements of the Argentine democratic state. Policy issues that mattered to the armed forces were taken up by different agencies and branches of government. Each of those decision-making sites processed political inputs in a different way. No two policies received the same treatment or experienced the same fate because no two sites exposed those policies to the same set of institutional guidelines. Accordingly, when the issue changed, so too did the organized context, which in turn produced different results. The military could not wield influence uniformly from issue to issue because it could not penetrate all corners of the state with equal proficiency; some agencies were simply more invulnerable than others. And chief executives could not achieve all they had set out to do because on certain matters they were forced to share authority with other branches of government. Everywhere politicians and soldiers turned they had to contend with institutional arrangements that were not of their own choosing, that were not easily altered, and that stood between them and the goals they were pursuing.

Naturally, institutions matter when political protagonists agree to work within them. In few countries of the Third World do politicians and soldiers observe institutional protocol with perfect regularity. Both sides may occasionally be tempted to step outside official channels if they believe doing so could more expeditiously advance their interests. Argentina has certainly experienced its share of institutional circumventions, most recently during the military mutinies of 1987, 1988, and 1990. But a focus on institutions does not presume constant and irrevocable allegiance. Insubordinate behavior has, now and then, been a feature of civil-military life in advanced democratic states, including our own.[7] It does require that subordination be the norm, not the exception, however, and that political contestants haven't the capacity to repeatedly disregard official channels by fulfilling their wants outside of them. In the current postauthoritarian era, Argentina appears to satisfy these minimal conditions.

The focus on institutions does not represent an effort to write off the armed forces as a political actor. Undoubtedly, they will remain part of the

---

7. Military defiance is not foreign to the United States. General MacArthur's public rebuke of President Truman during the Korean War is perhaps the best known instance, but there have been others. Air Force General John D. Lavelle authorized secret bombings of North Vietnam after Lyndon Johnson had ordered a halt to such operations in October 1968. And most recently, a two-star air force general was forced to retire after belittling President Clinton in public, while the former chairman of the Joint Chiefs of Staff, Colin Powell, openly contested the president on the issue of allowing avowed homosexuals to serve in the military. See Kenneth W. Kemp and Charles Hudlin, "Civil Supremacy over the Military: Its Nature and Limits," Armed Forces and Society 19 (Fall 1992): 16–17; Richard Kohn, "Out of Control: The Crisis in Civil-Military Relations," The National Interest 35 (Spring 1994): 3, 13.

political equation for some time to come. Nor does it preclude military rebel-lion, since, as Chapter 4 will show, it is the very workings of a democracy that can sometimes have the perverse and paradoxical effect of triggering their own resistance. And one final caveat. It should be acknowledged that the military's utilization of legal channels to voice its concerns does not in itself constitute subordination to civilian will. Institutions, in theory, could be exploited by the armed forces in a manner that would undermine the authority of elected leaders. While that has not occurred during the period under review here, it could occur. And whereas for now democratic leaders have the cooperation of the armed forces, they cannot be sure of their uncon-ditional allegiance. Consequently, civilian supremacy over the armed forces remains an Argentine aspiration, not an achievement. Will the armed forces submit themselves to civilian control? The question persists. And yet as the nation prepares to enter the twenty-first century, it should be encouraged by a growing military willingness to live under democratic administrations.

The rest of the book is organized as follows. Chapter 2 provides the theo-retical framework for the empirical discussions that ensue. In departing from conventional thinking, the focal point for the discussion of civil-military affairs is moved from society to the state, and from the military to civilian institutions. By doing so we are able to observe the impact of democratic structures, norms, and procedures on the fortunes of soldiers and politicians. More specifically, we can predict how each side fares in the struggle to defend its interests by examining key institutional features that shape how military-related policies will emerge.

Chapter 3 discusses changes in the Argentine polity in the aftermath of the dictatorship. The *Proceso* managed to harm the interests of practically every social and political group, thereby widening public opposition to au-thoritarian forms of rule to an unparalleled degree. The armed forces were adversely affected as well, raising the costs to them of a return to de facto rule. But avoidance of the past must be matched by a commitment to the present. Thus, we examine the current attitudes and behavior of the general electorate, the conservative elites, the political parties, and organized labor. In each case the findings are similar: while there are complaints about spe-cific policies and policymakers, there is substantial support for the demo-cratic regime. In this context coup mongerers cannot prevail.

The next three chapters look at institutional mediation and policy gains and setbacks across three issue areas. In Chapter 4 we discover that Alfon-sín's human rights program got off to a good start but then floundered for institutional reasons. The president decided to rely primarily on the judiciary to resolve the human rights problem. On the one hand, the courts' unwavering resistance to any form of intervention or intimidation made possible the completion of trials against the ex-leaders of the dictatorship, handing Alfonsín a major political victory. On the other hand, that same spirit of judicial independence meant a loss of presidential control. When the court decided to pursue officers at lower ranks—something Alfonsín had hoped they would not do—the president was forced to watch the wheels of justice turn ever so slowly, grinding out more indictments that would implicate more officers and that made it ever more likely that trials would persist into the indefinite future. This created a state of deep anxiety and fear that provoked unrest within the ranks of the armed forces.

Chapter 5 turns to the issue of defense budgeting. Here, too, institutional traits matter. The procedures governing budget formulation afforded maximal authority and independence to a few key civilian decision makers within the economics ministry. It was they who set strict limits to defense expenditure based on macroeconomic, not security-related, criteria. The armed forces and the defense ministry itself were largely out of the decision-making loop. Legally, the military could appeal to the Congress for help. But the Argentine legislative branch has little sway over federal budgets and could not overturn decisions made in the executive branch. Concentrated executive authority and high levels of autonomy combined to subordinate the needs of the military organization to the political and economic objectives of civilian officeholders.

In Chapter 6 the failures of defense reform are considered. After the crushing defeat in the Malvinas War, few doubted the need for a fundamental restructuring of the armed forces. The question became who would lead the effort? Legal authority was invested in the office of the president and its defense ministry to propose a scheme for enhancing defense readiness. But operationally, the defense ministry, which was long a victim of political neglect, could not and would not fulfill its mandate, while the president failed to demonstrate enough leadership. The executive branch turned the tasks over to the army, navy, and air force themselves. This meant that the unused authority at the top was dispersed below to a deeply divided institution. But in the absence of any clear directives and coordination from above, each service chose to do very little or nothing at all, leaving unfulfilled the goal of defense reform.

The final portion of the book is devoted to comparisons and conclusions. To see whether institutional designs have an impact beyond the borders of Argentina, we turn to two of that country's neighbors, Uruguay and Chile.

In Uruguay policy successes were uneven owing to institutional constraints and opportunities. On the one hand, the defense ministry was organized so as not to permit civilian leadership on issues of military organization, strategy, doctrine, and social function. On the other hand, military budgets were in the hands of civilian-run, executive-branch agencies and the Congress, while the military was left out of the fiscal loop. In Chile we find that President Aylwin used the powers conferred upon his executive office to great advantage by establishing a special commission to investigate the violation of human rights under the dictatorship. But the Congress and the courts, both victims of an institutional design imposed by the outgoing Pinochet regime, obstructed the president's bid to further his human rights agenda. Finally, the conclusion summarizes the major findings of this study while drawing out their implications for civilian control and democratic consolidation.

CHAPTER 2

Institutions, Policy, and Civil-Military Relations

Requisites for A Civil-Military Equilibrium

Civil-military relations in Argentina are in a state of equilibrium. Conflicts persist but are bounded by a higher order of cooperation. The scales of power do tip one way or the other but not far enough to either undermine the democratic regime or to make civilian supremacy a certainty. This means that occasional policy triumphs by the armed forces do not translate into catastrophic losses for civilians, nor do policy gains by civilians foster the political demise of the military. Politics is no longer an all-or-nothing proposition. Between the poles of neutrality at one end and domination at the other is an area where soldiers influence but do not threaten, coerce, or control. It is on this middle ground that the civil-military interaction unfolds. This chapter provides some theoretical guidance for understanding the politics of military affairs in a context of relative stability.

No matter how stable a civil-military relation is, power and influence are still the name of the game. "Regardless of the nature of the political culture in which he lives," write Amos Perlmutter and Valerie Bennett, "the modern military officer is oriented toward maximizing his influence in politics and/

or policy."[1] "In all countries ruled by civilians, the armed forces may try to convert the rulers to their own point of view. They have both the right and the duty to attempt this," says S. E. Finer.[2] And besides, argues Claude Welch, "no military can be shorn of political influence, save through the rare step of total abolition."[3] This is true in first-world democracies; it certainly must be true in nations like Argentina where the armed forces have been political animals for longer than anyone would care to remember. The issue is always one of limits. How far can the military push the political envelope without upsetting the equilibrium? While there is no blueprint for stability, scholars generally agree that military restraint must be exhibited both in its choice of means and ends.

Officers must move through constitutional channels yet observe their official position in the hierarchy.[4] They can neither make end runs around government by colluding with societal interest groups, nor can they hurdle over the chain of command by appealing directly to those with highest authority. And the military's concerns must be military in nature. Whatever influence it enjoys is to be used to advance a professional agenda. Substantively, it must resist the temptation to enmesh itself in debates about policies that lie beyond its professional confines. Procedurally, it must also respect the fundamental democratic axiom that it is for civilians alone to decide when and to what degree the armed forces should be involved in the shaping of defense policy. *Who* decides who will decide cannot be a question in the military mind; it must be a foregone conclusion.[5] If not, then the mere observance of protocol will only thinly veil the underlying perversion of the

1. Amos Perlmutter and Valerie Plave Bennett, eds., *The Political Influence of the Military: A Comparative Reader* (New Haven: Yale University Press, 1980), p. 3.

2. S. E. Finer, *The Man on Horseback: The Role of the Military in Politics*, 2d ed. (Boulder, Colo: Westview Press, 1988), p. 127.

3. See Claude E. Welch Jr., *Civilian Control of the Military: Theories and Cases from Developing Countries* (Albany: State University of New York Press, 1976), p. 2.

4. See Finer, *Man on Horseback*, pp. 127–34.

5. Simply because they are instruments of the state does not mean that the armed forces are relegated to obscurity. In modern democracies they are often entrusted to advise, sometimes even participate in, decision-making sessions pertaining to defense and security. But one thing has to be clear from the outset: it is the political authorities who determine the limits to their influence. This also extends to the conduct of war. It is not enough to say that the armed forces execute war on behalf of a civilian foreign policy goal. Problems arise when officers extend the boundaries of a conflict, or change its form, thinking that they are simply making an operational adjustment, when in fact they are interfering in the formulation of policy. Thus it is for civilians alone to determine where the line should be drawn between means and ends. See Kenneth W. Kemp and Charles Hudlin, "Civil Supremacy over the Military: Its Nature and Limits," *Armed Forces and Society* 19 (Fall 1992): 7–26.

civil-military relation. Accordingly, Claude Welch has said that the key is to set limits within which members of the armed forces, and the military as an institution, accept the government's definition of appropriate areas of responsibility.[6]

Why would the military accept these limits? And why does an institution that is well organized, disciplined, and lethally armed, and that could, if it so desired, easily turn its lethality against the unarmed civilian authorities, choose not to do so? Professionalism, Samuel Huntington thought, would subdue the military by guaranteeing its political neutrality, thereby allowing it to "carry out the wishes of any civilian group which secures legitimate authority within the state."[7] But there is now widespread agreement among scholars that Huntington had greatly overemphasized the salutary effects of professionalism. The more professional armies of the Third World have not always been cooperative and some in fact have been more prone to challenge civilian rule.[8]

Professionalism, Finer reminds us, is never enough. The military "must also have absorbed the principle of supremacy of the civilian power."[9] It is thought that in advanced democratic states, restraint is ingrained. By virtue of age-old laws, customs, or culture, the armed forces have so internalized the norm of subordination that they do not give it a second thought.[10] So deep-rooted is this habit of compliance that civilian control is not only irrevocable but, for all intents and purposes, taken for granted.

Unfortunately, in South America compliance is anything but principled or habitual. Armies there do not obey because it is the right thing to do. They have bitten into the fruit of politics too often in the past to be expected to vow political abstinence. It was not too long ago that they themselves had occupied public office, enjoying the spoils of power. Why would they have suddenly emerged from the transition as true believers in democratic constraint? In a region periodically plagued by military intervention, utter devo-

6. Claude E. Welch Jr., *No Farewell to Arms: Military Disengagement from Politics in Africa and Latin America* (Boulder, Colo.: Westview Press, 1987), p. 13.

7. See Samuel Huntington, *The Soldier and the State: The Theory and Politics of Civil-Military Relations* (Cambridge, Mass.: Harvard University Press, 1957), p. 84.

8. The more professionalized the military, the more well defined its prerogatives are, and the more vigorous its resistance against the loss of those prerogatives will be. As Bengt Abrahamsson argues, professionalization breeds corporate interests, and where those interests and the interests of civilians diverge or collide, political conflict is possible—even probable. See Bengt Abrahamsson, *Military Professionalization and Political Power* (Beverly Hills: Sage Publications, 1972).

9. Finer, *Man on Horseback*, p. 24.

10. Welch, *No Farewell to Arms*, p. 13.

tion to democratic authority is an acquired taste, one that comes *after* patterns of authority and conflict resolution have long been ritualized, not *before*. This is why full civilian control, as traditionally defined, remains un-achieved in a place like Argentina.

It is too soon to tell just how devoted the armed forces are to the principle of civilian supremacy, nor need a judgment be made now. It begs the funda-mental fact that loyalty is not the only basis of compliance. Conformance may spring from utilitarian rather than normative considerations.[11] Officers may conclude that current institutional arrangements are not optimal but satisfactory; that they are more acceptable than the alternatives; or that there simply are no achievable alternatives.[12] So it is in Argentina, where the armed forces, while not as yet wed to the idea of subordination, are in no position to upset the equilibrium. They have neither the strength nor the desire to do so. There are a number of reasons why this is so.

First, the objective conditions for coup d'état are simply not in place. Coup-prone officers would find themselves internationally isolated. The United States has renounced dictatorship as a viable political option, even where the most obsequious of such regimes might offer the West unwavering support. Multilateral lending agencies increasingly prefer working with dem-ocratic, Third World borrowers, and have come out strongly against excessive military spending. Regional, trade, and investment accords, which hold out the promise of economic reward to its members, have been signed thanks to the tireless, diplomatic efforts of democratic governments. Combined, these elements create an international climate ill-conducive to military reinter-vention.

Domestically, conditions are no better. The armed forces cannot over-throw constitutional regimes unless they receive significant support from, or at the very least the acquiescence of, civil society.[13] But revulsion over the

11. In choosing not to defect, a participant need not pledge unswerving allegiance to the demo-cratic system and its values, although there must be a "clear and uncompromising rejection of violent means to achieve or maintain power." See Juan Linz and Alfred Stepan, *The Breakdown of Demo-cratic Regimes: Crisis, Breakdown, and Reequilibration* (Baltimore: The Johns Hopkins University Press, 1978), p. 36. On the different bases of compliance, see Harry Eckstein and Ted R. Gurr, *Patterns of Authority: A Structural Basis for Political Inquiry* (New York: John Wiley & Sons, 1975), pp. 71–77.

12. See Adam Przeworski, "Some Problems in the Study of the Transition to Democracy," in *Transitions from Authoritarian Rule: Comparative Perspectives*, ed. Guillermo O'Donnell, Philippe C. Schmitter and Laurence Whitehead (Baltimore: The Johns Hopkins University Press, 1986), p. 52; Eckstein and Gurr, *Patterns of Authority*, pp. 72–73.

13. The number of scholars who accept this thesis are too numerous to mention. The following is a sample: Samuel Huntington, *Political Order in Changing Societies* (New Haven: Yale University

horrors inflicted by predecessor regimes has served to inoculate citizens against the temptation to conspire against elected officials, or to condone those who do.[14] The radical left, which previously treated democracy as a system with no inherent worth, as merely a means to a socialist end, has now reconsidered its position. The left suffered enough under dictatorial rule to inspire in it a newfound respect for democratic ideals. And it is not just the legacy of human rights abuse that pits so much of the public against tyranny. It is the haunting memories that some have of economic ruin, and their inability to do much about it, that causes them to question the wisdom of again casting their lot with autocrats. Right-wing propertied sectors in particular now realize they cannot leave their interests unattended at the military doorstep, and that a system more vulnerable to political influence may be preferable.

Furthermore, the authoritarian legacy is one that many men of arms would also prefer disassociating themselves from. This is particularly so in countries where the failed policies and immoral practices of the dictatorship redounded to the disfavor of the armed forces. When the line between the regime and the profession becomes blurred, as it was in a thoroughly militarized state like Argentina's, then the officer corps not only suffers the effects of poor governance but may be unwittingly forced to choose sides in policy disputes that could erode professional integrity, unity, and discipline. In the end, María Ricci and J. Samuel Fitch conclude, "military government is a contradiction in terms; the armed forces cannot govern without subverting their own essence."[15] Anxious to protect themselves from the corrosive influences of political office, many military institutions have since practiced coup avoidance.

Military aversion to authoritarianism also manifests itself in another, more subjective way. The armed forces no longer adhere as well to doctrines that license political intervention. For years they were bonded by a sacred mission: to rid the region of the "scourge of Marxism-Leninism" that they be-

---

Press, 1968); José Nun, "The Middle Class Military Coup Revisited," in *Armies and Politics in Latin America*, ed. Abraham F. Lowenthal and J. Samuel Fitch (New York: Holmes & Meier, 1986), pp. 59–95; Alain Rouquié, *The Military and the State in Latin America* (Berkeley and Los Angeles: University of California Press, 1987), pp. 275–76.

14. The full extent of this societal repudiation of authoritarianism as it pertains to Argentina is explored in Chapter 3.

15. María Susana Ricci and J. Samuel Fitch, "Ending Military Regimes in Argentina: 1966–73 and 1976–83," in *The Military and Democracy: The Future of Civil-Military Relations in Latin America*, ed. Louis W. Goodman, Johanna Mendelson, and Juan Rial (Lexington, Mass: Lexington Books, 1990), p. 68.

left ← Scale → rt

Marxism_____ Military-Auth's

lieved was wreaking havoc on the nation's security. This sense of purpose derived from national security doctrines (NSD) that justified military involvement in internal political affairs of the nation in order to combat "subversion."[16] Now, however, the NSD are in disrepute. The old security fears of communist subversion that hitherto served as a focal point for military coalescence have been rendered nearly obsolete by dramatic changes in the Soviet Union and Eastern Europe. Local guerrilla movements have been defeated, left-wing political parties have renounced violence, and elected governments have nearly all been centrist or rightist in their convictions. The receding threat of left-wing extremism has undermined one of the central premises of the NSD: that only a permanent military vigilance could render the nation impenetrable against its marxist foe.

Since the transition to democracy there has been, according to J. Samuel Fitch, a "substantial disarticulation in the various components of national security thinking, especially in Argentina."[17] The absence of doctrinal coherence by no means assures military compliance or civilian control. But it does remove another justification for antidemocratic conspiracies. Moreover, no doctrine has of yet fully supplanted the NSD, and so there is a greater diversity of positions within the officer corps.[18] With the institution less sure about its central missions, intervention seems improbable, although still possible.

Keeping all these factors in mind, officers calculate that the costs to resistance far outweigh the costs to cooperation. Were they to seriously contest the democratic order (assuming that they could) they would invite international condemnation, domestic, public repudiation, as well as internal division, all of which would do lasting damage to their institution. These are costs they would rather not incur. And so they consistently submit, even if

16. Doctrines establish the priorities through which the military can determine their essential missions, deploy their troops, and procure their supplies. For important discussions of the NSD, see Genaro Arriagada Herrera, *El pensamiento político de los militares* (Santiago, Chile: Centro de Investigaciones Socioeconómicas, 1981); Jorge A. Tapia Valdéz, *El terrorismo del estado: La doctrina de la seguridad nacional en el Cono Sur* (Mexico City: Editorial Nueva Imagen, 1980); Roberto Calvo, "The Church and the Doctrine of National Security," *Journal of Interamerican Studies and World Affairs* 21 (February 1979): 69–87; David Pion-Berlin and George Lopez, "Of Victims and Executioners: Argentine State Terror, 1975–79," *International Studies Quarterly* 35 (March 1991): 63–86.

17. J. Samuel Fitch, "Military Role Beliefs in Latin American Democracies: Context, Ideology, and Doctrine in Argentina and Ecuador," paper prepared for delivery at the 1995 meeting of the Latin American Studies Association, Washington, D.C., September 28–30, 1995, p. 63.

18. There is some movement toward a new international security doctrine where the armed forces place themselves at the service of foreign policy objectives by engaging in peacekeeping missions while also fully accepting their apolitical role within the nation. See ibid., pp. 52–53.

they have not as yet sworn allegiance to, the terms of democratic authority.[19] The equilibrium persists.

An Institutional Approach

However calm the civil-military relation may be, it is not static or problem free. Even within democratic confines, the relation is still fundamentally a political one. This may be harder to discern when the two sides are in complete agreement, since politics is so often about conflict and its resolution. But more commonly there are areas of discord. The Argentine military profession has its own peculiar standards, interests, and vision. Consequently, its priorities and those of the political class will not necessarily be the same. It may very well find itself at odds with the government over a host of military and defense-related issues. The point is that while disputes do occur, they do not escalate out of control. The reason is that the contemporary civil-military order in Argentina constitutes a relation of mediated power. It is one where the attempt by politicians and soldiers to convert wants into gains occurs indirectly. It is a relation guided and transformed by a shared recognition that there are boundaries to permissible action, norms of conduct, and official channels of influence that neither side can easily transgress. Civil-military conflicts are restrained and rule driven. The interface features limits and standards, and is exercised in organized, policymaking settings. It is, in short, a relationship that has been institutionalized.

When thinking about institutionalized relations, a number of words come immediately to mind: stability, conformity, regularity, moderation.[20] To one

19. Civilian control is a loaded term because it connotes not just a behavioral conformity but a value orientation that makes subordination permanent and irrevocable. Hence, if civilian control is to be fully realized in Argentina, cost-benefit calculations will have to give way to perceptions of legitimacy. Scott Mainwaring argues that at the beginning, instrumental adhesion to democratic rules is likely and permissible, although in the longer term instability will result unless participants are induced to believe in the system. See "Transitions to Democracy and Democratic Consolidation: Theoretical and Comparative Issues," in *Issues in Democratic Consolidation: The New South American Democracies in Comparative Perspective*, ed. Scott Mainwaring, Guillermo O'Donnell, and J. Samuel Valenzuela (Notre Dame: University of Notre Dame Press, 1992), p. 309.

20. To be stable and moderated is not to be conflict free. Civil-military relations, particularly in the Third World, are often conflictual in nature. Differences in interests, values, and perceptions between politicians and soldiers color the interaction and precipitate disputes about roles, spheres of influence, issues, and policies. But for civil-military relations to be normalized, disputes needn't be settled—only subjected to a higher order of restraint predicated upon a *mutual* acceptance of institutional rules of the game.

degree or another, all of these terms are applicable. To institutionalize a relation is to normalize it: to make it predictably adhere to acceptable, indeed legitimate, conventions of political life. Underlying this normalcy are two dimensions, one formal, the other behavioral. Most Latin American countries are lawful states, if by that one means that they have constitutions, statutes, codes, regulations, and other legal instruments intended to establish order, rules, and consequences for the polity. Through law these states erect the foundations upon which political activities unfold. But the degree to which members of society subscribe to these formalities is another matter entirely. Where democracies are fragile, rules are often observed only in the breach. For political relations between any principal actors in society to become institutionalized, adherence to democratic conventions must become a behavioral adaptation, not just a legal fact. In the new civil-military order of Argentina, there is a much greater (although not perfect) adhesion to constitutional norms than in the past.

So long as the armed forces abide by democratic rules of conduct, the organizations that embody those rules must become the subject of inquiry. Contacts between military commanders and political rulers occur within governmental agencies—the decision-making centers within which policies are formulated, debated, implemented, or defeated. These agencies are institutions, and institutions are "collections of standard operating procedures and structures" that shape political behavior within their confines.[21] At each decision-making site there are features of the institutional design that regulate the interaction between politicians and soldiers and in that way help configure their policy fortunes.

Policies constitute the substance of the civil-military relation—the issues over which politicians and soldiers may agree or disagree. One noted authority on the subject may be going too far when he says that policy is "whatever

---

21. James G. March and Johan P. Olsen, "The New Institutionalism: Organizational Factors in Political Life," *The American Political Science Review* 78 (September 1984): 738. For related definitions, see James G. Ikenberry, "Conclusion: An Institutional Approach to American Foreign Economic Policy," *International Organization* 42 (Winter 1988): 223. Jack Knight says that an institution is foremost a "set of rules that structure social interaction" and that "knowledge of these rules must be shared by the members of the relevant community or society." See Jack Knight, *Institutions and Social Conflict* (Cambridge: Cambridge University Press, 1992), pp. 2–3. Also see Sven Steinmo, Kathleen Thelen, and Frank Longstreth, eds., *Structuring Politics: Historical Institutionalism in Comparative Analysis* (Cambridge: Cambridge University Press, 1992), pp. 5–7; Kathryn Sikkink, *Ideas and Institutions: Developmentalism in Brazil and Argentina* (Ithaca, N.Y.: Cornell University Press, 1991), p. 23.

governments choose to do or not to do."[22] But governments are in the business of authoritatively allocating scarce resources among competing needs. Policies are the packages within which those tough choices are made. In a democratic society the armed forces are but one among many groups trying to feed at the public trough. Policy outcome, then, is a critical measure of how adroit these different groups are at converting their preferences into perquisites at the expense of rivals.

As already stated, that conversion process is indirect, one that is mediated by institutions. Institutional design may either facilitate or inhibit military attempts to influence policy processes that affect its corporate well-being. As these designs change, so too should policy outcomes that pertain to military interests. But similarly, they constrain or enhance the ability of political leaders to see their initial programs through to completion. Neither side is in a position to ensure its own success by somehow tampering with, circumventing, or dominating the institutional order. To the contrary, they must submit to its rules and then hope for the best. As Adam Przeworski has pointed out, the "capacity of particular groups to realize their interests is shaped by the specific institutional arrangements of a given system." But, he quickly adds, "outcomes of conflicts are not uniquely determined."[23] Hence, while institutional norms set the procedural ground rules for interaction, they do not *guarantee* substantive gains or losses for either side.

For the authorities, policy failure is perfectly compatible with the notion of civil-military normalcy. In fact, as the chapter on human rights will show, objectionable policies often fail not because democratic institutions crumble under the weight of military pressure but because they function so well. Moreover, institutions do not stifle military influence; they only routinize it. So long as legitimate avenues of influence remain open to the armed forces, civilian leaders can never be certain about the fate of their military-related programs. If civilians confront uncertainty, so too do the armed forces. Under democratic administration they can no more ensure that policy outcomes will fulfill their wants than can anyone else. Frustration may result, but intimidation, obstruction, evasion, or subversion are not remedies normally available to them in a democratic, institutional environment that is relatively stable.

22. Thomas R. Dye, *Understanding Public Policy*, 6th ed. (Englewood Cliffs, N.J.: Prentice-Hall, 1987), p. 3.

23. Przeworski, "Some Problems in the Study of the Transition to Democracy," p. 58.

The approach taken here fits within the "new institutional" school of thought and represents its first application to Latin American civil-military relations.[24] Institutionalists are often pitted against rational-choice theorists. The former put their stock in the endurance of organizational structures, rules, patterns, and traditions, all of which affect the behavior of individuals. By contrast, the latter begin with the individual; it is his interests, values, calculations, and actions that determine how institutions emerge and perform.[25] Any organization, they claim, can be reduced to its component parts; its members, whose strategic choices and interactions taken in the aggregate constitute the life force of the institution itself. Institutionalists, on the other hand, believe the whole is greater than the sum of its parts. Institutions are not only actors in their own right but are fully capable of compelling rational individuals to behave in ways they might not have chosen on grounds of pure self-interest. As James March and Johan P. Olsen state: "In contrast to theories that assume action is choice based on individual values and expectations, theories of political structure [which are collections of institutions] assume action is the fulfillment of duties and obligations."[26]

While not underrating the theoretical and philosophical differences between these two schools, I will argue that they are complementary, and can combine forces to help analyze civil-military affairs from a policy perspective. Let us begin with the normal distinction that is made between the formulation and implementation of policy. Inarguably, a chief executive *formulates* policies to further his own personal, political agendas and those of his political party, whether these be narrowly or broadly construed. Self-interest dictates that he do what he must to survive in office, firm up his political base, ensure either his own reelection or barring that the reelection of the party faithful, all the while contributing to the consolidation of the democratic

24. See the works cited in footnote 21. The following is a selective list of other institutional titles: James G. March and Johan P. Olsen, *Rediscovering Institutions* (New York: The Free Press, 1989); Peter Hall, *Governing the Economy: The Politics of State Intervention in Britain and France* (New York: Oxford University Press, 1986); Paul Dimaggio and Walter Powell, eds., *The New Institutionalism in Organizational Analysis* (Chicago: University of Chicago Press, 1991); Douglas C. North, *Institutions, Institutional Change, and Economic Performance* (Cambridge: Cambridge University Press, 1990).

25. A useful overview of rational-choice theory can be found in Kristen Renwick Monroe, ed., *The Economic Approach to Politics: A Critical Assessment of the Theory of Rational Action* (New York: HarperCollins Publishers, 1991), pp. 1–31. Major rational-choice works are too numerous to mention in detail, but here are two: Kenneth J. Arrow, *Social Choice and Individual Values* (New Haven: Yale University Press, 1951); Jon Elster, *Ulysses and the Sirens: Studies in Rationality and Irrationality* (Cambridge: Cambridge University Press, 1979).

26. March and Olsen, "The New Institutionalism," p. 741.

system. The policy preferences that are driven by these interests are usually shaped outside of the chief executive's immediate governmental surroundings, and oftentimes in advance of his assumption of office.

As candidate for president, Raúl Alfonsín knew that to win he must strike a resonant chord with a broad, multiparty, multiclass, coalition of citizens outraged over the abuses recently suffered at the hands of the military state.[27] He helped write the Radical Civic Union (UCR) Party platform, which called for the eradication of all forms of torture and severe punishment for those found guilty of such transgressions.[28] As president, he attempted to make good on this pledge by ordering several former military leaders to stand trial for human rights abuses. Carlos Menem had his own motives. He knew early on that to succeed as president, as well as to secure the future electoral viability of his party, he would have to stabilize the economy by first bringing government deficit spending under control. This was his motivation to deepen the cuts in defense expenditures initiated by his predecessor.

As the coercive arm of the state, the Argentine military (like all militaries) has obligations to the constitutional authorities. But as a professional fighting force it also must look out for its own organizational interests. Its core objective is to preserve total control over the means of coercion; maintain a strong sense of professional ethics, pride, and conduct; and ensure a sense of discipline, cohesion, and esprit de corps within the ranks.[29] Surrounding the core are functions that are also of importance: upgrading living standards, equipment, and educational materials; maintaining defensive readiness; fulfilling assigned missions; and protecting budgetary shares, to name a few. These needs will then generate either support for or opposition to proposed policies.

Based on self-interest, politicians and soldiers alike will devise strategies to advance their cause most effectively and efficiently within the democratic order. But however much either side may start out intending to maximize its gains, it soon resigns itself to muddling through as best it can. It wades through the thick institutional waters, making means-ends adjustments along the way and hoping for the best. It is no longer a question of optimal

---

27. Manuel Mora y Araújo, "The Nature of the Alfonsín Coalition," in *Elections and Democratization in Latin America, 1980–85*, eds. Paul Drake and Eduardo Silva (San Diego: Center for Iberian and Latin American Studies, 1986), pp. 175–99.

28. Jorge Camarasa, Rubén Felice, and Daniel González, *El juicio: Proceso al horror* (Buenos Aires: Sudamericana/Planeta, 1985), p. 24.

29. Defense of professional, core interests is paramount for the armed forces. See Eric Nordlinger, *Soldiers in Politics: Military Coups and Governments* (Englewood Cliffs, N.J.: Prentice-Hall, 1977); on the specific features of military professionalism, see Huntington, *The Soldier and the State*.

choice but rather of satisfactory choice compelled by institutional processes it may have little control over.[30] Politicians and soldiers choose, but institutions constrain. Even if policy is formulated in response to individual or group interests, the facility with which it is implemented depends on organizational factors.

Policy positions are set mostly outside of the institution; policy fortunes are figured within them. Rational-choice theory is vital to help us uncover the underlying motivations behind the desire to pursue or contest a policy. Institutional theory is critical if we are to understand why some programs are fulfilled while others are not. The two theories work in tandem by providing a more comprehensive picture of the forces that shape military-related policy.

Naturally, there are those actors who may wish to reform or overturn institutions that frustrate their wants. Can institutions be overhauled, and if so, how often? There are some theorists who maintain that institutions are objects of a continuing choice, perpetually at the mercy of instrumental actors (i.e., politicians or soldiers) wishing to discard or revise the rules of the game each time it is to their advantage to do so.[31] Since institutions were set up to advance the goals of those individuals or social groups who built, sustained, or comprised them, they should be perpetually servile to their desires. Should they (for whatever reason) fail to be, then they can and will be subject to continuous modification until their structures, rules, and norms are made compatible with the goals that they were supposed to have served.[32]

This perspective takes us too far. While organizations are subject to reform, this occurs episodically, not continuously. Institutions do have a tendency to persist over time. Change, even when needed, is difficult to achieve because, as Stephen Krasner says, "altering established routines will be costly and time consuming, and the *consequences of change cannot be fully predicted*" (emphasis mine).[33] Uncertainty is the issue. How sure can proponents of change be that the as yet unseen and untested institutional alternative will

---

30. See Herbert A. Simon, "A Behavioral Model of Rational Choice," *Quarterly Journal of Economics* 69 (1955): 99–118.

31. A view criticized by Robert Grafstein, "Rational Choice: Theory and Institutions," in *The Economic Approach to Politics: A Critical Assessment of the Theory of Rational Action*, ed. Kristen Renwick Monroe (New York: HarperCollins Publishers, 1991), p. 263.

32. A position espoused by Richard D. McKelvey and Peter C. Ordeshook, "An Experimental Study of the Effects of Procedural Rules on Committee Behavior," *Journal of Politics* 46 (1984):182–205.

33. See Stephen D. Krasner, "Sovereignty: An Institutional Perspective," in *The Elusive State: International and Comparative Perspectives*, ed. James A. Caporaso (Newbury Park, Calif.: Sage Publications, 1989), p. 88.

yield greater benefits than the order they wish to reform or overturn? What is the probability that they can succeed? If they do, is it worth the sacrifice? If they don't, what are the consequences of failure?[34]

Aside from uncertainty, there is also the matter of power. Do change advocates have the collective strength to transform governing institutions? Opposition to the current order must overcome the coalition of political appointees, civil servants, and members of society who are the beneficiaries of the status quo and who want to see its arrangements persist into the future.

If disenchantment with the existing institutional framework is deeply felt, if the coalition for change is sizable and forceful enough, and if reformers conclude that the benefits of going forward into an uncertain future outweigh the costs of standing still, then institutional change is possible, even probable. These are precisely the kind of cost/benefit calculations that rational-choice theorists tell us political protagonists make deciding on a course of action. Thus while the institutional argument that governing organizations have a tendency to linger is persuasive, equally valid is the rational-choice claim that when change does occur, it occurs largely for instrumental reasons; individuals or groups are seeking to benefit themselves, believe institutional arrangements stand in their way, and are strategically assessing the probability that those arrangements can be overhauled with the forces at their disposal. Here, too, we find important bridges between the two theoretical traditions.

To recap, this is a policy-oriented, institutional approach to the study of civil-military affairs. Policy is the substance and democratic institutions the mediating ambience of the relation. Programmatic preferences are set by politicians and soldiers rationally calculating how to further their own ends. Programmatic outcomes (the main concern in this study) that measure whether or not politicians prevail over soldiers on a given issue at a given point in time are set largely by the organizational features of those governmental units charged with policy implementation. By moving democratic governance to center stage, our orientation takes a certain exception to conventional thinking about the armed forces and politics in nations like Argentina. It is to that literature that we now turn.

Rival Approaches

For years the focus has been on the military organization, not civilian-led, governing institutions. Whether seen as a force for modernization, a pre-

---

34. See Przeworski, "Some Problems in the Study of the Transition to Democracy," pp. 53–56.

server of oligarchical interests, a defender of the middle class, an instrument for transnational capitalists, an organizer of state terror, or an obstacle to democratic reconstruction, the military actor almost always occupies center stage in the field of Latin American studies. By contrast, democratic policy-makers and institutions are usually found offstage. If they show up at all, they play small, bit parts, clearly outperformed by the more formidable military protagonists.

This bias was forgivable during the mid- to late 1960s and throughout the decade of the 1970s when practically all of Latin America was under the grip of dictatorship. The political class had been shunted to the side, its leaders ousted from office, its parties censored or outlawed, and its legislative bodies closed. But a perusal of landmark writings on civil-military affairs during the late 1950s and early 1960s—a time once characterized as the twilight of the dictators—reveals the same general trend. The emphasis back then was on the political role of the armed forces: Was it an agent of change or a preserver of the status quo?[35] Authors like Edwin Lieuwen dismissed transitions from military to democratic, civilian rule as epiphenomenal, secondary to more fundamental underlying social transformations, changing patterns of development, and shifting military roles.[36] If we jump ahead to the 1980s—the decade of democratic rebirth—and on to the early 1990s, there is a return to military-centered literature.[37] Despite the solidity with which democracy has regained a foothold on the South American continent, the current fixation is still on the power and prerogatives of soldiers.[38]

---

35. The two best examples of these writings are Edwin Lieuwen, *Armies and Politics in Latin America* (New York: Frederick A. Praeger, 1960), and John Johnson, *The Military and Society in Latin America* (Stanford: Stanford University Press, 1964).

36. In fact, Lieuwen argues that even in those countries in which democracies flourish and the armed forces are, as he described them, "non-political," civilian control exists only where "substantial social change has taken place," resulting in a "new social equilibrium." See Lieuwen, *Armies and Politics in Latin America*, p. 169.

37. The following is a sample of the military-centered literature of recent years: Robert Wesson, ed., *New Military Politics in Latin America* (New York: Praeger Publishers, 1982); George Philip, *The Military in South American Politics* (London: Croom Helm, 1985); Robert Wesson, ed., *The Latin American Military Institution* (New York: Praeger Publishers, 1986); Augusto Varas, ed., *Democracy Under Siege: New Military Power in Latin America* (New York: Greenwood Press, 1989); Louis W. Goodman, Johanna S. R. Mendelson, and Juan Rial, eds., *The Military and Democracy: The Future of Civil-Military Relations in Latin America* (Lexington, Mass.: Lexington Books, 1990); Daniel M. Masterson, *Militarism and Politics in Latin America: Peru from Sánchez Cerro to Sendero Luminoso* (New York: Greenwood Press, 1991); Frederick M. Nunn, *The Time of the Generals: Latin American Professional Militarism in World Perspective* (Lincoln: University of Nebraska Press, 1992); Paul W. Zagorski, *Democracy vs. National Security: Civil-Military Relations in Latin America* (Boulder, Colo: Lynne Rienner Publishers, 1992).

38. Studies that reveal the interests, behavior, beliefs, and perceptions of the armed forces are

Contemporary thinking on civil-military affairs finds its inspiration and its reference in a bygone era. It was a time when societies seemed strong and states exceptionally weak. Societal actors—be they landed, industrial, or union in nature—lorded it over the political class. They dominated the democratic process or they simply dispensed with it when it was convenient to do so. State institutions were regarded as superfluous since they could be easily evaded or overrun. Interest groups knew no restraints. In the politically charged atmosphere of the time, rivals settled their scores by whatever means were at their disposal; rules were devised only to be broken. Taken to its limits, this situation would often degenerate into classic praetorianism, where "social forces confront each other nakedly" while political leaders and institutions look on helplessly.[39]

Although the military has always officially been a part of the state, it has often acted *as if* it were outside of it. Much like a pressure group, it has marshaled its considerable resources for the benefit of social class allies or for its own gain. As an instrument of defense policy, the Latin American armed forces were supposed to faithfully fulfill their missions if and when they were called upon to do so by the political authorities. War, if it came to that, was to be the continuation of policy by other means.[40] But in a peculiar and perverse inversion of Carl von Clausewitz's theorem, armies often departed from the norm by forcing politicians to serve their own ends. As self-anointed guarantors of national security, they unilaterally defined what were the nation's vital interests, how best to defend these, and against whom. They would then insist that elected or nonelected governments respond to their call to arms or suffer the consequences. In short, they transformed themselves from instruments to advocates of policy.[41] Understandably, then, a multitude of scholars has treated the military as an all-powerful interest group willing and able to violate institutional lines of authority to suit its own needs.[42]

---

important and should continue. But for reasons offered in this chapter, equal attention to the civilian side of the ledger is now warranted and in fact essential.

39. Huntington, *Political Order in Changing Societies*, p. 196.

40. Carl von Clausewitz, *On War*, edited and translated by Michael Howard and Peter Paret (Princeton: Princeton University Press, 1976), p. 87.

41. A perfect example of how the armed forces appropriated these privileges for themselves is detailed in Osiris Villegas, *Políticas y estrategías para el desarrollo y la seguridad nacional* (Buenos Aires: Editorial Pleamar, 1969).

42. The very first sentence of Alain Rouquié's book *The Military and the State in Latin America* reads as follows: "We cannot understand the power and role of the military in Latin American public life without a knowledge of the *societies* in which the military establishments are situated and the forces they control" (emphasis mine, p. 17). Military disdain for the political class that officially ruled over them is well documented in Brian Loveman and Thomas M. Davies Jr., eds., *The Politics*

Whether interest groups clashed among themselves or with governments, the results were equally harmful to democratic institutions, which were either ignored, mocked, or abused. This vision of the strong society and weak state that conformed so well to the realities of Argentine politics in decades past now seems peculiarly out of place in the current period, marked by what is so far a profound, sustained movement toward and deepening of the competitive system of government. Democratic institutions are not defenseless or dispensable. To the contrary, they are quickly becoming important, permanent fixtures on the political landscape. Whether they want to or not, soldiers must contend with governmental characteristics that either predate them, are not of their own choosing, or are not easily circumvented.

Institutions are "givens." True, they can and have been overhauled. But as suggested earlier, this kind of dramatic change occurs infrequently—usually during periods of acute crisis—and only when the balance of power has shifted decisively in favor of those clamoring for change. During periods of relative stability, political, social, and military actors must cope with the institutions at hand, adjusting their expectations and strategies accordingly.

Latin American scholars, by contrast, have long treated democratic institutions as too fragile to be of any real consequence. Samuel Huntington referred to the "feeble state surrounded by massive social forces" when mentioning Argentina.[43] Douglas Chalmers described the "politicized state" where "everything is possible" owing to the fact that nothing is sacred.[44] Because there is no deep-seated, cultural respect for decision-making procedures, these can be abruptly disabled and then reinvented each time powerful groups decide it is in their interests to do so. Guillermo O'Donnell agreed, suggesting that winning political coalitions will establish new rules or overhaul the political system entirely in order to secure advantages for themselves while imposing constraints on the losers.[45] And Charles Anderson described political systems as "tentative," meaning they were based on a "flexible coalition among diverse power contenders which is subject to revision at any time."[46]

---

of Antipolitics: The Military in Latin America, 2d ed. (Lincoln: University of Nebraska Press, 1989). Other works that treat the military as if it were a social force include: Samuel Huntington, Political Order in Changing Societies; and José Nun, "The Middle Class Military Coup Revisited," pp. 59–95.

43. Huntington, Political Order in Changing Societies, p. 84.

44. Douglas Chalmers, "The Politicized State in Latin America," in Authoritarianism and Corporatism in Latin America, ed. James M. Malloy (Pittsburgh: University of Pittsburgh Press, 1977), p. 26.

45. Guillermo O'Donnell, Modernization and Bureaucratic-Authoritarianism: Studies in South American Politics (Berkeley: Institute of International Studies, 1979), p. 75.

46. Charles Anderson, "Toward a Theory of Latin American Politics," in Politics and Social Change

Like *some* contemporary rational-choice theorists, these scholars reached the logical conclusion that if institutions could so easily be undone, then real power must lie beyond them. To sort out critical questions about resource allocation and distribution, to understand who gets what, when, and how, why not turn to the groups that manipulate institutions to their advantage? Why not treat governments as objects of conquest by competing social forces?

This is precisely what has been done. "The institutions of government," David Truman once wrote, "are centers of interest-based power."[47] The very *process* of government, he argued, could not be understood apart from organized interests. The father of interest-group theory has found a flock of admirers within the field of Latin American politics.[48] Echoing his views are those of Chalmers, who wrote that the control and manipulation of the state apparatus is "a major element in the political struggle . . . to promote the power and goals of one group over another."[49] Political actors operate essentially on the basis of pressures and threats from strong-willed societal groups, argued O'Donnell.[50] And for Anderson the political process is nothing more than manipulation and negotiation among power contenders.[51] These views seem more symptomatic than exceptional; much of the theoretical thinking on civil-military relations and state-societal relations in Latin America displays the same interest-group prejudices.

Within this framework state institutions are conceived of as spectator arenas in which an all-out struggle for control between societal actors ensues.[52] At most, governments can only referee the contest, ratify the victors, and record the outcomes. The groups who prevail then exploit the state: public-sector jobs, services, salaries, and finances are perquisites to be extracted by

---

in *Latin America: Still a Distinct Tradition?* ed. Howard J. Wiarda (Boulder, Colo: Westview Press, 1992), pp. 242–43.

47. David B. Truman, *The Governmental Process: Political Interests and Public Opinion* (New York: Alfred A. Knopf, 1960), p. 506.

48. Of course Truman's laboratory was the United States, where as he readily pointed out, pluralism reigns supreme. Diversity, overlapping membership, and widespread respect for rules of fair play ensure that no single group dominates. In Latin America, however, some organizations have achieved near monopolistic status in their respective sectors, earning them the name corporate interest groups. See Edward C. Epstein, *The New Argentine Democracy: The Search for a Successful Formula* (Westport, Conn.: Praeger Publishers, 1992), pp. 63–170.

49. Chalmers, "The Politicized State in Latin America," p. 31.

50. O'Donnell, *Modernization and Bureaucratic-Authoritarianism*, p. 68.

51. Anderson, "Toward a Theory of Latin American Politics," pp. 242–43.

52. Some marxists share this perspective as well. See Nicos Poulantzas, *Political Power and Social Classes* (London: Humanities Press, 1968).

the most formidable groups for the enrichment of their supporters; coercive instruments are to be used to suppress their adversaries. Weak public officials would design policies to aid and abet this appropriation of resources by placating those who impose on them. Policy, then, is a *direct* reflection of the will and preferences of those in the system who dominate.

If policy were simply the product of organized pressure, then institutional rules and procedures would be irrelevant. Policy outcomes could be deduced by identifying the agenda of those groups who most effectively take advantage of the state. Nowhere is the temptation to do just this greater than in the area of civil-military affairs. In the past the armed forces were the agitators, moderators, and arbitrators that stirred political life. With a monopoly on the means of coercion, they could push the system down the slippery slope toward political anarchy and eventually regime demise. Too often they did just that. Civilian officials could do little more than try to stave off military intervention. Acquiescent public policy was merely one means to achieve that end. If this were still true, then whenever or wherever the balance of power tilts in favor of the armed forces, policymakers should, out of sheer instinct for survival, respond directly and positively to their wants.

Yet this proposition is neither true in practice nor necessary in theory. As will be documented in subsequent chapters, it cannot account for the curious mix of policy outcomes observed in contemporary Argentina. Within a narrow frame of time, the armed forces simultaneously observed policy success and failure, with results varying not according to the exertion of power but to the mediums through which power was expressed. The evidence simply does not conform to an image of helpless policymakers overwhelmed by military might at every turn. To the contrary, it is the armed forces who have been terribly weakened by the legacy of dictatorship and defeat in war. Their numbers and resources have dwindled, their social and political alliances have frayed, and they haven't the organizational muscle to mobilize resistance against the constitutional authorities.[53] As a result, political institutions now have the upper hand.

This empirical observation speaks to two important theoretical points. First, institutional capacity is relational—not absolute—in quality.[54] States, which are sets of institutions, are either strong or weak in comparison to

---

53. Chapter 3 will detail the reasons why this is so.

54. Alfred Stepan, "State Power and Civil Society in the Southern Cone of Latin America," in *Bringing the State Back In*, ed. Peter Evans, Dietrich Rueschmeyer, and Theda Skocpol (Cambridge: Cambridge University Press, 1985), p. 331; Theda Skocpol, "Introduction," in *Bringing the State Back In*, p. 19; Huntington, *Political Order in Changing Societies*, pp. 78–80.

nonstate actors.[55] It is in the balance of power between the two that one finds answers to the questions about capacity, autonomy, and stability. To paraphrase Huntington, stability is predicated upon the ratio of institutionalization to interest-group mobilization, not on the absolute value of either. Should that ratio remain high, *even in systems plagued by institutional weaknesses*, then stability results.[56] In this sense the contemporary Argentine state has an advantage (for reasons stated above) despite what some have rightfully claimed to be its historic fragility.[57]

Second, in a democracy, power—in or outside of the state—is divisible, not monolithic. No organization or individual can exhibit strength with equal effectiveness from one setting to the next. Contexts shift, and as they do, so too does the mix of opportunities and constraints confronting any political actor, the armed forces included.[58] Institutions comprise varied, organized contexts where arrangements enable some and disable others, where rules provide "procedural advantages and impediments for translating political power into concrete policies."[59] Thus, even in systems where the military maintains a considerable store of power, institutional arrangements should be observed closely to understand where military influence makes a decisive impact and where it does not.

The state itself is not monolithic. In states that are thought to be vulnera-

---

55. Skocpol, "Introduction," p. 22.

56. See Huntington, *Political Order in Changing Societies*, pp. 79–80. Joel Migdal argues that states often become stronger during times of social upheaval brought on by exogenous shocks (e.g., war) to the system. The temporary disorientation of once powerful social groups that results from that shock offers the state a window of opportunity to reclaim control. See Joel S. Migdal, *Strong Societies and Weak States: State-Society Relations and State Capabilities in the Third World* (Princeton: Princeton University Press, 1988), pp. 271–72. The lessons for Argentina are transparent. The crushing defeat in the Malvinas War contributed decisively to the debilitation of the armed forces, allowing democratic officeholders to recoup influence lost years before.

57. Historically, Argentines shared a "chronic distrust" of the state, often regarding it as ineffectual and weak. Despite its great size, the Argentine state never operated with any great proficiency. It suffered from a host of maladies, including poor coordination, inadequate infrastructure, a lack of rigorous entrance requirements for civil servants, poor training facilities, and a high personnel turnover rate. These afflictions, the product of long-term neglect and abuse at the hands of political leaders, reduced the state's performance capacity. See Sikkink, *Ideas and Institutions*, pp. 188–95.

58. We should remind ourselves that this field of study is aptly labeled civil-military *relations*. The vernacular is plural, not singular, and whether intended to or not, calls attention to the idea that there may be multiple equations of power between politicians and soldiers, depending on the context.

59. Ellen M. Immergut, "The Rules of the Game: The Logic of Health Policy-Making in France, Switzerland, and Sweden," in *Structuring Politics: Institutionalism in Comparative Analysis*, ed. Sven Steinmo, Kathleen Thelen, and Frank Longstreth (Cambridge: Cambridge University Press, 1992), p. 59.

ble to societal pressure certain agencies or branches of government may nonetheless display high degrees of insularity.[60] That is why Theda Skocpol concludes that one can find "islands of state strength in an ocean of weakness."[61] Civilians need not relent to the demands of special interests so long as they are ensconced within a governmental unit that operates independently and efficaciously. Military influence is brokered by the norms and rules of procedure that guide policymaking within the unit. Hence, the military effect cannot be known apart from the organizational contexts in which it is expressed.

Institutional designs influence the degree, direction, and effectiveness of pressures brought to bear on the policy process by political contestants. Interest-group theorists contend that institutions are only as effective as pressure groups allow them to be.[62] In a reversal of that logic, it is maintained here that pressure groups are only as effective as institutions permit them to be. As such, far from being spectator arenas in which the tug of war between political competitors unfolds, institutions are the very agents who arbitrate that tug of war.[63] They are, in short, autonomous political actors in their own right.[64]

By contrast, the more recent scholarship places the emphasis on military autonomy. Power, it argues, has taken on a new identity. No longer is there a need to overturn the regime. Armies can dominate by placing themselves beyond the pale of governmental authority. Their mission is to preserve if not enlarge the perquisites they acquired while in office. To do so they exercise a kind of sovereignty within a self-defined and self-regulated sphere of influence resistant to political oversight.[65] In this way they reduce the scope

---

60. See Stephen D. Krasner, "U.S. Commercial and Monetary Policy: Unravelling the Paradox of External Strength and Internal Weakness," *International Organization* 31 (August 1977): 635–71.

61. Skocpol, "Introduction," p. 13.

62. See Truman, *The Governmental Process*.

63. To claim that institutions can be treated as political players demands that we impute to them some coherence and autonomy—a notion I am quite comfortable with. See March and Olsen, "The New Institutionalism," pp. 738–39. On altering preferences, see Hall, *Governing the Economy*, p. 233.

64. March and Olsen, "The New Institutionalism," pp. 738–39.

65. Juan Rial warns against the new armies of the region that are autonomous from the state and segmented from society. See his chapter, "The Armed Forces and Democracy: The Interests of Latin American Military Corporations in Sustaining Democratic Regimes," in *The Military and Democracy: The Future of Civil-Military Relations in Latin America*, ed. Louise W. Goodman, Johanna S. R. Mendelson, and Juan Rial (Lexington, Mass.: Lexington Books, 1990), pp. 277–80. Paul Zagorski, identifies a postnational security state where the military has managed to preserve and defend a broad array of prerogatives accumulated during past eras (see his *Democracy vs. National Security*). Also see Felipe Agüero, "The Military and the Limits to Democratization in South America," in *Issues in Democratic Consolidation: The New South American Democracies in Comparative Perspective,*

of civilian power by rendering government policy inapplicable with respect to most vital military issues. Since these issues cannot be placed on the policy agenda, they never come up and never enter the decision-making stream. It is the *nondecisions* that are of import because they reveal the disguised yet potent nature of military force.

Several objections can be raised. First, governmental decisions that have adversely affected the military organization *have* repeatedly been made. Some of these, such as defense budget cuts, will be examined in this book. If in fact the armed forces have been unable to keep these kinds of issues off the agenda, then they obviously do not enjoy as much veiled power as some experts would attribute to them.

Second, civilians may avoid problems not out of reverence for military autonomy but out of self-interest or disinterest. More politically pressing concerns consume their time and attention. The needs of the armed forces are of a lower priority to them. Politicians are in the business of gathering votes and building electoral coalitions. But in South America voters are usually not animated by most military and defense-related matters even if ultimately they are affected by them. In this scenario policymakers need not attach a great priority to defense, and may in fact avoid the issue without incurring a political cost. If, however, a military issue does capture public attention, policymakers will not only place the issue on their agenda but may be moved to contest the armed forces if there is political gain to be had.[66]

And third, the concept of autonomy itself is poorly specified within this literature.[67] In the rush to condemn the armed forces while pronouncing the new democracies practically dead on arrival, it is often forgotten by these scholars that not all expressions of military strength are necessarily injurious. Often escaping notice is the fact that there are both benign as well as malignant forms of military autonomy. The malignant form expresses the mili-

---

ed. Scott Mainwaring, Guillermo O'Donnell, and J. Samuel Valenzuela (Notre Dame: University of Notre Dame Press, 1992), pp. 153–98; Varas, ed., *Democracy Under Siege*, pp. 1–15. All of these studies have in common the presumption that military corporateness stands in the way of civilian control and therefore, ultimately, of democratic consolidation.

66. The argument that politicians will engage and even contest the military when they have electoral incentives to do so is persuasively made by Wendy Hunter in *Eroding Military Influence in Brazil: Politicians Against Soldiers* (Chapel Hill: University of North Carolina Press, 1997). Also see by the same author, "Politicians Against Soldiers: Contesting the Military in Postauthoritarian Brazil," *Comparative Politics* 27 (July 1995): 425–43.

67. For a full elaboration on the meaning and usage of the term military autonomy, see David Pion-Berlin, "Military Autonomy and Emerging Democracies in South America," *Comparative Politics* 25 (October 1992): 83–102.

tary's determination to extend its influence and control over matters that lie beyond its institutional confines. The military transgresses those boundaries in an attempt to strip the political class of *political* powers that it then claims for itself.[68] The benign manifestation is, by contrast, more *institutionally* centered. It is aimed at furthering professional advancement by building protective layers around the organization to ward off harmful, divisive interventions from political or civil society.[69] Institutionally autonomous armies do not interfere with policymakers; rather, they ensure that policymakers do not interfere with the internal functioning of their organization. Although reversions to more politically minded autonomy cannot be ruled out, institutional ones currently prevail in Argentina, and pose no real hazard to democratic rule.

Taken as a whole, the alternative scholarship assumes that armies are strong, governments are weak, policies are simply pressured into existence, and rules of the game are made to be broken. Our set of theoretical assumptions are noticeably different. We argue there is a ceiling to power above which the armed forces cannot go and a floor below which they need not go. In between they enjoy a margin for maneuver but one that is constrained by democratic structures, norms, and procedures. Policy is a function of process as much as pressure. And since processes unfold within government, governing institutions matter—a fact that implores us to take a closer look at them to reveal the critical dimensions that may shape the civil-military relation.

Institutional Design and the Mediation of Civil-Military Relations

There is no single civil-military balance of power, as is commonly thought, but rather multiple ones. The equation shifts as we move from one decision-

68. As one expert put it, the armed forces wield "substantial negative power over many of the most important national political decisions." This is, in his view, tantamount to a "new form of military intervention" that may not strike as suddenly as the coup d'état but whose impact will, in the longer run, be equally destructive. See Varas, *Democracy Under Siege*, p. 2.

69. S. E. Finer summed up the differences this way: "The military is jealous of its corporate status and privileges. Anxious to preserve its autonomy, it provides one of the most widespread and powerful of the motives for intervention. In its defensive form it can lead to something akin to military syndicalism—an insistence that the military and only the military are entitled to determine on such matters as recruitment, training, numbers and equipment. In its more aggressive form it can lead to the military demand to be the ultimate judge on all other matters affecting the armed forces." See Finer, *Man on Horseback*, p. 41.

making locus to another. Whatever policy advantage soldiers may enjoy in one arena may be nonexistent elsewhere. Therefore, it is essential that we unpackage the civil-military relation to reveal it in its myriad forms across diverse institutional settings. Not all governing institutions are of the same design. Depending upon the issue at hand, political leaders will submit their program proposals to different branches of government, or to different agencies within a branch. Since each location features its own structure, norms, and personnel, we might expect policy outcomes to differ as well.

To know a policy's fate, we must know which portals of state it passes through en route from conception to delivery. Those doors lead to chambers where programs are designed, debated, and dispatched. For example, in Argentina budgeting is lodged within the executive branch, and more specifically within the economics ministry. While decisions there are subject to congressional approval, the legislative oversight is weak and approval of executive requests almost certain. Defense and internal security laws are written in congressional chambers, not at military quarters, although armed forces can and do send their lobbyists to the Congress in hopes of influencing the legislation. Human rights strategies are presidential in origin, but deliberation about human rights transgressions will occur within the judicial branch, while certain programmatic changes may require congressional approval. Defense reform, if and when it is undertaken, resides in the ministry of defense and the armed forces. Since these policies take alternate paths through diverse agencies, their end results may differ as well.[70]

Depending upon whether the institutional mediation either facilitates or restricts military entrance, it serves to alternately narrow or expand the policymaker's margin. The scope, frequency, and intensity with which the armed forces can press their claims depends on whether or not they are "in or out of the loop." As channels of access to the inner policy chambers vary by decision site, so too will military influence. In some instances refurbished ministries have revamped formal lines of authority to the benefit of executive decision makers. Military appeals cannot usually be dismissed out of hand. But they can and have been subjected to a new hierarchy that privileges "top-down" over "bottom-up" flows of influence. In other instances and for various reasons institutions have been ineffectual tools for policy implementation.

There are a number of structural and procedural characteristics of deci-

---

70. The impact of institutional structures on policy implementation as it relates to economic development strategies is persuasively discussed in Sikkink, *Ideas and Institutions*.

sional sites that affect whether policymakers will achieve their goals in the face of military resistance. For purposes of simplification we will concentrate on two of the most important of these: the relative concentration or dispersion of decision-making authority, and the relative insularity or vulnerability of decision makers.[71]

The concentration of decision-making authority refers to the number of actors/units involved in formulating and implementing policy. The greater the concentration, the more power resides in the hands of a single, key decision maker or agency who can impose his (its) preference and will on the outcome. Structurally unified organizations have advantages over less unified competitors because they can speak with one voice and manage dissent.[72] The benefits of concentrated authority, or conversely the drawbacks to dispersed authority, are actually twofold. The first involves relations between civilian actors; the second involves relations between civilians and soldiers.

If in a democracy there is a separation of powers, then one branch of government is not bound to follow the dictates of another. Should the legislative or judicial branch have or rightfully claim some jurisdiction over a policy initiated by the chief executive, then who is to say they will fulfill presidential wishes? If political actors—even presidential allies—within those centers of power do not feel obliged (i.e., out of party loyalty) or are not bound (i.e., by custom) to dutifully sign off on all executive recommendations, then why would they? They may or may not, depending upon their own unique interests, motivations, and circumstances.

What is conceived is not necessarily delivered. The best-hatched plans can be subverted by civilian state actors who have either political agendas or bureaucratic (i.e., ministerial) turfs to protect that are distinct from the president's. As the significant players in a policy process multiply, so too do the occasions upon which policies can be tampered with, delayed, or derailed by their detractors.[73] The wider the array of organizational and personal in-

---

71. On institutional concentrations of power as it pertains to military regimes, see Karen Remmer, *Military Rule in Latin America* (Boston: Unwin Hyman, 1989), pp. 34–42. I think Remmer's formulation has applications to democratic regimes as well. The scholarship on institutional autonomy is too numerous to mention in its entirety. One example from the statist literature would be Eric Nordlinger, *On the Autonomy of the Democratic State* (Cambridge, Mass.: Harvard University Press, 1981), pp. 27–38. In the Latin American literature, see Barbara Geddes, *Politician's Dilemma: Building State Capacity in Latin America* (Berkeley and Los Angeles: University of California Press, 1994), pp. 2–13.

72. Huntington, *The Soldier and the State*, p. 87.

73. On the other hand, political figures may not be in a position to act on their own accord.

terests and points of view to contend with, the more difficult it will be for central decision makers to preserve their original designs intact by engineering consensus along the policy route.[74]

Enter the armed forces. For them this scenario is a blessing. On the lookout for means of redressing unfavorable decisions, they appeal to the unique sensibilities of rival agencies. They exploit and perhaps exacerbate the rifts that already exist between competing state actors, be they ministers of defense and finance or legislative and executive arms of government.[75] And so the dispersion of authority across decision sites avails the armed forces of the opportunity to play off one center of civilian power against another. In short, to the extent that the commander in chief can manage military policies on his own, he can avert the undesirable military *and* civilian affects of decentralized power.

The second principle variable to be considered here is decision-making autonomy. A decision site's autonomy will be defined in structural, procedural, legal, and functional terms. Autonomy refers to an agency's capacity to act independently from others, to fulfill its mandate while adequately insulating itself from unwanted external pressures. Structures define points of access and barriers to entry for those who would attempt to shape policy outcomes. Procedures determine who will deliberate over policy and who may or may not influence the deliberators. Highly autonomous decision-making units reduce the number of options an opponent has to defeat policy

---

Clearance of policies is eased where agents act like decision takers rather than decision makers. Even when political actors have the legal authority to act independently, political, organizational, or historical conventions may persuade them not to. The norms that prevail in a given institutional setting may force political appointees to conform strictly to the desires of the chief executive. In those instances the will of those at the top can be enforced along each link of the policy chain, making passage more likely even where those links are many. See Aaron Wildavsky and Jeffrey L. Pressman, *Policy Implementation* (Berkeley and Los Angeles: University of California Press, 1984), p. 109.

74. Winning passage through the checkpoints at which those individuals are stationed along the route is the problem Wildavsky and Pressman identified as policy clearance (see ibid., pp. 102–9). Policy roadblocks exist when agents charged with implementation are at worst antagonistic toward the stipulated goals or at best disinterested. If checkpoints and points of view are arrayed across institutions, then bureaucratic politics will only compound the problem, as organizational and individual self-interests merge to constitute a "formidable obstacle course for the program" (p. 102).

75. As one commentator on U.S. civil-military relations said, "Each military service has at some time appealed to Congress to restore budgets cut by the Secretary of Defense." See Michael D. Hobkirk, *The Politics of Defense Budgeting: A Study of Organization and Resource Allocation in the United Kingdom and the United States* (London: Macmillan Publishing Co., 1984), p. 50. As the military successfully curries favor with the legislature, it dilutes the powers of the central executive authorities.

measures.[76] Thus, even the diffusion of authority across multiple decision sites does not necessarily benefit the armed forces if each of those sites remains impregnable.

Other sites are more porous for various reasons. For example, to design and fulfill a program, government planners might depend on information that only the military is privy to. They will have no choice but to elicit cooperation from knowledgeable officers. While formally in charge, these officials must informally delegate some of their authority to outsiders who in this instance monopolize a valued resource like expertise.

Then there are legal bases to autonomy. Agencies that are authorized by law to act independently from and with authority over the armed forces have a natural advantage over agencies not similarly mandated. It is more difficult for the military to ignore institutional prerogatives when those are codified. It is also more difficult for the military to take issue with those within an agency who enjoy the legal right to demand compliance from their subordinates.

And yet formal authority is not enough. Public officials must have the skill, desire, and perseverance to see controversial policies through to completion by using the laws at their disposal. But oftentimes those within a ministry (or any organization for that matter) are more absorbed with preserving their own niche than they are with fulfilling a larger cause. While an organization is supposed to be the institutional embodiment of purpose, the fact is, writes James M. Burns, that "most organizations lack central unifying goals."[77] It is, he adds, up to the chief executive to instill a sense of mission into an agency by tapping into and activating the motivational bases (income, security, status, etc.) of its employees. It is the president's leadership, in other words, that helps legally chartered institutions respond to a calling. But it is also his failure to lead that causes institutions to weaken.

Autonomy can be enhanced in a number of ways. Structurally, the creation of additional bureaucratic layers establishes vertical distance between the chief executive and his subordinates, placing the centers of political power further out of the military's reach. Aside from distance there is also direction. Procedures that ensure that the net flow of influence is from the top down, not the bottom up, will reinforce the executive's independence. Autonomy can also be increasingly codified into law. And functional auton-

---

76. Some scholars refer to veto points, which are "areas of institutional vulnerability where mobilization of opposition can thwart policy innovation." See Immergut, "The Rules of the Game," pp. 64–68.

77. James MacGregor Burns, *Leadership* (New York: Harper & Row, 1978), p. 376.

omy is enhanced through one brand of leadership known as democratic empowerment. Civilians are empowered when they equip themselves to deal knowledgeably and confidently about military affairs, something they must do if they are to increase their capacity for control.[78]

Combining these two institutional features produces the typology arrived at in Figure 2.1.

In quadrant A there are high levels of concentrated authority and autonomy. Policy can be designed and carried out more easily because there are fewer chances for it to be mired down in interpersonal, interbureaucratic squabbles. The armed forces will be less effective because it will have fewer intragovernmental divisions to exploit. Policy is unlikely to be deflected from course by forces outside of government because the decision makers are capable and sites are well insulated.

In quadrant B, each agency involved in the policy process is also relatively well insulated from military pressures. But central decision makers are either many or spread across two or more branches of government, complicating the quest for policy consensus. So here benefits to insularity will be to some extent offset by the dispersion of authority, producing moderate success rates.

In quadrant C there are fewer decision makers but each one is vulnerable

Fig. 2.1. Policy outcomes and institutional design

		Concentration of Authority	
		High	Low
		A. High Success	B. Moderate Success
Decision-Making Autonomy	High		
	Low	C. Moderate Success	D. No Success

78. Alfred Stepan, *Rethinking Military Politics: Brazil and the Southern Cone* (Princeton: Princeton University Press, 1988), pp. 33–145.

to outside influence. So here, too, a moderate level of success is predicted. And, finally, in quadrant D there are a significant number of decision points that must be navigated and ample opportunities for the opposition to make its presence known. Consequently, success is unlikely.

The theoretical framework developed here will enable us to resolve the puzzle as to why Argentine politicians who were grappling with military questions encountered significantly different levels of policy success across issue domains. The issues to be explored are human rights, military budgets, and defense reform. All of these matters go to the heart of contemporary civil-military affairs.

The human rights dilemma tended to be contentious and even explosive because all sides were so deeply affected by its outcomes. For soldiers accused of transgressions, nothing less than their military careers and freedom hung in the balance; for the families, some form of justice was needed to ease the suffering of loss; and for the politicians, a reasonable solution was sought to avert losing margins of political support and military cooperation simultaneously.[79] Thus, how or whether or not the human rights quandary would be resolved would impact decisively on the course of civil-military affairs.

The defense budget is the sine qua non of military corporate interests. Salaries, housing, operations, maintenance, training, and arms procurement depend on it. Sustaining or enlarging it is one of the central objectives of any military organization. "Changes in the size of the defense budget are a telling indicator of the political power and prestige of the armed forces," says Eric Nordlinger.[80] In the Third World the loss of budget shares has often been the prelude to military intervention.[81] While intervention is currently improbable in Argentina, budget decisions can still give rise to unwanted tensions and conflict.

And budget cutbacks can seriously harm military readiness if not accompanied by structural reform to foster greater efficiency, speed, and interservice cooperation. The need for reform in Argentina became especially evident in the wake of the Malvinas defeat, which exposed the military's fighting deficiencies. Yet many military officers have mixed feelings about transformations of this kind, fearing that they could cause them to lose perquisites and positions. Hence, the question of reform weighs heavily on politicians and soldiers alike.

79. For more on this, see David Pion-Berlin, "To Prosecute or to Pardon? Human Rights Decisions in the Latin American Southern Cone," *Human Rights Quarterly* 16 (February 1994): 105–30.
80. Nordlinger, *Soldiers in Politics*, pp. 68–71.
81. Ibid.

It is hypothesized that certain features of governmental, institutional design yield specific policy results. The higher the concentration of authority and decision-making autonomy, the more likely it is that civilian policymakers will see their military-related programs through to completion. The more dispersed the authority and the lower the autonomy, the less likely it is that civilians will prevail.

The expected findings are as follows. Budget-cutting endeavors should have met with great success because fiscal powers were centered within one ministry which itself was well insulated from external pressures (quadrant A). The human rights program should have been only moderately successful. On the one hand, the executive and judicial branches of government, in whose hands most of the human rights decisions rested, enjoyed considerable autonomy from the armed forces. On the other hand, the justice system had its own norms, rules of procedure, and agenda, making it less likely that the president's singular preferences would prevail (quadrant B). And genuine defense reform should not have gotten off the ground. The defense ministry, upon which the president must rely for knowledge and enforcement of policy, was a historically weak, nonautonomous institution unprepared to assume the new responsibilities suddenly thrust upon it. Chief executives failed to provide the ministry with effective leadership, thereby allowing authority to disperse to the separate service branches (quadrant D).

Methodology and Case Selection

Although its focus is mainly on Argentina, this book is more than a single-nation study. It is a controlled, comparative study in two senses. First, it is comparative because it cuts across three important, civil-military issue areas (already mentioned) to see if the central hypothesis will hold in each instance. Those issues were selected because each one corresponds to its own institutional site(s) of implementation. Those sites vary in concentrations of authority and decision-making autonomy, the two key independent variables in the study. Hence the policy-specific narratives found in Chapters 4 through 6 allow us to comparatively examine different institutional configurations within a single country.[82]

82. Issues are not the focus of this book; institutions are. Other policies could very well have substituted for the three chosen, so long as they served the same methodological cause: to produce data points for the various mixes of institutional autonomy and authority.

Unlike the traditional case study that relies on one observation of the independent and dependent variables, here several data points are produced on each. By observing different values (high or low) for the causal agents, it is easier to assert that institutions have some measurable impact on the dependent term, policy outcome (success or failure). Moreover, because that impact is measured against a single military establishment during a brief span of time, our research design controls against wide fluctuations in organizational attributes, preferences, and power. With built-in variance and control, this case study then can serve an explanatory and not just descriptive, exploratory, or heuristic purpose.[83]

This study is also cross-nationally comparative. It moves beyond Argentina to examine the impact of institutions on policy in two other Southern Cone states. While equal attention is not granted to Argentina's neighbors, the brief journey north to Uruguay and west to Chile should prove useful. It would expose our thesis to additional tests, this time in other country settings. The replication of the Argentine findings would strengthen the theory that institutional mediation shapes civil-military policy outcomes.

Because these three nations are all members of the same geographical subregion called the Southern Cone, are linked historically, and are broadly matched on a host of social-economic variables, they are often thought of as "most similar systems."[84] In a general sense they are, and it is against the backdrop of systemic commonality that the comparative nature of this study unfolds. But they are simultaneously different with respect to certain key political variables,[85] ones that could potentially aid and abet alternative hypotheses to our own.[86] If the impact of institutional mediation on civil-

83. Harry Eckstein, "Case Studies and Theory in Political Science," in *Handbook of Political Science*, ed. Fred Greenstein and Nelson W. Polsby, vol. 7 (Reading, Mass.: Addison-Wesley, 1975); Alexander L. George, "Case Studies and Theory Development: The Method of Structured, Focused Comparison," in *Diplomacy: New Approaches in History, Theory, and Policy*, ed. Paul Gordon Lauren (New York: The Free Press, 1979).

84. Others concur that these three countries share underlying socioeconomic structural features, causing them to be frequently lumped together. See Ruth Berins Collier and David Collier, *Shaping the Political Arena: Critical Junctures, the Labor Movement, and Regime Dynamics in Latin America* (Princeton: Princeton University Press, 1991), p. 14. The terminology "most similar systems" was coined by Adam Przeworski and Henry Teune in *The Logic of Comparative Inquiry* (New York: John Wiley, 1970).

85. Argentina, Chile, and Uruguay are neither inherently nor irrevocably alike or different; they converge or diverge depending upon the issues raised and the questions asked. On the adoption of a more flexible method that simultaneously observes similarities and differences, see Collier and Collier, *Shaping the Political Arena*, pp. 12–18.

86. See Theda Skocpol, "Emerging Agendas and Recurrent Strategies in Historical Sociology,"

military relations were to remain significant, despite the potentially con-
founding effect of other factors, then our central hypothesis would have been
strengthened.

Consequently, Uruguay and Chile were chosen as comparative cases precisely because they are also different and because those differences pose
rather difficult hurdles for an institutional thesis to clear. The difficulties are
twofold. First, both of these democracies were reborn only after civilians
made concessions to outgoing dictators. Many of the "rules of the game," so
to speak, were either stipulated by a military-drafted constitution (Chile) or
agreed to in direct negotiations between the politicians and the armed forces
(Uruguay). These founding conditions contrast sharply with those in Argentina, where following the total collapse of the *Proceso* dictatorship, the armed
forces were in no position to either ordain or transact the terms of democratic restoration. A rival theory would suggest that because the present is
firmly anchored in the past, today's civil-military policies are solely a function of historical antecedents. Since the circumstances surrounding regime
transition were substantially different in Uruguay and Chile than they were
in Argentina, we would not expect to turn up any unifying cause for policy
outcomes across these national boundaries.

Second, post-transitional levels of military power were considerably higher
in Uruguay and Chile than in Argentina. It could easily be maintained that
policies are determined not by institutional design but by the sheer exertion
of military will; pressure, not process, it might be argued, is the key to understanding why some policies advance while others founder. If the overall
balance of power favored the armed forces over civilian leaders, and if a
pressure-politics thesis could tell us all we needed to know, then institutional
arrangements should have been irrelevant. More precisely, the impact of military opposition to undesired policies should have had equally deleterious
consequences *from one decision site to the next*.[87] If that were so, then the
survival rate of controversial policies should have varied little from one
branch or agency of government to the next.

Was this indeed the case? Or were military pressures more or less effective,

---

in *Vision and Method in Historical Sociology*, ed. Theda Skocpol (Cambridge: Cambridge University
Press, 1984), p. 378.

87. After all, it was Chile's outgoing Pinochet regime that single-handedly wrote the 1980 constitution that defined the new, comprehensive rules of the game. Its intent was to reconfigure a future
democratic, political system to its liking. Legislative, judicial, and electoral regimes were revamped
to assure that the presence of the armed services would be felt everywhere. Military pressures should
have been somewhat less in the pacted democracy of Uruguay but nonetheless considerable and
uniform throughout the political system.

depending upon the institution? If in fact we find that military influence was unevenly exerted, due to the same or similar features of the institutional design as observed in Argentina, then we will have guarded against the rival thesis that policy results were whatever the armed forces wanted them to be.[88] The potential discovery, through cross-national comparison, that institutional arrangements matter *despite high levels of military power* takes on added significance because it represents both a stronger refutation of a pressure-politics thesis as well as a stronger confirmation of the institutional approach.[89]

88. Two scenarios are plausible. First, Chilean and Uruguayan civilian-led institutions could have been rendered completely irrelevant by informal military influence. Soldiers simply evaded institutional channels while utilizing their considerable powers to compel civilian leaders to abandon undesirable programs. Alternatively, rules were observed, but institutions were totally vulnerable to persistent and legal military pressure. Veto points were numerous, and executive attempts to push through objectionable policies were repeatedly confounded by the military's lobbyists or its political allies. The control feature of this design resides in the fact that levels of military power varied from low (Argentina) to moderately high (Uruguay) to very high (Chile). If the same causal relationship can be found cross-nationally between institutional design and policy outcome, then we can discount military power as a principal causal agent. Again, the choice of policy areas was critical only insofar as that choice permitted variation in the independent term.

89. If there are some institutional openings that civilian policymakers could exploit, even after beginnings as inauspicious as those found in Chile, then we would have discovered some semblance of civil-military normality in a place where it was least likely to be found. This possibility will be explored in Chapter 7.

CHAPTER 3

The Changing Political Landscape in Argentina

This chapter lays the foundations for the policy discussions that will follow by demonstrating that since the demise of the Argentine military regime known as the *Proceso* a newfound respect for democratic normality has emerged. This is true not just among the political class but within military and civil society as well. Politicians, soldiers, and citizens express their preferences and displeasures via democratic institutions. Institutional circumventions still do occur on occasion but with much less frequency than in the past.

A fundamental difference between the pre- and post-*Proceso* era is the shift in the civil-military focal point. Before, the politically weighty decisions were made between the military and societal interest groups. These contacts were informal, secretive, and injurious to the democratic regime. Now, the civil-military center of gravity has shifted from society to the state. Civil-military interaction now pivots around the activities of government officials and the armed forces *within state-centered arenas* (as subsequent chapters will explain). These contacts are formal, open, and largely respectful of the regime. What explains this turn of events? This is the question to be resolved here.

The evolution of civil-military collusion—first on behalf of democratization and then in opposition to it—will be briefly recounted. From there we turn to a discussion of the *Proceso* and its sobering effects on society and the armed forces itself. As a result of having lived through the political and economic horrors of that regime, the public's aversion toward authoritarianism has grown, as has its preference for democratic solutions. These attitudinal changes will be analyzed in the final section of the chapter.

Argentine Civil-Military Relations and Democratic Stability

It is difficult under any circumstances to speculate on the chances for a lengthy and stable period of democracy during which the armed forces are placed securely under the authority of elected officials; more so in the case of Argentina where democracy has often been a brief and unstable interlude between periods of military rule. From 1930 to 1976 the armed forces had cut short the tenure of every democratically elected head of state. The coup had become so familiar a practice in Argentina as to take on the appearance of normality. One noted scholar put it succinctly when he said, "nothing is more foreign to Argentina than anti-militarism."[1] If by militarism we mean the phenomenon whereby the progressive insertion of the armed forces into the political arena becomes regularized, widespread, and even socially accepted, then Argentina certainly qualified. No doubt it is a greater challenge to exorcise the demon of militarism from the body politic once society itself succumbs to it. As Alain Rouquié asserts, "it is in the whole society, in its divisions, its conflicts and contradictions where one must look for the origins of military power."[2]

During the late nineteenth and early twentieth centuries Argentine society underwent rapid change. The population of the country doubled between 1895 and 1914, as immigrants from Europe landed on its shores by the tens of thousands. Lured there by a buoyant economy expanding at more than 6 percent annually, these foreigners soon constituted a sizable proportion of the now rapidly growing, upwardly mobile, middle class. From the shopkeepers at its lower end to the professionals and public administrators at its upper

---

1. Alain Rouquié, *Poder militar y sociedad política en la Argentina* (Buenos Aires: Emecé Editores, 1982), 2: 342.
2. Ibid., p. 379.

end, this middle class was making impressive economic headway.[3] What it, along with the working class lacked, were rights of political representation.

Standing in their way was the collection of wealthy landowners, bankers, and investors known as the oligarchy. Through massive electoral fraud, Argentina's dominant social-political elites effectively disenfranchised the rest of society. To assure that its presidential and congressional candidates (all of whom were handpicked by the governors of the nation's fourteen provinces) would win, the oligarchy tampered with registration lists, intimidated opponents, and bribed those they couldn't scare into voting "correctly."[4]

Rather than participate in this charade, the Radical Civic Union Party (Unión Cívica Radical, UCR), which represented the rising middle class, ignited rebellions at the turn of the century in attempts to unseat the oligarchy from power and install a legitimate, popular, competitive democracy. In the cast of characters joined to these plots, the military played a supporting role only. Some of its members, whose families were of modest means and of immigrant status, were persuaded to go along. Inspired by civic ideals and led by civilian conspirators, they were, as the rebellious leader of the UCR, Hipólito Yrigoyen, had said, the "armed branch of [public] opinion."[5]

None of these rebellions succeeded in toppling the regime. The majority of officers still remained loyal or noncommittal, heeding the call of the oligarchy's National Autonomous Party to tend to their professional affairs while leaving the political and economic management of the country to the elites in power.[6] But they did generate pressures for change, finally compelling President Roque Sáenz Peña (himself elected fraudulently in 1910) to revamp the nation's electoral system in exchange for a UCR pledge to abandon its armed insurrections. The new law, passed in February 1912, established compulsory, universal male suffrage and put an end to systemic improprieties by ordering the secret ballot, by creating electoral rolls from military conscription lists, and by assigning custodial powers to the armed forces on election day.[7]

Yrigoyen was the first presidential candidate to benefit from this new, politically open system when he was freely and fairly elected president of

---

3. See David Rock, *Argentina, 1516–1987: From Spanish Colonization to Alfonsín* (Berkeley and Los Angeles: University of California Press, 1987), pp. 163–75.

4. Ibid., p. 184; Rouquié, *Poder militar*, 1: 62.

5. Rouquié, *Poder militar*, 1: 136.

6. Miguel Angel Scenna, *Los militares* (Buenos Aires: Editorial de Belgrano, 1980), p. 122.

7. D. Rock, *Argentina*, p. 189.

Argentina in 1916. The man who had once exhorted soldiers to revolt in the name of democracy now, as head of state, desired a more acquiescent military . . . acquiescent to him. At the time, the armed forces preferred to remain detached from political conflict. Since the beginning of the twentieth century they had turned inward, preoccupied as they were with the challenges of professionalization. A 1901 law moved the Argentine military from a private force dedicated to parochial causes to a more professional, national force committed to defending "la patria." Advances were made in recruitment, training, and the development of a hierarchical system of rank and promotions. Universal conscription was put in place, and commissions were granted to only those officers who had completed their course work at the military academy. Promotions to higher rank were predicated on graduation from superior war schools, while those who failed to make the grade were retired from the services.[8]

If soldiers were to concentrate on professional development, they could not enmesh themselves any further in rebellious activities. In 1905, months after the last in the series of ill-fated civil-military insurrections had taken place, an amendment to the original statute prohibited all commanders of troops from directly or indirectly participating in political activity.[9] But legal restrictions could not prevent them from being drawn into the political fray once Yrigoyen assumed power. The president never hesitated in using the armed forces to further his own partisan ends. When on some twenty occasions he sent federal authorities in to constitutionally seize control from provincial governments he disliked, the military were ordered to collaborate. And when in January 1991 a confrontation between striking workers and security forces turned violent, leaving the nation's capital paralyzed with fear, he sent the armed forces in to restore order.[10]

The armed forces were more professional now, and they resented their assignment to policelike functions. But they were even more deeply offended by the president's meddlesome tactics. In blatant disregard of standard military practice, Yrigoyen passed over senior officers eligible for promotion in favor of others who were less worthy but who had previously been denied ascension because of their participation in the UCR revolts. Despite the fact that many of those so favored had already been retired, the president not

---

8. Robert Potash, *The Army and Politics in Argentina, 1928–1945: Yrigoyen to Perón* (Stanford: Stanford University Press, 1969), pp. 2, 3.

9. Ibid., p. 9.

10. Rouquié, *Poder militar*, 1: 142–43, 151.

only reinstated these "revolutionaries" with full pensions but honored them for great service to the nation.[11]

Ironically, Yrigoyen's support for past military revolts came back to haunt him in 1930 during his second term in office, when he was overthrown by a military coup. This was the first successful coup led by professional soldiers. Argentine history turned an important page in 1930: one chapter had drawn to a close, another was about to begin. Before, a disenfranchised public had stood at the barrack doors, imploring the military to help it bring democracy to its nation. Now, that same military had turned against the democratic tide, storming the gates of the presidential palace and stripping the elected leader of all powers. Over the next half-century or more the armed forces would remain politically engaged, either as moderators, guardians, or rulers of the political system.

The 1930 coup, like those that would follow in the 1940s, 1950s, 1960s and 1970s, was, as Robert Potash noted, "much more than a military operation."[12] It was a result of the combined efforts of soldiers and civilians alike to bring down the regime. The instigators would probably not have proceeded were it not for the support of disgruntled conservatives, socialists, and even disaffected members of the Radical Party itself, especially since the military was not solidly aligned with them. In fact, General José Uriburu, who led the charge, had a devilish time stirring up unrest within the ranks and in the end could commit only 1,400 servicemen to the cause.[13] He quickly realized that with a divided military to contend with, his new government would not survive long without public backing. Fortunately for Uriburu there were enough civilians across the political spectrum who were sufficiently upset with Yrigoyen's assaults on provincial governments and his personalistic style of rule to make the coup attempt worth his while.

The military intervention of 1930 certainly differed in several respects from those carried out decades later. Most notably, the officers under Uriburu's command had no clear, unified notion of how they would govern, on behalf of what cause, or for how long. In contrast, the *golpistas* of 1966 and 1976 were committed ideologues determined to stay in power long enough to see their visions of a transformed society fulfilled. Whereas the military of the 1930s shamelessly sponsored bogus elections that denied entry to the Radical Party, the generals of the late 1960s and 1970s dispensed with the

11. Ibid., 1: 136; R. Potash, *The Army and Politics in Argentina, 1928–1945*, pp. 10–11.
12. R. Potash, *The Army and Politics in Argentina, 1928–1945*, p. 54.
13. A. Rouquié, *Poder militar*, 1: 197.

democratic veneer altogether by canceling elections, curbing or outlawing political party activity, and ruling via authoritarian means.

But all of these coups had one thing in common: they were societal in nature, launched only after some significant portion of the public had turned its back on the democratic regime while signaling its complacency with, if not outright support for, a praetorian intervention. The determination with which the military would trample upon constitutionality was always in proportion to society's eagerness to rid itself of its own governments.

Indeed, the episodic return to dictatorship has not been an unwelcome tradition in Argentina. That it has occurred so regularly without significant levels of public protest attests to the firm beliefs of numerous political and socioeconomic constituencies that they stood to gain from the abrupt transfer of power from democrats to despots. For them the coup represented the hope of a return to the past, a new beginning, or a form of sweet revenge against their political foes. They looked forward to the prospect of military rule.

The middle class that had so enthusiastically championed the democratic cause during the first part of the twentieth century rejoiced at the toppling of the freely elected government of Juan Perón (1946–55). Perón was a populist who built a huge political following upon an expanding labor union base. Although he promoted a sizable redistribution of national income toward poor wage earners, he did so while simultaneously stimulating economic growth, credit, and investment. The middle income sectors, it turned out, were miffed more by official corruption, press censorship, political harassment, and anticlericalism than they were by Perón's economic program.[14] The Radical Party gave voice to their concerns while welcoming in the new military regime that displaced Perón in September 1955.

Working-class followers of Peronism returned the favor in June 1966, when they stood behind the armed forces as they unseated the UCR government of Arturo Illia (1963–66).[15] In the eight years leading up to the coup the Radicals, along with other political parties, had been willing participants in what could charitably be referred to as a limited democracy. As the all-

---

14. William Ascher, *Scheming for the Poor: The Politics of Redistribution in Latin America* (Cambridge, Mass.: Harvard University Press, 1984), pp. 59–64; Potash, *The Army and Politics in Argentina, 1928–1945,* 170–71.

15. Says Guillermo O'Donnell, "the 1966 coup has the support of, at least the acquiescence of, a considerable part of the popular sector, and was endorsed by a majority of political and union leaders." See his *Bureaucratic-Authoritarianism: Argentina, 1966–1973, in Comparative Perspective* (Berkeley and Los Angeles: University of California Press, 1988), p. 40.

powerful arbiters of this new political system, the military had established a simple rule: elections could be held so long as Peronist candidates were proscribed from running. Illia had won the presidency under these restrictive terms. Peronists became deeply embittered by their exclusion and vengeful toward those who had risen to power at their expense. Without the wherewithal to compete electorally, they resorted to more combative forms of protest, calling on their working-class brethren to engage in widespread, disruptive labor practices. These actions eventually had the intended effect of destabilizing the Illia government just enough to draw in the armed forces, who were angered over the president's failure to deal firmly with labor's onslaught.[16]

Sometimes it was political leaders who brought on their own demise not only because of errors committed in handling the military but because of an unwillingness to build bridges and broad coalitions of support for their programs. Their policies became self-defeating, as would-be adherents turned away, withheld their cooperation, and ultimately defected from the legal process.[17] Soon there were calls for draconian political remedies.

Yrigoyen's blunders have already been mentioned. Perón's 1950 *Ley de Desacato*, which exacted unreasonable penalties for libel and slander against public officials, was designed with his Radical Party congressional opponents principally in mind. The law sent Ricardo Balbin, head of UCR, to prison for five years. Perón followed with a state of internal war under which he rounded up numerous political opponents.[18] These kinds of measures, along with reprisals against the Catholic Church and exhortations to his followers to commit violence, were finally too much for Argentina's middle sectors to take. They found ready allies within the navy and then the army who were willing to overthrow the great populist.

Arturo Frondizi (1958–62) hurt himself by making key foreign policy blunders, by weakening his political base, and by antagonizing his erstwhile Peronist allies, only to suddenly reverse course by allowing Peronists to compete for gubernatorial office, gambling that they would not win and that consequently the military would remain calm. He was wrong on both counts, and after refusing to annul the election results, the military deposed him in

---

16. Rock, *Argentina*, pp. 345–46; David Pion-Berlin, *The Ideology of State Terror: Economic Doctrine and Political Repression in Argentina and Peru* (Boulder, Colo.: Lynne Rienner Publishers, 1989), pp. 79–80.

17. An argument persuasively made by Gary Wynia in *Argentina in the Postwar Era: Economic Policymaking in a Divided Society* (Albuquerque: University of New Mexico Press, 1972).

18. Rock, *Argentina*, pp. 303, 306.

March 1962. Arturo Illia entered office with a weak mandate, having captured only 25 percent of the vote. But rather than broaden his support base once in office, he narrowed it with economic policies that discouraged agricultural investment and with political strategies aimed at dividing and then co-opting organized labor. And Isabel Perón's (1974–76) numerous blunders—her abandonment of the social pact and embrace of economically liberal solutions, her repression of union leaders, and her submission to the will of Lopez Rega and his ferocious campaign to liquidate "enemies" of the state—undoubtedly set the stage for the military coup of March 1976.[19]

But the fortunes of elected leaders would always deteriorate in step with the unraveling of political support for their governments. And so at the eleventh hour, as he held onto power by the barest of threads, Frondizi could not count on one single opposition party to go along with his last-minute maneuvers to save his administration.[20] As political officeholders would lose the public's confidence, the bond between soldiers and citizens would grow stronger. And as military-societal alliances were forged, military-government relations would worsen. At the end of this triangular "dance" it was usually the head of state who was left without a partner.

To the extent that these have not been mere singular occurrences, but patterns in Argentine political life, they are cause for concern. The more ingrained a behavior, the more it is replicated and the more difficult it is to unlearn. Each military coup makes the succeeding one that much easier to execute and to accept. A self-fulfilling prophecy is then created: citizens expect governments to fail and rather than rally to defend them, they withhold their support, thus ensuring that they do fail. It is the nation's history of democratic failure, despite its liberal traditions and its literate and cultured society, that has repeatedly captured the attention of scholars.

The country seems to have served as a prototype for a host of theories about democratic demise. Samuel Huntington pointed to Argentina when he argued that social mobilization in the face of politically petrified institutions would cause system overload, instability, and praetorianism.[21] Peter

---

19. On Frondizi, see Robert Potash, *The Army and Politics in Argentina, 1945–1962: Perón to Frondizi* (Stanford: Stanford University Press, 1980). On Illia, see Rock, *Argentina*, pp. 344–46, and Paul H. Lewis, *The Crisis of Argentine Capitalism* (Chapel Hill: University of North Carolina Press, 1990), pp. 280–81. On Isabel Perón, see Pion-Berlin, *The Ideology of State Terror*, pp. 82–89.

20. Frondizi agreed to form a coalition cabinet at the military's urging. But neither the rival UCRP nor the Progressive Democrats, Democratic Socialists, or Conservative Federation of Center Parties would serve. See Potash, *The Army and Politics in Argentina, 1945–1962*, p. 364.

21. Samuel Huntington, *Political Order in Changing Societies* (New Haven: Yale University Press, 1968), pp. 83–84.

Smith took issue with this theory, arguing that democracy failed, not because an accumulation of social demands outstripped the capacity of political institutions to deal with them, but because political elites failed to resolve problems that were inherently manageable, thus throwing the nation into cycles of crisis.[22] Guillermo O'Donnell had Argentina in mind when he wrote that with the ascendancy of populist classes and the shrinking of an import substitution industrialization (ISI) economy, a crisis would result that could only be resolved through authoritarian means.[23] And others have pronounced the imminent death of Argentine democracy due to the nation's deeply embedded culture of respect for "caudillismo."[24]

Once taken together, these studies of particular chapters in Argentine history tell a story of a nation that seems to be inflicted with incurable spells of violence, crisis, systemic breakdown, and dictatorship. But it is no longer clear how seriously ill the patient is or whether the affliction is in fact irreversible. Argentina is in the midst of a sustained recovery and may be less of a least likely case for democratic institutionalization than imagined. The reason could be found in the country's most recent bout with autocratic rule. The self-styled *Proceso de Reorganización Nacional* (PRN: 1976–83) was not simply the latest in a long line of Argentine dictatorships. The *Proceso* was different. It may have been one of those defining moments in a nation's history when virtually all sectors of society are so adversely affected that each is compelled to question his own age-old assumptions and practices.

Representing the accumulation of decades of frustration about grievances unattended, the *Proceso* went to political and economic extremes hitherto unwitnessed to "cleanse" the nation of its problems. Unprecedented levels of state terror directed at a cross-section of the population, coupled with sweeping economic changes that left industries and trade unions paralyzed, were primary features of this de facto regime. In its wake the *Proceso* left so many victims it is difficult indeed to find its beneficiaries. It widened public opposition to authoritarian forms of rule to an unparalleled degree. Although it would be going too far to claim that the cycle of military interventionism has been permanently broken, it may been handicapped by events in the recent past that have significantly raised the costs to praetorianism for

22. See Peter H. Smith, *Argentina and the Failure of Democracy: Conflict Among Political Elites, 1904–1955* (Madison: University of Wisconsin Press, 1974).

23. Guillermo O'Donnell, *Modernization and Bureaucratic-Authoritarianism: Studies in South American Politics* (Berkeley: Institute for International Studies, 1979).

24. As an example, see Susan Calvert and Peter Calvert, *Argentina: Political Culture and Instability* (Pittsburgh: University of Pittsburgh Press, 1989).

citizens and soldiers alike. What follows is an appraisal of those costs and their implications for civil-military relations.

The *Proceso*'s Legacy: The Civilian Effect

The *Proceso* has the ignominious distinction of having managed to alienate practically all of the Argentine people all of the time. While wage-earning sectors were decimated by the regime's version of neoliberal orthodoxy, landed elites, industrialists, and financiers were adversely affected as well. If blue-collar workers were disproportionately victimized by the state's security forces, businessmen, middle-class professionals, and other members of society were similarly shocked to find the regime's repressive policies unexpectedly directed against them too. We will review how the economic and human costs of authoritarianism were spread to the privileged sectors of Argentine society. Then we will examine the harm done to the military itself. The cumulative result of all this has been to disarm the pro-coup coalition between soldiers and citizens, strengthen civil society's support for democratic institutions, and diminish the military's desire for rule, thus permitting the normalization of civil-military relations.

The dictatorship was inaugurated on the morning of March 24, 1976, when Isabel Perón conceded the presidency to the military forces led by General Jorge Videla. The junta's opening proclamation seemed to forecast yet another period of prosperity for capital and misery for labor. It accused the previous Peronist government of "manifest irresponsibility in the management of the economy which had destroyed the productive apparatus."[25] Its mission would be to rebuild the economy by reducing state intervention, revitalizing competitive markets, and restoring investor confidence. The power of monopolistic, rent-seeking organizations such as organized labor would have to be diminished if these objectives were to be realized.

Not surprisingly, the organized working class suffered dreadfully under the junta's rule. Real wages declined by 32 percent in the first year and experienced practically no growth for the remainder of the *Proceso*, despite productivity increases of nearly 5 percent annually.[26] And the industrial, blue-collar

---

25. *Review of the River Plate*, May 31, 1976, p. 405.
26. Monica Peralta-Ramos, *The Political Economy of Argentina: Power and Class Since 1930* (Boulder, Colo.: Westview Press, 1992), p. 73.

work force shrank from 1.1 million in 1974 to 800,000 in 1981. One noted authority described these and other setbacks as "the most devastating reversal of its [working-class] position in the twentieth century."[27] These economic measures were buttressed by a salvo of repressive actions that stymied labor's resistance. Collective bargaining was suspended and strikes forbidden. Unions were ordered closed, assets were seized, elected leaders disqualified, and union membership made voluntary. The General Confederation of Labor (Confederacíon General de Trabajodores, CGT) was taken over and then in 1979 outlawed altogether, thus decapitating the movement.[28]

As it turned out, however, the economic burdens were not borne by the industrial working class alone. The costs of adjustment unexpectedly spread to other classes, sectors, and income groups. Industrialists and agrarian elites alike were repeatedly stunned by the twists and turns of economic policy undertaken without consultation and with little regard for their interests. A new and powerful entrepreneurial group did develop around financial capital. But it too was sucked into the vortex of economic ruin by state policies that resulted in the sudden collapse of major banks in 1980.

First of all, both labor and capital were penalized by a program that led to the "progressive destruction of the productive apparatus in the industrial sector."[29] The junta's "open" economy left Argentine producers completely vulnerable to international competition. From the across-the-board reductions in tariffs and import duties, to the elimination of subsidies on the importation of inputs, the military's program showed no mercy in its relentless attacks on domestic firms.[30] The lowering of tariffs allowed the Argentine market to be flooded with cheap imports, hitting hardest those firms with no access to foreign credit.

The results? Negative rates of industrial growth and an unprecedented 15 percent reduction in manufacturing establishments along with a 140 percent increase in bankruptcies between 1975 and 1980.[31] The decline did not limit itself to medium and small firms, since giant auto, iron, and steel industries experienced significant losses. Nor were losses restricted to domestic produc-

27. Peter Ranis, *Argentine Workers: Peronism and Contemporary Class Consciousness* (Pittsburgh: University of Pittsburgh Press, 1992), p. 37.

28. Pion-Berlin, *The Ideology of State Terror*, p. 116.

29. Victor E. Tokman, "Global Monetarism and Destruction of Industry," *CEPAL Review* 23 (August 1984): 109.

30. Tax exemptions on capital goods and two-tier exchange-rate systems that had traditionally permitted the importation of these same items at lower prices were eliminated, hurting key industrial sectors. See Peralta-Ramos, *The Political Economy of Argentina*, pp. 73–74.

31. Ibid., pp. 108, 110, 112.

ers. Foreign-owned, transnational corporations suffered a combined annual growth rate of negative 3.4 percent.[32]

As advertised, the neoliberal program was to have restored the pampa bourgeoisie to a preeminent, economic position. It started out that way, as the elimination of slaughtering quotas for meat producers and export taxes for wheat and cereal growers boosted exports by 22 percent annually. But a reversal of the exchange rate policy in December 1978 trimmed agriculture's largess. The economic minister, Dr. José Martínez de Hoz, decided to trail the rate of devaluation behind the domestic rate of inflation, in effect revaluing the currency. This would, in theory, provoke a convergence of domestic prices with international ones, as cheaper foreign products entered the Argentine market. But it would also cause export earnings to drop. By 1980 the volume of Argentina's grain exports had declined 28 percent from the previous year, while foreign sales of meat and fish fell 35 percent over the same period. Agricultural sector growth as a whole declined by 6.5 percent that same year.[33]

Even the financial sector, which had for a short time benefited from the neoliberal economic program, soon fell on hard times. In the spring of 1980 several large banks went under when they became saddled with insurmountable debts. By the fall of that year several others followed suit. Industries that were pushed to the wall by foreign competition borrowed funds but could not meet their repayment obligations, and their subsequent collapse left these banks in an untenable situation. The Central Bank was forced to audit or liquidate some sixty-two financial institutions that controlled 20 percent of all the nation's deposits.[34]

The dominant classes in Argentina had thrown their weight behind military coups before in hopes of establishing a strong regime that could withstand the assaults of the popular classes. This bureaucratic-authoritarian regime would, they expected, allow a coherent set of policies aimed at accumulating capital to emerge uninterrupted and unobstructed by popular protest while at the same time being responsive to the bourgeoisie's own needs. The state would disarm social and political groups that challenged the dominant economic project while remaining open to unofficial flows of influence from the privileged classes. It was thought that the state "moved in time with the upper fractions of the bourgeoisie," consequently limiting the regime's

32. Pion-Berlin, *The Ideology of State Terror*, p. 121.
33. Ibid., p. 189.
34. Peralta-Ramos, *The Political Economy of Argentina*, p. 81.

autonomy and ensuring that its policies adhere to the demands of the proper-tied elite.[35]

But the government was unresponsive to the specific complaints lodged by entrepreneurial representatives. The *Unión Industrial Argentina*, representing some of Argentina's largest industrial firms, pleaded with the government to enforce antidumping legislation to protect local business against unfair competitive practices of foreign corporations. Although such measures were finally approved, they came much too late for Argentine companies. The *Sociedad Rural Argentina*, representing the largest cattle ranchers and wheat growers in the nation (including the family of Martínez de Hoz), cited the exchange rate policy of December 1978 as a "great error," saying "urgent" corrective measures must be taken to forestall further economic decline.[36] None were. The *Confederación Rurales Argentina* explained to the economics minister the fact that interest rates (which were 98 percent in nominal terms and 26 percent in real terms by 1980) were prohibiting farmers from financ-ing the purchase of new equipment to raise yields and forcing many into debt and bankruptcy.[37] The minister responded with a ghastly logic: if there are those who are selling out, others must be buying. The high cost of bor-rowing will challenge the new owners to avoid the inefficiencies of the past.[38]

Despite repeated appeals for economic adjustments by representatives of the pampa bourgeoisie as well as medium and large industrial establishments, the regime remained intractable; it made no economic changes at the re-quest of interest groups or in conformance with their wishes. The most eco-nomically powerful groups in Argentine society quickly learned a universal truth: there is little accountability under authoritarian rule, and less still with a regime as autonomous and insular as this one.[39] Much like a heavy, inert object, the de facto regime would not be budged from the ground on which it stood—at least not by forces external to itself. The military had become impervious to societal pressures.[40] The dictatorship showed its dark

35. Guillermo O'Donnell, "State and Alliances in Argentina, 1956–1976," *Journal of Develop-ment Studies* 15 (October 1978): 25.

36. Sociedad Rural Argentina, *Boletín de la Sociedad Rural Argentina* 469 (April 15, 1981): 2, 3.

37. Pion-Berlin, *The Ideology of State Terror*, p. 190.

38. *Latin American Economic Report*, October 26, 1979, p. 42.

39. See William C. Smith, *Authoritarianism and the Crisis of the Argentine Political Economy* (Stan-ford: Stanford University Press, 1989), p. 262.

40. The economics minister had promised the private sector early on that his administration would not veer from its original plan. Initially the bourgeoisie was all smiles, but ironically it was precisely that commitment to stay the course that later revealed to them the inherent dangers of authoritarian rule. It is far easier for powerful social classes to set the armed forces loose against weak civilian leaders than it is to rein them in.

side when it turned its back on the entrepreneurial class.[41] The business community's sense of betrayal ran deep, and many of its members came to believe that their interests could no longer be left unguarded at the doorstep of the military. They now preferred a politically more open system, one susceptible to influence.[42]

There is another reason why the business community and the propertied classes in general may prefer democracy to dictatorship. Evidence compiled by the Argentine National Commission on the Disappeared (CONADEP) details a pattern of repression that was widespread and that crossed over socioeconomic lines.[43] Members of the propertied classes soon discovered to their utter horror that they were not immune from state-sanctioned terror. Their sense of vulnerability, their loss of personal security were every bit as unnerving to them as they were to members of the wage-earning sectors.

As time elapsed the regime seemed increasingly capricious in its assaults on individual freedoms. What began as a seemingly well-directed attack on armed insurgents and trade unionists quickly degenerated into a vaguely defined witch hunt for "subversive" agents of all stripes. This could have explained why the state's *Dirty War* extended to middle- and upper-class as well as working-class neighborhoods.

But a more concrete motivation was at work as well. The commission, which took 7,380 depositions from families of the disappeared, described official looting of victim residences as a "modus operandi," a normal part of the terror process.[44] Eyewitnesses recounted work teams that abducted their victims and ransacked their homes, carting away entire households of possessions and unloading their enormous war booty into huge army vans waiting outside. With an insatiable thirst for state-sanctioned theft, these special forces would increasingly attack families with financial means.[45]

Other practices were less commonplace but equally disturbing. Members of the navy were not satisfied simply with the confiscation of household belongings; they wanted the homes themselves. They went so far as to establish an agency charged with rebuilding and readying for sale homes that were

41. Key economic groups were "deprived of an autonomous voice" by the *Proceso* regime, according to William C. Smith, *Authoritarianism*, p. 263.

42. This was made apparent in a poll taken in August 1985, indicating a substantial erosion of support for the military and for military intervention within the upper class. See *Latin America Weekly Report*, August 16, 1985, p. 10.

43. Argentine National Commission on the Disappeared, *Nunca Más: Report of the Argentine National Commission on the Disappeared* (New York: Farrar, Straus & Giroux, 1986).

44. Ibid., p. 271.

45. Ibid., pp. 272–83.

partially damaged during abduction raids. Once imprisoned, the owners of those homes would be forced to sign over powers of attorney authorizing the sale of their property to military families. Where former occupants had been executed, the military would regularly forge titles, deeds, and other documents necessary to establish a transfer of ownership from middle- and upper-class victims to military beneficiaries.[46]

Political repression had become a big business for some members of the military. Tearing out a page from the guerrilla group known as the *Montoneros,* officers began to kidnap Argentine entrepreneurs for personal gain. Jacobo Timmerman, the famed Argentine journalist and editor of *La Opinión,* witnessed the torture of Dr. Rafael Andrés Perrotta, the director-owner of *El Cronista Comercial* (another well-respected Argentine daily) who had been held by the authorities for a large ransom. In other instances soldiers would extort money by intervening in the legitimate sale of an enterprise. Typically, the sellers were either secretly imprisoned or forced to flee the country. The buyers were then required to deposit their money in a vendor's account at a bank. At the point of transfer the authorities would move in to confiscate the funds, claiming the sale was invalid because it had been "discovered" that the sellers were engaged in subversive activity.[47]

If there is a civilian effect to the *Proceso,* it is that its terrible blunders and unspeakable atrocities may have ironically strengthened the democratic process. The *Proceso* stands as a stark reminder to the public, and to the privileged, propertied sectors in particular, of what can happen should it again place its faith in despotic solutions to problems. Rather than freezing into position past behaviors, the experience of authoritarian rule has transformed them.[48] Citizens, frightened by the prospects of an authoritarian revisitation, have eschewed extremist solutions, moved to the political center, toned down the rhetoric, and learned to play by the institutional rules of the game.

The *Proceso*'s Legacy: The Military Effect

At the time of the transition a profound gulf separated the armed forces from society. Military incompetence, self-aggrandizement, and repression in office

---

46. Ibid., pp. 270–71, 281.
47. Ibid., pp. 274–75, 281.
48. Karen Remmer, "Redemocratization and the Impact of Authoritarian Rule in Latin America," *Comparative Politics* 17 (April 1985): 253–75.

contributed to an unprecedented repudiation of the profession at the hands of civil society. The military found itself discredited by and ostracized from the larger Argentine community to a degree not previously experienced. The public's moral repudiation of and disgust for the illicit practices of the Argentine armed forces rebounded back into the barracks to bruise the military's self-image.[49] But the armed forces had brought on this identity crisis themselves, through their connivance with regime policies.[50] Now, many officers would prefer to disassociate themselves from the practices of the past.

The failed policies and immoral conduct of the 1976 to 1983 military government directly harmed the military institution itself. Military stature, unity, and self-confidence declined measurably in Argentina by the time power was transferred to civilian hands. There were military, ethical, and political components to the crisis afflicting the armed forces. Among the military elements, the most outstanding was the Malvinas defeat itself.[51] Vanquished armies are always haunted and traumatized by the ghosts of defeat. The nation and its men in arms had to endure the embarrassing revelations of deficient, improvisational, and error-ridden military conduct as critically recounted by young combatants who fought in the Malvinas. The measures taken by the high command of the army immediately following war's end did nothing to calm the "spirits." After having been imprisoned by the English, the returning junior officers and soldiers were treated very poorly and, for all practical purposes, quarantined by their superiors. More serious still, nothing was done to analyze and evaluate the war experience. Instead of trying to extract lessons through a genuine examination of the conflict, army leaders reviewed the facts superficially. And rather than propose profound changes in military structure and behavior, their solutions were cosmetic, designed to protect the institution's image.[52]

49. Studies of modern democratic societies find that military institutions must be "sensitive and responsive to the values and perceptions of society" or risk a loss of legitimacy. See Sam Sarkesian, *Beyond the Battlefield: The New Military Professionalism* (New York: Pergamon Press, 1981), p. 90. Where congruence between military and societal values breaks down, as it did in the United States during the Vietnam War, the armed forces lose their sense of purpose and hence find it more difficult to deploy themselves effectively. It seems plausible that military behavior must conform to certain minimal societal norms even in a militarized, Third World country such as Argentina.

50. On public repudiation of the military in Argentina, see *Latin America Weekly Report*, August 16, 1985, p. 10, and Walter Little, "Civil-Military Relations in Contemporary Argentina," *Government and Opposition* 19 (Spring 1984): 207–24. On the crisis of military identity, see David Pion-Berlin and Ernesto López, "A House Divided: Crisis, Cleavage, and Conflict in the Argentine Army," in *The New Argentine Democracy: The Search for a Successful Formula*, ed. Edward Epstein (Westport: Praeger Publishers, 1992), pp. 69–73.

51. This section borrows from Pion-Berlin and López, "A House Divided," pp. 69–73.

52. Ibid., p. 71; Ernesto López, *El último levantamiento* (Buenos Aires: Editorial Legasa, 1988), pp. 23–24.

The ethical components to the crisis, which grew out of the military's participation in the *Dirty War*, were twofold: economic improprieties and human rights violations. The previously mentioned seizure of victims' personal belongings during their abduction came to symbolize how far the armed forces had slid from their obligations to serve the fatherland to the practice of serving themselves. This professional moral decay was underscored by the fact that officers of every rank engaged in economically exploitative practices.

No military ethical standard could have escaped unscathed from the infinite barbarism portrayed by the inhumane treatment of political prisoners. This unspeakable practice included the torture, disappearance, and assassination of detainees and the stealing of their children. Originally, the military took no responsibility for specific violations of human rights. In its final political document released to the public in April 1983, the military argued that while regrettably some excesses had been committed, these were inevitable—indeed pardonable—under the "nearly apocalyptic" battlefield conditions of the countersubversive war.[53] But in 1995 those justifications gave way to startling admissions of wrongdoing. Revelations of misdeeds by underlings led senior commanders to acknowledge that their services committed legally and morally unacceptable horrors. The army chief went furthest, saying that both those who gave the orders *and* those who followed them were delinquent.[54] This mea culpa reflects just how much the armed forces felt pressured to come to terms with their own disreputable past.

The political facets of the crisis were several. First, the thorough mismanagement of the war effort itself left a nagging political question in the minds of Argentine soldiers: Had the junta, under General Galtieri's leadership, responded to a historical dispute with Great Britain or to its own political needs? Aside from the unsettling suspicion that they had been mere instruments of the political appetite of the generals and admirals, the officers had to contemplate a series of contradictions: that they had fought against NATO and at the same time endorsed an economic policy of openness and subordination to the powers of the Western world; and that they had performed an act of service for the United States in Bolivia and Central America only to discover at the moment of truth that Washington had placed its bets with its principal West European ally.

Second, the political failures of the *Proceso* itself contributed to the decline in military self-confidence. The *Proceso* represented the last link in a

---

53. *La Nación*, April 29, 1983, pp. 13–14.
54. *La Clarín Edición Internacional*, May 2–May 8, 1995, pp. 6–7.

chain of military interventions characterized by the recurrent absence of success. The messianic images and promises that accompanied the military intervention in the end failed to deliver any credible results. Should performance be ruled unsatisfactory—even within the biased set of indicators chosen by the regime itself—this will weaken the confidence of the ruling coalition, promote divisions within the ranks of the military, and dissuade officers from engaging in future conspiratorial activities. The junta's policy failures and its loss of faith in its programmatic objectives did just that.[55]

Fissures that had been nearly invisible during the first phase of the *Proceso* surfaced as the regime neared its end. Each new cleavage cast a new, disturbing light on an organization torn by conflict and self-doubt, and contributed to its own loss of power. Fault lines seemed to run in several directions. The politically conservative, economically liberal officers behind General Leopoldo Galtieri feuded with the politically moderate, economically nationalist supporters of General and then President Roberto Viola. The struggle culminated when the Galtieri forces ousted Viola in a palace coup on December 11, 1981.[56] The changing of the guard did nothing to reunite the armed forces, and in fact only exposed the bitter internal power struggle that had been going on for months prior to the coup. Galtieri's plunge into war with the British four months later was a desperate act designed to reunify a badly split institution.

But with defeat in the Malvinas War, unity would continue to elude the military. This was best symbolized by the refusal of the air force or navy to join the postwar government of army general Reynaldo Bignone. Once abandoned, Bignone could do little more than schedule elections according to a timetable proposed by the democratic, multiparty coalition.[57] Later still, after the transfer of power to civilian hands, it would be horizontal divisions between rank that would prove to be decisive as well as destructive. This was brought most prominently into public view with the *Semana Santa* uprising of April 1987.

In sum, the *Proceso* shattered the confidence, self-image, and unity of the Argentine armed services. Although it has since made something of an institutional recovery, the military is unlikely any time soon to contemplate a

55. See Pion-Berlin and López, "A House Divided," pp. 71–72.

56. On these internal regime squabbles, see David Pion-Berlin, "The Fall of Military Rule in Argentina: 1976–1983," *Journal of Interamerican Studies and World Affairs* 27 (Summer 1985): 64–68.

57. David Pion-Berlin, "Military Breakdown and Redemocratization in Argentina," in *Liberalization and Redemocratization in Latin America*, ed. George A. Lopez and Michael Stohl (Westport: Greenwood Press, 1987), p. 222.

return to rule, having fallen so far from grace. Anxious to protect themselves from the divisive and corrosive influences of political office, most professional soldiers have since practiced coup avoidance. Remembrances of the past have, to date, inoculated the military against the temptation to reintervene. Still, there is a distinction to be made between coup avoidance and support for democratic procedure. While the military as a whole had renounced direct intervention, some officers within the army continued to exceed the law to air their grievances (see below). These soldiers were slower to fully conform to institutional protocol, although since the end of 1990 they have.

The New Democracy in Argentina

Authoritarian failures may provide auspicious beginnings for electoral regimes. Ultimately, however, democracy must win on its own terms. Public attitudes, behavior, and voting must reflect a newfound and solidly rooted respect for competitive rules and an avoidance of subversive tactics even under the worst economic conditions. To what extent has this political learning taken place in Argentina? And how does it shape the new civil-military relation?

The General Electorate

The Argentine voting public has maintained a steady distinction between the efficacy of public policy and the legitimacy of democratic institutions. Policy wise, Argentines had much to complain about under Alfonsín. With the exception of a brief period between June 1985 and March 1986, the economic news was not good. The president's *Plan Austral* had raised expectations of an economic breakthrough, but never delivered. Despite several "corrections" in the plan, consumer prices continued to accelerate, real wages declined, purchasing power eroded, the fiscal deficit worsened, economic growth declined, and unemployment grew.[58] Average monthly inflation, which was 7 percent in January 1987, rose to 150.4 percent in June

58. William C. Smith, "Hyperinflation, Macroeconomic Instability, and Neoliberal Restructuring in Democratic Argentina," in *The New Argentine Democracy: The Search for a Successful Formula*, ed. Edward C. Epstein (Westport: Praeger Publishers, 1992), pp. 27–41.

1989—Alfonsín's final month in office.[59] These results were quite dismaying to a public that, according to every poll conducted, considered inflationary control to be a pressing priority of the nation.[60]

Expectations ran high on the eve of the democratic rebirth, when the public anticipated a future free from political and economic instability. A majority (66 percent) were optimistic when asked about the general state of affairs in the country in May 1984. But by June 1988, after three years of *Plan Austral*, 74 percent disagreed with the notion that things were getting better.[61] Expressions of personal discontent regarding economic fortunes rose steadily during the democratic period as well. Those who thought their own financial situation had deteriorated from the year before increased from 26 percent in May 1984 to 62 percent in June 1988.[62]

Traditionally, indicators such as these are important because they signal frustration that if deeply felt and widespread enough could precipitate social unrest, violence, and calls for regime change. However, Alfonsín's economic failures did not translate into doubts about the democratic regime but only about the policies and those who made them. Between 1984 and 1988 no more than 4 percent of those polled believed the government was solving the nation's economic problems. In the year before Alfonsín's departure only 22 percent believed that the government, if given the time, could correct these deficiencies.[63] The president's own standing with the public had declined as well. In 1989 hyperinflationary price movements wreaked havoc on family budgets, creating enormous feelings of anxiety about the future. But the public vented its displeasure at the polls by voting the Radicals out of office in May.

Despite systemic as well as personal economic misfortunes, public support for a competitive and participatory democracy was unflinching. In May 1984, 83 percent agreed that the best political system was one based on periodic elections. By 1988, with inflation running at 343 percent by year's end, with the fiscal deficit at 10 percent of GDP,[64] and with unemployment in the Buenos Aires area having increased to a record level of 14 percent (from 8.6

---

59. Ibid., p. 38.
60. See Edgardo Catterberg, *Los Argentinos frente a la política: Cultura política y opinión pública en la transición Argentina a la democracia* (Buenos Aires: Planeta, 1989), p. 44.
61. Ibid., p. 52.
62. Ibid., p. 48.
63. Ibid., p. 45.
64. World Bank, *Argentina: From Insolvency to Growth* (Washington, D.C.: World Bank, 1993), pp. 329, 291.

percent in 1984),[65] still 79 percent of those polled supported democracy over all other alternatives.[66] A solid majority disagreed with the notion that democracy is dangerous because it can breed disorder. Public dissatisfaction with governmental performance never spilled over into doubts about the democratic regime as it had in the past. With regime legitimacy no longer in doubt, there was not then and is not to date any foundation for civil-military collusion against elected officials.

Conservative Elites

Within the general electorate the political right has, since 1930, cast its lot with tyranny. In that year a coalition of mainly conservative parties representing landed and industrial interests, called the *Concordancia*, threw its support behind the military coup against the government of Hipólito Yrigoyen. Seventeen months later it backed the candidacy of General Agustín P. Justo, who prevailed in an election held under a state of siege, with strict exclusions for Argentina's then most popular party, the UCR. Anxious to regain the political clout it had lost since 1916, the political right and the oligarchy suppressed any discomfort they may have felt with such electoral irregularities. For decades hence they would support political practices that would either make a mockery of democratic procedures or that would dispense with such procedures altogether.

Argentine conservatives of a free-market persuasion time and time again had offered their technocratic services to despotic regimes, believing that the military would provide the coercive backing needed to implant their vision of an open economy liberated from state interference. But with the 1966 *Revolución Argentina* and again with the 1976 *Proceso* they were dismayed to find that the state's role in the economy had expanded.[67] Their military partners in power often embraced market doctrine on a rhetorical level while reneging on those very principles in practice. Finally the lesson born from this betrayal seems to have been learned by the Argentine right, resulting in a "profound conservative disenchantment with the armed forces as political ally."[68]

As a result, politically conservative, economically liberal elites have made

---

65. Smith, "Hyperinflation, Macroeconomic Instability and Neoliberal Restructuring," p. 32.

66. Catterberg, *Los Argentinos frente a la política*, p. 64.

67. Edward L. Gibson, "Democracy and the New Electoral Right in Argentina," *Journal of Interamerican Studies and World Affairs* 32 (Fall 1990): 190–91.

68. Ibid., p. 185.

a concerted effort to distance themselves, politically and philosophically, from the military regimes they once faithfully served. They have reunited behind an effort to promote free-market economics through democratic means. Says Edward Gibson:

> If *liberalismo* was to regain its influence in Argentine democratic politics, a new political project was needed, one which unambiguously renounced the failed paths of liberal-military coalitions and made clear to the Argentine public the distinction between the *liberales en el gobierno* of the past, and the proposals of the argentine liberalismo in the new age of democratic politics.[69]

In this new age the right has discovered some of the advantages of political openness. Its ideas flow easily and are widely disseminated through the public domain. State shrinkage, privatization, deficit reduction, and market competitiveness—concepts held dear by the right—are now common currency in the television and print media. It has also achieved unprecedented recognition within policymaking circles as well. The Peronist administration not only embraced "liberalismo" but invited its leading advocate, Alvaro Alsogaray, to be its chief policy advisor. Alsogaray accepted the invitation and in doing so placed himself and fellow technocrats from the *Unión del Centro Democrático* (UCD)—Argentina's largest conservative party—in a historic alliance with the once national populist party. These are strange bedfellows to be sure, but their relation is one that has borne fruit for conservatives.

Neither the UCD nor any other conservative political party has yet to generate enough mass voter support to become a contender to the throne. The Peronist and Radical parties have dominated the field, while the UCD's fortunes at the voting booth have waned. But at the elite level the UCD has scored a victory: its ideas have found expression in the policies of state, its interests defended at the highest levels. The commitment of recent democratic governments to economic solutions favored by the right seems solid and genuine. The betrayal of such ideals by de facto regimes of the past stands in sharp contrast with current policy and serves as a reminder to conservative voters that their lot may be better protected under democratic auspices.

69. Ibid., p. 192.

Trade Unions

Since the exile of Perón in 1955 organized labor has always been at the forefront of social and political agitation against incumbents. Trade unionists assumed the mantle of leadership within the Peronist movement once prohibitions on political party activities were imposed. As discussed earlier, they provided the organizational muscle for a movement that had lost its right to participate in the political process. For example, the *Plan de Lucha* (battle plan) launched by the *Confederación General de Trabajadores* (CGT) in 1964 embodied a well-coordinated, simultaneous occupation of 1,436 work places. More than an attempt to address economic grievances, the plan was "aimed at creating a climate of disorder that would help bring about a coup," argues Guillermo O'Donnell.[70] Eventually it did just that.

Labor would resort to all means necessary—up to and including the use of violence—to bring about favorable economic conditions and a return to power of Peronism. If such actions helped precipitate military coups, so be it; labor showed no remorse. Defense of democracy was not their priority; gaining economic and political advantage was.

Undoubtedly, workers were enormously sobered by the horrors of the *Proceso*. They realized that the demise of constitutional regimes could also mean the demise of organized labor itself. The narrow pursuit of trade union interests was no longer worth any price. Accordingly, labor attitudes have changed in profound ways since the fall of the dictatorship.

A 1985 to 1986 survey of rank-and-file workers in the largest unions in and around Buenos Aires found a deep-seated preference for democratic, pluralist forms of government.[71] Although workers were "extremely critical of the socio-economic policies of the Radical Government," to which they directly attributed their fall in living standards and loss of income shares, they remained "very appreciative of being given the right to give full voice to their opposition."[72] Peter Ranis, the author of this study, adds: "Despite the decline of purchasing power among the working class under Alfonsín,

labor prefers democracy

---

70. O'Donnell, *Bureaucratic-Authoritarianism*, p. 48.

71. The survey sampled the opinions of 110 rank-and-file workers from seven of the largest unions in Greater Buenos Aires—those seven comprising 46 percent of all organized workers in the country. See Peter Ranis, *Argentine Workers: Peronism and Contemporary Class Consciousness* (Pittsburgh: University of Pittsburgh Press, 1992), p. 11.

72. See ibid., p. 198. Real wages in Argentina declined by 26 percent from 1984 to 1988, while labor productivity had actually increased in the industrial sector by 8 percent during the same time period. See Smith, "Hyperinflation, Macroeconomic Instability, and Neoliberal Restructuring," p. 53. Income distribution, which turned sharply against the wage-earning sector during the *Proceso*, did not recover under Alfonsín. See Ranis, *Argentine Workers*, p. 54.

despite the deterioration of public services, poor retirement benefits, the lack of improvement in educational and medical services, and the stagnation of social welfare coverage, the workers strongly endorsed the democracy that Alfonsín's government restored."[73]

Within the working class, democracy is not simply a means toward a social-economic end. Ranis finds that "workers value democracy as a good in and of itself without any direct manifestation in specific social policies."[74] For the worker, democracy guarantees him a personal freedom that cannot be traded for social or economic gain. Nor is there any confusion concerning what he means by democracy. The unionist defines democratic practice in narrow political terms, not social terms. Moreover, those surveyed overwhelmingly favored democracy (68.3 percent) over populist (16.7 percent), socialist (5.0 percent), or military (3.3 percent) forms of governance.[75] Ranis's results seem to dispel the notion that authoritarian currents still run deep within the working class or that workers have an affinity for military leadership. To the contrary, most laborers professed strong, antimilitary sentiment. No group, including landowners and businessmen, received more negative ratings from laborers and employees than did the armed forces.[76]

It is difficult to know whether these prodemocratic attitudes among the rank and file explain why labor has been markedly less combative in recent years than before. Although attitudinal adjustments matter, undoubtedly the pragmatic calculations of union leaders come into play. Argentine trade union leaders are opportunistic and will invariably choose those strategies that can best maximize their personal power, taking stock of government and rank-and-file reactions.[77] In large measure labor has opted for negotiation and conciliation because disruption has simply not worked. Under the militant leadership of Saúl Ubaldini, labor called thirteen general strikes during the Alfonsín presidency—four in 1986 alone. Yet a badly divided labor movement never threw its weight solidly behind these stoppages. Many of them were poorly attended, and none of them succeeded in changing the Radical government's course.[78]

---

73. Ranis, *Argentine Workers*, p. 205.
74. Ibid., p. 204.
75. Six percent had no preference (ibid., p. 152).
76. Ibid., p. 136.
77. See Edward C. Epstein, "Labor-State Conflict in the New Argentine Democracy: Parties, Union Factions, and Power Maximizing," *The New Argentine Democracy: The Search for a Successful Formula*, ed. Edward C. Epstein (Westport: Praeger Publishers, 1992), pp. 124–56.
78. James W. McGuire, "Union Political Tactics and Democratic Consolidation in Alfonsín's Argentina, 1983–1989," *Latin American Research Review* 27, no. 1 (1992): 46.

With the coming to power of Carlos Menem, the combative wing of labor was decimated. Menem engineered the displacement of Ubaldini from the CGT Azopardo while reuniting labor under a leadership that would go along with his harsh, neoliberal economic program.[79] To date, the "collaborationists" have prevailed, and a more compliant labor movement has absorbed the costs of austerity without a fight. Whatever the underlying motivation for compliance may be, the effect on the democracy has been beneficial. Elected officials are no longer traumatized by the prospect of losing control to an unforgiving labor movement. Neither are they haunted by the vision of a breakdown of public order that often accompanies persistent labor agitation. Whether actual or perceived, such a breakdown would assuredly foster doubts about their governing skills and invite calls for an authoritarian revisitation. In the current climate of relative stability such calls have not been made.

Political Parties

The frailties of the Argentine political party system are many, but there is one that protrudes prominently: democratic infidelity.[80] Political parties are disloyal to democracy when they are willing to defect from the competitive political game—even temporarily—to explore other options for achieving power, up to and including the military coup.[81] When the political organizations in the opposition forsake the rules of the game, the seeds of democratic destruction are sown.[82] Unfortunately, this has occurred all too often in Argentine history, as Peter Snow and Luigi Manzetti state: "Throughout this century, the parties out of power in Argentina concentrated much of their energies on convincing the general public, and especially the leaders of the armed forces, that the current administration lacked legitimacy and thus had no right to govern."[83]

As discussed above, numerous political organizations and leaders across the ideological spectrum have participated in the betrayal of democratically elected administrations. Parties and their opponents have frequently traded places—as each one takes its turn to discredit the government in power. Political parties are especially willing to engage in this unscrupulous behavior

79. See Epstein, "Labor-State Conflict," pp. 142–45.
80. On the various defects in the Argentine political party system, see Peter G. Snow and Luigi Manzetti, *Political Forces in Argentina*, 3d ed. (Westport: Praeger Publishers, 1993), pp. 76–86.
81. Ibid., p. 81.
82. See Juan Linz and Alfred Stepan, *The Breakdown of Democratic Regimes: Crisis, Breakdown, and Reequilibration* (Baltimore: The Johns Hopkins University Press, 1978).
83. Snow and Manzetti, *Political Forces in Argentina*, p. 82.

because they have less vested in the institutional process itself. The primary function of Argentine parties has always been to mobilize voters, not to govern or to influence the governing process.[84] Decision making has been the province of powerful chief executives and their advisors, who often ignore party platforms, principles, and politicians. Legislative representatives have not played an influential role, either, because historically the Argentine Congress has been a weak institution.

Here, too, change is under foot. Party disloyalty has declined—a trend that can be traced to the historic agreement between Juan Perón and Ricardo Balbin in 1970. Called the "Hour of the People," this accord signaled a commitment to end the mutual acrimony, disrespect, and suspicion that had for decades poisoned relations between Argentina's two principal parties.[85] With the restoration of democracy in 1983, the trend continued. The Radical Party's stunning defeat of the Peronists that year was its first in a totally unrestricted election. The legitimacy of the contest and the margin of victory meant that the Peronists could not and would not cry foul, however crushing a defeat it might have been for them. Nor would the Radicals take issue with the Justicialist's clean, commanding victories that followed in 1989 and again in 1995.

In each instance the losers have not only respected the outcomes but have continued to work—and at times even collaborate—within the system. Witness the extraordinary success Alfonsín had in steering his legislation through the Congress. According to one study, Radical and Peronist legislators cooperated to approve some 65 percent of executive bills, not to mention 89 percent of all bills that came to the floor for a vote.[86] More recently, the two parties put aside their differences to endorse important amendments to the constitution later approved by the Argentine electorate. Included among these is a provision that would subject the authors of coups to charges of treason (the penalty being life imprisonment) and deny them the right to be pardoned for their crimes.[87]

On substantive grounds the parties disagree. But on procedural grounds they concur that democratic methods must be respected, defended, and employed. Perhaps no greater test of party loyalty can be found than that which manifests itself when the regime is perceived to be under siege. That oc-

---

84. Ronald H. McDonald and J. Mark Ruhl, *Party Politics and Elections in Latin America* (Boulder, Colo.: Westview Press, 1989), p. 153.

85. Snow and Manzetti, *Political Forces in Argentina*, p. 60.

86. Ibid., p. 83.

87. *Latin American Special Report*, February 1995, p. 11.

curred in April 1987, in the midst of the first of several military uprisings. As will be shown, affirmations of solidarity with the democratic system were widespread, extending far beyond the political parties themselves.

The *Semana Santa* Rebellion

During Holy Week (*Semana Santa*) of April 1987, Lieutenant Colonel Aldo Rico and a group of army co-conspirators barricaded themselves inside the *Campo de Mayo* military base in apparent protest against the continued prosecution of active officers for human rights abuses committed during the Dirty War.[88] The military rebels, who were called *carapintadas* (so named for the camouflage paint they smeared on their faces), faced no resistance from other soldiers, who sympathized with their demand for an end to the trials and for the resignation of General Ríos Ereñú, Alfonsín's trusted chief of staff.[89] Rico gambled that the government would not or could not suppress the rebellion. As it turned out, he was proven right, as orders issued by the second army corps chief to surround the base were ignored by his subordinates. Some troops moved hesitantly toward *Campo de Mayo* but once there refused to fire on the rebels.

These mutinous acts, which were described by the participants as purely internal matters of the military, had a way of quickly spilling onto the political playing field, causing fears of another military coup. While Rico insisted his efforts were not aimed at destabilizing the regime, his call for the removal of General Ríos Ereñú was an attack on the civilian authorities themselves. And even if the rebels had no immediate intention of overturning the government, a victory here could set the stage for more adventurous plots later on. So the authorities took the incident quite seriously, as did the society at large.

Evidence of public repudiation of this military action was everywhere. Upon hearing of Rico's rebellion, thousands of citizens immediately gathered outside the *Campo de Mayo* base, chanting slogans against the soldiers and in support of the democracy. The authorities urged them to disperse, but

---

88. Accounts of the military uprisings can be found in various issues of *La Nación* and *Clarín* between April 17 and 20, 1987.

89. For an excellent analysis of the origins and nature of this rebellious faction within the army, see Deborah L. Norden, *Military Rebellion in Argentina: Between Coups and Consolidation* (Omaha: University of Nebraska Press, 1996).

they refused.[90] A crowd of one hundred thousand rallied in front of the *Casa Rosada* on April 16, where the president told them, "the democracy of Argentina cannot be negotiated."[91] Three days later their numbers had swelled to two hundred thousand as people waited for Alfonsín's return from *Campo de Mayo*, where he had flown by helicopter to meet with Aldo Rico in a personal attempt to put an end to the hostilities.[92]

The impressive outpouring of popular support for the regime was in part spontaneous, in part a response to official calls for solidarity by political and social leaders across the spectrum. In an unprecedented show of unity, leaders of all parties, labor organizations, and business associations signed the Act of Democratic Compromise. Pledging to defend the constitutional democracy with every means at their disposal against efforts to subvert it, the signatories promised that "no pressure or threat could bend our inflexible decision to comply with the law."[93] They also affirmed their commitment to rally their constituents in defense of the democratic order. Signatories included at one end the often truculent, left-wing labor leader Saúl Ubaldini (then secretary general of the CGT), and at the other end former right-wing coup apologists like UCD president Alvaro Alsogaray.[94]

The importance of these expressions of institutional solidarity cannot be overstated. They were offered at a time when the government's control over the armed forces was, to say the least, precarious. It is not only that the loyalist forces had failed to crush the rebellion. It is that the president had failed to persuade Argentines that he, as commander in chief, had stipulated rather than negotiated the terms of Rico's surrender. In fact, less than a week after the rebellion was quieted the president submitted a bill to Congress (subsequently approved) that exonerated all officers at the rank of lieutenant colonel or lower charged with human rights offenses. Although this measure had been under consideration by the administration before *Semana Santa*,

90. *New York Times*, April 18, 1987, p. 1.

91. Ibid., April 17, 1987, p. 1.

92. Ibid., April 20, 1987, p. 1.

93. *La Prensa*, April 20, 1987, p. 4.

94. Ubaldini said, "If necessary we (the workers) will defend the democracy with our lives," adding "the ills of democracy must be cured with more democracy," and "we do not want any more governments chosen by force rather governments elected by popular will." See ibid., April 19, 1987, p. 5. Three business leaders, including Rolando Pietrantueno, then head of the CAI (Consejo Argentino de la Industria), the group representing the largest industrial enterprises, signed on as well, condemning the work of a "minuscule group of officers of authoritarian persuasions." See ibid., April 20, 1987, p. 10.

the uprising undoubtedly hastened its passage while indicating that Alfonsín had probably been more conciliatory than demanding in his encounter with Rico.[95] This fostered a perception of presidential weakness which in turn invited junior officers to become even more adventurous and insubordinate later on.

For the moment, the civil-military balance of power had turned decisively against the Alfonsín administration. And yet, paradoxically, the prospects for a military coup were now more remote than ever (not withstanding the palpable *fear* of intervention that had been generated at the time). With political and social figures of every persuasion standing firmly against them, the rebels could not have launched a successful coup attempt even if they had so desired. While these defiant soldiers certainly created a stir, their uprising revealed more about the limitations of military praetorianism in the post-*Proceso* age than they did about its possibilities. In the absence of societal support, rebel armies can only push the political envelope so far. And since the public has disavowed regime destabilization, military subversives are left to operate in relative isolation.

Moreover, with military nervousness over judicial action having been substantially quieted after *Semana Santa*, rebel elements found themselves without a persuasive, institutional cause, and increasingly isolated within the ranks of the armed services themselves. The leadership of the rebel movement passed to officers who were less pragmatic and more political and ideological, and therefore less able to win the allegiance of the bulk of the officer corps, which was professional in orientation.[96] This is one reason why subsequent rebellions launched in 1988 and 1990 were so ineffectual.[97] Few of the new rebel demands were met, as the political leadership and its army commanders turned against the *carapintadas* with a vengeance. The mutineers may have caused moments of fear and panic, but without significant bases of support from within civil and political society, not to mention the full backing of the military, they hadn't the capacity to inflict more permanent damage on the regime. With the benefit of hindsight, it now seems that the rebellions had momentarily disrupted but had not fundamentally altered the institutionalized civil-military relation.

95. *Clarín Edición Internacional*, May 25, 1987, p. 1.
96. On the change in *carapintada* leadership, see Norden, *Military Rebellion in Argentina*, pp. 132–33.
97. On these other uprisings, see Pion-Berlin and López, "A House Divided," pp. 63–96.

Conclusion

The events of April 1987 and beyond offered further and more compelling evidence that civil-military relations have changed. The social connections that military conspirators had come to rely upon and had drawn sustenance from were now severed. Although many members of Argentine civil society continue to find government leaders and their policies objectionable, they are unwilling to jeopardize the democratic system in exchange for some uncertain gain to be won through military pressure. The armed forces are unlikely to topple elected officials unless they can command some significant public allegiance to or, at the very least, acquiescence in their conspiracy against the constitutional regime. Neither is forthcoming in today's environment, making military intervention improbable, though not impossible.

The public expresses its dismay at the balloting box, where incumbents who fail to perform may be thrown out of office. The preference for electoral solutions to problems brings into sharper relief the limits to military power in the new Argentine democracy. There seems to be a ceiling to power above which the armed forces cannot go and below which they desire to extend their influence within the democratic order.[98]

Not only has military influence been restricted, but it has also been largely institutionalized. Civil-military interactions are now centered within governing institutions. A fundamental difference between the pre-*Proceso* and post-*Proceso* Argentina is the shift in the focal point for civil-military relations from society to the state. At the state level the armed forces make their case to public officials, observing the norms and conventions of democratic procedure. Military liaison officers are seen scurrying around the halls of Congress and darting in and out of the defense ministry. There they meet with their political counterparts in hopes of influencing policy. Disagreement is common, but contacts between civilian and military figures are generally cordial and respectful. This is the new political landscape of Argentina. In the next chapter, one portion of this landscape will be observed in detail, as we trace President Alfonsín's human rights policy through the corridors of power.

---

98. See, for example, David Pion-Berlin "Military Autonomy and Emerging Democracies in South America," *Comparative Politics* 25 (October 1992): 83–102; and Wendy Hunter, "Back to the Barracks? The Military in Post-Authoritarian Brazil," Ph.D. diss., University of California, Berkeley, 1992.

CHAPTER 4

Settling Scores
Human Rights Gains and Setbacks Under Alfonsín

In assuming office on December 10, 1983, President Raúl R. Alfonsín had embarked upon a historic mission: to be the first Latin American head of state to bring members of his own armed services to trial for human rights abuses. How successful would that mission be? And could he achieve this goal while protecting the democracy against harmful military retribution? Although the president was within his power to set the policy course, he could not singularly control it. Other political actors would have their say. The presidency is powerful in a country like Argentina, but it is not monarchical. Separate agencies of government enjoy varying levels of autonomy and have their own political as well as institutional axes to grind. They will not grovel at the feet of the executive. This was especially so of the judicial branch, which Alfonsín had entrusted to fulfill most of his human rights plan.

But the civilian courts were not the only actors the president had to contend with. Military tribunals, the Congress, human rights organizations, and ultimately the armed forces themselves all played a role. When there are multiple institutional actors involved in the process, each bound by its unique norms of procedures and determined to assert its rightful prerogatives, the final policy product may not turn out to be what the original designer had in mind. Alfonsín was to discover that fact all too soon.

Clearly the president would not and could not afford to back down from his commitment to justice. He had personally defended families of the disappeared and protested government policies at great personal risk. He had helped write the Radical Party platform, which called for the eradication of all forms of torture and severe punishment for those found guilty of such human rights transgressions.[1] Five months before his election he said that a democratic system could not be reborn by forgetting the past and that to do so would be to build the new system upon an "uncertain ethical foundation."[2] But he also had voters in mind. Given the palpable sense of outrage expressed by the electorate in the immediate aftermath of the *Proceso*, it would have been impossible for him to avoid the questions of truth and justice.

Still the limits to policy needed to be set: Precisely how far should the president go? Could he go? These questions framed the political and moral dilemmas as well as opportunities facing Alfonsín and his advisors. On the one hand, the balance of power had tipped decisively in favor of the democratic incumbents in the aftermath of the *Proceso*'s collapse. That shift opened up new policy "spaces" hitherto unseen. On the other hand, this enormous and unprecedented window of opportunity was sure to close eventually. The newly installed leaders could reasonably predict that in the medium term the distribution of power might shift as memories of the Malvinas War faded and as the officer corps regained its composure and regrouped to defend its corporate interests.[3] Thus, it was essential that Alfonsín take maximum advantage of an ephemeral moment by launching some form of inquest into the disappeared (which he did) and by prosecuting some members of the military and security forces responsible for the abuses of the recent past (which he also did).

It also seemed reasonable to think that the moral imperative that so visibly affected the politics of the transition would recede, as the public's recollection of the *Proceso* horrors receded from view and as its focus on present social economic difficulties sharpened. Thus, we could envision an inverse

---

1. Jorge Camarasa, Rubén Felice, and Daniel González, *El juicio: Proceso al horror* (Buenos Aires: Sudamericana/Planeta, 1985), p. 24.

2. Ibid.

3. The point made about the opening and the closing of a unique window of opportunity is echoed by Marcelo Cavarozzi and María Grossi, "Argentine Parties Under Alfonsín: From Democratic Reinvention to Political Decline and Hyperinflation," in *The New Argentine Democracy: The Search for a Successful Formula*, ed. Edward C. Epstein (New York: Praeger Publishers, 1992), p. 175.

relationship between ethical obligations and military pressures, which was in one respect ideal for Alfonsín. During the first phase of his administration he would face moral pressures for justice at a time of military weakness. Then, as military power returned and public moral outrage subsided, he could focus less on the human rights agenda and more on the pragmatic goals of military professionalization, modernization, and subordination to civilian authority.

In short, Alfonsín could use this political moment to his advantage by first raising the costs to military defiance and then by increasing the benefits to military compliance. This was by no means an easy balancing act to achieve. The president would have to carefully time and calibrate his policies so that the more punitive measures would impact earlier and then be phased out. There had to be a kind of planned obsolescence to judicial policies that if left to linger would most assuredly deepen the anxiety, restlessness, and anger already felt within the officer corps. With their careers and reputations hanging in the balance, how long would soldiers comply with court orders, or with their political superiors for that matter?

Did Alfonsín actually have these considerations in mind? And if so, to what extent could he control policy events as they unfolded to ensure that the strategy of planned obsolescence would prevail? Or would the process slip from his grasp as other actors in other institutional settings took over? These are questions to which we now turn.

Designing Human Rights Policy

It was during the 1983 campaign, while speaking at the Argentine College of Law, that Alfonsín first made clear that if there were to be trials they would have to be limited in scope and duration; the entire military institution could not be dragged into court.[4] His was a midcourse that would steer between a wholesale indictment of the armed forces on the one hand and an amnesty on the other. In consultation with his legal advisors he eventually proposed a trifold distinction between (1) those in command of the *Proceso*, (2) those who had strictly followed orders and were presumed to be mistaken

---

4. Carlos Nino had helped to organize this reunion at the college. He spoke with the author during an interview in Buenos Aires on July 2, 1993.

about the legitimacy of the orders (unless evidence to the contrary could be produced), and (3) those who had clearly exceeded the orders given.[5]

The president's distinction both followed from and amended the Code of Military Justice. Article 514 of that code had stated that when a crime is committed by virtue of following an order, only the superior who issued that order could be considered responsible; the subordinate could be punished only where he had acted on his own.[6] The presumption of error was added to convey the point that duty is not blind: officers could not be excused simply because they obeyed, since such compliance could have been in violation of Argentine and international statutes that prohibited crimes against humanity. But given the difficult environment that soldiers found themselves in—one framed by the ideology of national security whose practitioners spared no effort in justifying any actions in the name of defeating subversion—it is not difficult to imagine that many servicemen could have erred in regarding their commands as legitimate.[7] This proposed amendment to the military code became known as the principle of *obediencia debida*, or due obedience, and in modified form it was passed into law in February 1984.

There was an undeniably persuasive legal and political logic to the due obedience clause. It reasonably favored punishment for those who masterminded the *Dirty War* and for those who had committed excesses, while holding out the possibility of exoneration for those in subordinate positions. It understood the moral obligations all soldiers had under national and international law to question orders that would result in abhorrent abuses. And yet it excused officers if, under difficult circumstances, they had failed to make sound judgments regarding those orders.

As sensible as the government's trifold legal distinction appeared to be, *obediencia debida* was not without its problems. Alfonsín and his human rights advisors simply underestimated both the number of individuals within the state security apparatus in positions of authority and the number of officers entangled in gross violations of human rights. Not until later, through the revelations of the presidentially appointed National Commission on the Disappeared, and later still, during the presentation of facts at the trials, would

5. Alfonsín's proposed just obedience legislation, before its modification by the Senate in February 1984, can be found in Marcelo A. Sancinetti, *Derechos humanos en la Argentina post-dictatorial* (Buenos Aires: Lerner Editores Asociados, 1988), Appendix, pp. 185–89.

6. Dr. Oscar Igounet and Dr. Oscar Igounet (hijo), *Código de Justicia Militar* (Buenos Aires: Librería de Jurista, 1985), p. 158.

7. This argument was developed by Carlos Nino and Jaime Malamud-Goti and has precedent in the Nuremburg Proceedings following World War II. Interview with Carlos Nino, Buenos Aires, July 2, 1993.

it come to light that there were literally hundreds of security figures residing at many levels of the hierarchy who had exercised discretion. Many of these lorded the power of life or death over their detainees. For these operators the justifiable error defense would likely fail once the courts gathered evidence about their complicity, knowledge, and responsibilities. Others committed horrendous crimes under orders in the line of duty. Thus, their activities could not be construed as excessive.[8]

Additionally, the just obedience strategy was complicated by congressional action. An amendment to Alfonsín's bill was offered up by Senator Elias Sapag from a provincial party called the *Movimiento Popular Neuquino.* The amendment stated that junior officers could be exculpated on grounds of being in error regarding the legitimacy of orders except where they had committed "atrocious or aberrant acts."[9] Sapag had lost two children in the *Dirty War* and wanted to ensure that the due obedience defense not serve as a giant loophole through which offenders could go free. The new language, which found its way to Article 514 of the Military Code of Justice, would certainly make prosecution and conviction easier. With the term "aberration" so vaguely defined, whose presumption of innocence could not be rebuked? Even the most dutiful officer had no doubt at some point committed an action that could have been construed as deviant.

Still at the time, the Alfonsín administration did not strongly counter the Sapag revision. The amendment was introduced and passed easily, along with the other modifications to the Code of Military Justice first proposed by the executive branch. Unfortunately, Alfonsín did not fathom just how many military fish could be caught in the net of atrocious and aberrant behavior. Perhaps if he had, he would have reconsidered his position in order to ensure that some limits be placed on the number of officers likely to be indicted. In short, the president's original plan did build into it certain safeguards intended to prevent the trials from getting out of hand and to bring the moral phase of policy to closure. But these safeguards were not entirely adequate and were partially undermined by congressional action.

8. When designing his human rights policy, Alfonsín may have been under the impression that the junta's orders were to illegally detain suspects but to go no further. While the junta did not discourage the maltreatment and execution of detainees, he supposed, they never explicitly authorized it either. Those who tortured or murdered political prisoners did so on their own. Thus, Alfonsín reasoned, the distinction between pardonable offenses under orders and unpardonable excesses would hold up in court. In this regard the president had erred, according to Ricardo R. Gil Lavedra. Interview with author, Buenos Aires, November 3, 1994.

9. See Americas Watch, *Truth and Partial Justice in Argentina* (New York: Americas Watch, 1987), p. 19.

Be that as it may, the proposal to amend the Military Code of Justice was now law. For better or worse the human rights policy, fully crafted, would next make its way to the courts, as Alfonsín had originally intended it to. The first phase would transpire in the military tribunal, and then in the second phase it would move to civilian federal court. Once in the legal arena the policy would be subjected to the terms upon which those courts conducted their affairs. What were those terms and how did they affect the success of the human rights plan?

Phase One: The Military Tribunal

A month after his election and four days before his inauguration as president, Alfonsín had an important meeting with several cabinet appointees and trusted advisors to map out, in some detail, his human rights strategy. Attending the meeting on December 6, 1983, were Defense Minister Raúl Borrás, Interior Minister Antonio Troccoli, and Alfonsín's two human rights advisors, Carlos Nino and Jaime Malamud-Goti.[10] It was then that the formal decision was made to prosecute nine of the ex-leaders of the military dictatorship on charges of illegal detention, murder, and torture. The question was where to begin: In military or civilian court?

All who were in attendance at that December meeting, with the exception of Minister Borrás, were in favor of authorizing the civilian courts to handle the military human rights cases. They concurred with Nino and Malamud-Goti that as citizens, soldiers were subject to the penal codes, which outlawed all forms of atrocities—whether these were committed in the line of duty or not. They embraced the Radical Party's liberal precepts about the military: officers were individual citizens first, state functionaries second, but never members of a privileged corporation. As the president himself once said: "In a modern and democratic society, the military is merely citizens

---

10. This meeting was confirmed by Carlos Nino in my interview on July 2, 1993, in Buenos Aires; also see Horacio Verbitsky, *Civiles y militares: Memoria secreta de la transición* (Buenos Aires: Editorial Contrapunto, 1987), pp. 51–55. The president-elect would come to depend on Nino and Malamud-Goti for human rights advice. These two young lawyers were part of a team of "political technocrats" whose vision it was to transform the UCR into a forceful advocate for social justice. Often referred to by Alfonsín as "the philosophers," Malamud-Goti and Nino soon became trusted members of the president's inner circle and had a substantial influence on his policies.

taking up arms in defense of the nation's values and its legal and political organization in the face of external threats."[11]

This was a point of contention since Article 108 of the Argentine Code of Military Justice, prior to its modification by civilians in 1984, gave the military courts jurisdiction over members of the armed forces who had committed infractions while on active service, whether in times of war or peace.[12] If this law was valid, then altering it (thereby sending soldiers to civilian magistrates) would violate a soldier's constitutional rights to be tried only on the basis of statutes that predated his offense.

Raúl Borrás, the minister of defense designate, agreed. Borrás had known Alfonsín since 1966 when the two joined forces to rebuild the UCR in the province of Buenos Aires under the watchful eye of the Onganía dictatorship. He was perhaps the most trusted of Alfonsín's cabinet members and used that confidence to persuade the president-elect to reconsider his position and allow the armed forces to conduct their own trial.[13]

He argued that the military was not an ideologically monolithic institution; there were officers eager to distance themselves from commanders they considered to have been incompetent and corrupt. Given the diversity of views within the services, it was not unreasonable to believe that the ex-comandantes could be convicted if only the administration would give the armed forces a chance to "cleanse their own house."[14] Should the military choose not to, then the president had yet another recourse. Under Alfonsín's proposed amendment to the Military Code of Justice (later to become Law 23.049), the government could appeal unfavorable rulings to the federal court, should it be found that there were unwarranted delays or an obstruction of justice in the military judicial proceedings.[15] Borrás won the day, and Decree 158/83, issued that same month, ordered nine ex-comandantes to stand trial before the Military Supreme Council composed of retired officers from each branch.[16]

11. Dr. Raúl R. Alfonsín, "Discurso del Señor Presidente de la nación Argentina en la cena de camaradería de las fuerzas armadas" (Buenos Aires: Secretaría de Información Pública, July 5, 1985), p. 17. Translation from the original Spanish is mine.

12. Igounet and Igounet, *Código de Justicia Militar*, p. 27.

13. On the influence of Borrás upon Alfonsín's opinion, see Camarasa et al., *El juicio*, pp. 28–29.

14. Borrás also reasoned that this strategy would be less troublesome to the armed forces and involve a lower political cost for the government. An exercise in self-purification could be held in closed sessions, shielded from the hostile glare of public attention, allowing defendants and prosecutors alike to be more forthcoming. Under those conditions the armed forces could not allege that the trial was staged to humiliate the *Dirty War* participants.

15. Igounet and Igounet, *Código de Justicia Militar*, pp. 431–32.

16. But the government-sponsored law to modify the Military Code of Justice (Law 23.049) did state that for all future crimes in times of peace, military court jurisdiction would be limited to

By June 1984 it became evident that the Supreme Council was dragging its heels. After a 180-day limit to render verdicts had expired, the federal courts granted the court an additional 90 days to bring the proceedings to a close. But after that period had elapsed, the council, which had still not reached a single verdict, issued its explanation. Not only could it not convict the junta members for lack of sufficient evidence, but it would not do so. It found the orders of repression issued by the generals to have been "unobjectionable."[17] This was a particularly troublesome decision, coming as it did just days after the National Commission on the Disappeared released its report detailing the horrors of the *Dirty War* that had resulted from the junta's directives. The military justices washed their hands of the whole matter, tendering their resignations to Raúl Borrás in October.

In allowing the military court to conduct its own trials, Borrás and Alfonsín had miscalculated. The Supreme Council judges had never intended to prosecute their fellow officers. A warning about the council went unheeded by the government in March 1984. At that time a civilian judge had tried to indict Lieutenant Alfredo Astiz and Admiral Rubén Chamorro for the abduction and mortal wounding of Dagmar Hagelin, the daughter of a Swedish diplomat serving in Argentina. But the military court advised the judge that such a charge was impossible since it had already acquitted the two officers of all charges several years before. That acquittal took place during the dictatorship and in secret, with none of the key civilian witnesses to the crime ever called before the council to testify.[18]

Nonetheless, once the executive decision was made to grant the military jurisdiction, it was out of the president's hands. The tribunal was ill-prepared for the assigned tasks, being overworked, understaffed, and undermotivated. But most important, the judges that served on the tribunal could not be counted on to deliver justice. As retired officers their allegiance was first and foremost to the military institution they had faithfully served for so many years. At the end of the day they would act like soldiers, not independent magistrates.

Phase Two: The Civilian Tribunal

The Federal Court of Appeals assumed jurisdiction over the proceedings in October 1984 and then turned it over to the court's prosecutor, Julio Stras-

---

strictly institutional infractions such as insubordination, uprisings, etc. See Sancinetti, *Derechos humanos en la Argentina post-dictatorial*, p. 189. Also see Amnesty International, *Argentina: The Military Juntas and Human Rights* (London: Amnesty International Publications, 1987), p. 88.

17. Camarasa et al., *El juicio*, p. 65.

18. Amnesty International, *Argentina: The Military Juntas*, p. 14.

sera, who took the case to trial in April 1985. Strassera chose 709 crimes among the thousands presented with which to mount his legal attack.[19] The cases were limited to the most egregious crimes and chosen to establish a methodical pattern to the repression. Rejecting the defense's contention that if there were crimes they were committed by a few deranged officers, Strassera proved that the same kinds of offenses were practiced countrywide under numerous military commands. Over time, there was a sustained pattern of abduction, torture, and murder that could not have come at the hands of a few renegade officers, he claimed.[20]

Although the junta commanders did not themselves engage in or directly supervise the atrocities, they controlled the apparatus of state terror, issued the "general instructions calling for extraordinary measures to be used against all subversive elements," and were thus indirect, punishable authors of the crimes committed, according to the court.[21] On December 9 of that year, five of the ex-comandantes of the military junta were found guilty of flagrant violations of human rights, sentenced to long prison terms (with life imprisonment for ex-General Jorge Videla and ex-Admiral Emilio Massera, seventeen years for ex-General Roberto Viola, eight years for ex-Admiral Armando Lambruschini, and four and one-half years for ex-Brigadier Osvaldo Agosti), and stripped of their military status.[22]

Punishments for junta

The verdicts were enormously gratifying to Alfonsín and represented a significant policy success for his administration. The trials were unprecedented in Latin American history. Never before had a government in the region successfully prosecuted its military predecessors for human rights abuses, and not since the Nuremburg trials against the Nazi criminals of World War II had a trial of this nature anywhere in the world captured so much public attention and scrutiny. The verdicts rendered a blow to impunity, placing the armed forces on notice that future acts of repression in the name of national security would not be tolerated by a civil society.

Although these verdicts were welcome, they had not been delivered in

19. Invoking the seldom-used legal principle of opportunity, the Federal Court of Appeals had requested Strassera to sample from among the thousands of crimes committed those he would prosecute. However, this did not give Strassera a license to dismiss charges against others (especially lower-ranking officers) who may have been implicated in the crimes not prosecuted for this particular trial. The opportunity principle gives the Argentine prosecutor far less discretion than enjoyed by his counterparts in the United States. Gil R. Lavedra, interview with author, Buenos Aires, November 3, 1994.

20. Alejandro M. Garro and Henry Dahl, "Legal Accountability for Human Rights Violations in Argentina: One Step Forward and Two Steps Backward," *Human Rights Law Journal* 8, nos. 2–4 (1987): 323.

21. Ibid., p. 328.

22. *El libro de el diario del juicio* (Buenos Aires: Editorial Perfil, 1985), pp. 532–34.

timely fashion. Two years had elapsed since Alfonsín had first ordered the trials. The Military Supreme Council's purposeful obstruction had caused costly delays. The prolongation of the process was critical because unbeknown to the administration, the human rights task was far from completed. In the fall of 1985 members of the cabinet were confidently boasting that once the federal court established the guilt of the commanders, most subordinates would then be set free. Roque Carranza, the defense minister at the time, reasoned that in finding the political leaders of the Dirty War culpable, the judges would simultaneously exonerate those below, who were simply in error regarding the legitimacy of orders.

Item Thirty

This was not to be. As part of its December sentence the Federal Court of Appeals had also noted that

> the commanders secretly established a criminal method for fighting terrorism. Low-ranking officers of the armed forces were granted broad discretion to deprive of freedom whoever appeared to be, according to intelligence information, an agent of subversion. . . . The fate of the victims was decided by their captors . . . who enjoyed absolute discretion to decide whether to set them free or to kill them.[23]

It was the hierarchical yet decentralized nature of the terrorist state, according to the court, that placed considerable power and information in the hands of subordinates. By virtue of their positions and autonomy many officers (including those who were receiving orders) were fully aware of the unlawfulness of the commands and carried them out nonetheless.[24] It was therefore beyond doubt that guilt resided at lower echelons as well. The court added:

23. See Enrique Dahl and Alejandro M. Garro, "Argentina: National Appeals Court (Criminal Division) Judgment on Human Rights Violations by Former Military Leaders: An Introductory Note," *International Legal Materials* 26 (January–May 1987): 332.

24. Verbitsky, *Civiles y militares*, p. 147.

There is no doubt there were those who by their position in the chain of command knew of the illegality of the system and [there] were also those who executed, without due consideration, atrocities. Thus it follows that there exists subordinates who are not going to be exonerated by obediencia debida, and who are responsible for the known acts together with those who imparted the orders.[25]

The justices considered it their legal obligation to report all other criminal offenses that had come to their attention. In an *item thirty* of its final pronouncement the Federal Court of Appeals noted it was turning evidence over to the armed forces Supreme Council (which would resume jurisdiction over subsequent cases) so that it could commence proceedings against all "superior officers who were in command of the areas and sub areas of defense during the campaign against subversion and against all those who had operational responsibility in the actions."[26] As a consequence of this ruling, the prospect of a second wave of trials suddenly loomed on the horizon, with legal proceedings descending uncontrollably through the chain of command. This was bad timing, since the armed forces were beginning to lick their wounds, close ranks, and regain some measure of institutional confidence that had been lost in the previous three years.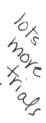

It is with *item thirty* that judicial autonomy first became a problem for the executive branch. Alfonsín and his human rights advisors were genuinely and unpleasantly surprised by this addition, believing that the spirit of their due obedience principles had been violated. It "opened the door for more prosecution," said Carlos Nino, at a time when the government expected the courts to begin closing it.[27] The president himself said "he was expecting that justice would establish a respect for the amendment to the military code of justice, . . . but they did not want to do so."[28] After the appellate court ruling Alfonsín hoped that the Supreme Court would restore the original intent of the due obedience amendment, but there too he was to be disappointed when on December 30, 1986, the highest tribunal upheld all of the lower court's rulings.[29]

From the viewpoint of the justices *item thirty* was nothing exceptional. For

25. *Diario del Juicio*, no. 30, December 17, 1985, p. 4.

26. See Americas Watch, *Truth and Partial Justice in Argentina*, p. 38.

27. Carlos Nino, interview with author, Buenos Aires, July 2, 1993.

28. Dr. Raúl R. Alfonsín, interview with author, Buenos Aires, July 20, 1993.

29. American Association of Jurists, *Juicios a los militares: Argentina* (Buenos Aires: Asociación Americana de Juristas, 1988), pp. 178–206.

a tribunal to ask for further investigation is "a common point in any decision," according to Andrés D'Alessio, the president of the Federal Court of Appeals at the time.[30] But it was one that also followed quite logically from the justices' own assessment of the voluminous evidence presented to them. Military officers were found to operate in a "mafiosa-like" environment, where nearly all were inextricably involved in atrocious behavior and bonded through pacts of blood. Even without the Senate-imposed language regarding "atrocious and aberrant behavior" Alessio doubted that "pardonable error" would have served as an effective defense, since all those cases considered by his court involved officers who had sufficient authority to have been fully aware of the illegality of orders and who themselves were accomplices to abhorrent crimes. As such, the justices would not likely have found them innocent.[31] In essence, Alessio was arguing that the Senate language never reduced the judges' powers of discretion since they had made up their own minds to convict the accused anyway.[32]

President Alfonsín was disappointed. Judges whom he had appointed, respected, and knew well would surely subscribe to the principles set forth in the due obedience clause of the Military Code of Justice and thereby dismiss charges against subordinates.[33] But the court had disdain for the idea that there could be a predetermined number of guilty parties that would preclude investigation and court proceedings. As interpreters and not creators of law, they argued that if the executive branch wanted more favorable rulings, they should change the legislation.

Finally, and perhaps most important, the justices were protective of the independence they enjoyed as members of a separate branch of government. They would not buckle under even subtle forms of external pressure. Said Gil Lavedra, a member of the appellate court that prosecuted the ex-comandantes: "With regard to my court, we were completely aware of the fact that judgment was something we rendered alone, and that the democratic system could function only if we acted with complete autonomy."[34]

30. Andrés José D'Alessio, interview with author, Buenos Aires, November 1, 1994.

31. Ibid.

32. The widely held presumption that the Sapag amendment restricted the judiciary's discretionary powers is false, according to one judge, because the justices had always believed that the excesses were the orders. And since all the cases before them involved atrocities of one form or another, all the accused fell outside the safety net of just obedience. Ibid.

33. This impression was conveyed to me in response to a question regarding the court's decision to prosecute others in the chain of command. Raúl R. Alfonsín, interview with author, Buenos Aires, July 20, 1993.

34. Ricardo R. Gil Lavedra, interview with author, Buenos Aires, November 3, 1994.

Judicial independence was nothing new in Argentina. There is a long (although spotted) history of judicial defiance of political pressure, sometimes under the most trying conditions. The Supreme Court, which is the nation's highest tribunal and the last refuge for those whose rights have been trampled upon, has, at times, stood up to tyrannical regimes. It was under the *Revolución Libertadora* of 1955 to 1958, the military regime that deposed then-president Juan Perón, that the Supreme Court first affirmed the right to *ámparo* (protection) that postpones enforcement of arbitrary acts if it can be established that irreparable harm might result to the accused. Under the military regime of General Juan Carlos Onganía (1966–70) the court reviewed a number of politically motivated arrests, declaring many of these unconstitutional.[35] No one was more surprised by these rulings than Onganía, since he had handpicked the justices himself. And some forty times during the *Proceso* (1976–83) the court demanded that the executive branch comply with writs of habeas corpus by producing arrest orders, by documenting the status of the prisoner, and by justifying prolonged detention without trial.[36]

Certainly if the judiciary could, on occasion, stand up to the executive branch under a dictatorship, it would have little difficulty doing so under the more benign, libertarian conditions of a democracy. Although the justices on the bench of the Federal Court of Appeals charged with handling the trial had each been appointed by Alfonsín, they were not beholden to him. All had served in the judiciary during the *Proceso*. So too did the prosecutor, Julio Strassera, who actually received a promotion under military rule.

But neither were the men of the Argentine bench beholden to military interests. To the contrary, the judicial system enjoyed a high degree of autonomy from the armed forces. Argentine judges did not fear the military and refused to be intimidated by provocations designed to halt their proceedings. For example, threats were called in regularly warning the justices that bombs would be exploded in the courtroom if the trial against the junta was not halted. While the justices took the necessary precautions, they never once

---

35. See Germán Bidart Campos, *The Argentine Supreme Court: The Court of Constitutional Guarantees* (Buenos Aires: Allende and Brea, 1982), p. 117.

36. This fact was brought to my attention by Andrés José D'Alessio in a letter to me dated November 15, 1994. Alessio in turn got the information from the former Supreme Court secretary, Dr. Jorge Barral. Details of specific habeas corpus cases tried by the Supreme Court during the *Proceso* can be found in Adolfo R. Gabrielli, *La Corte Suprema de Justicia y la opinión pública, 1976–1983* (Buenos Aires: Abeledo-Perrot, 1986), pp. 33–62.

suspended the trials, believing that to do so would have been to play into the hands of terrorism.[37]

Given these facts, it was unlikely that the judiciary would act with servility toward anyone, the armed forces and the executive branch included. But conversely, why would they have cause to obstruct administration policy? It was not apparent that they ever intended to do so. The judges were simply behaving as judges. However, as the political dynamics surrounding human rights changed, and as government priorities shifted, the executive and judicial branches increasingly became unwitting adversaries.

Alfonsín knew from the beginning that his human rights strategy faced two potential hazards. The first would be an uncontained expansion in the number of military officers charged with crimes. Too great a number could trigger allegations that the government was bringing the institution itself to trial. The second would be the undue prolongation of the judicial process. The inability to render speedy verdicts would only exaggerate the state of uncertainty and anxiety already felt by the accused. The government intended its due obedience clause to reduce the scope of prosecution by offering military subordinates the escape clause already described. This quickly proved to be grossly insufficient, prompting some of Alfonsín's appointees to urge that stronger legislative restrictions be imposed on the legal process as early as the fall of 1984. They feared that the judiciary would never set limits on its own activities. What about the legal process had them worried?

Judicial Norms of Procedure

There are some peculiar features of the judicial system of Argentina that had direct implications for the success or failure of Alfonsín's human rights strategy. A brief comparison with the judicial process in the United States is in order. Under our system of law a victim has no easy access to the halls of justice. He must first report a crime directly to the police. The police have ample discretion, choosing to either investigate or not. Should they launch a probe, they may still determine that there is insufficient evidence to warrant an arrest and go no further. Should the investigation turn up evidence

---

37. This was confirmed to me by Ricardo R. Gil Lavedra, interview with author, Buenos Aires, November 3, 1994, and by Andrés José D'Alessio, interview with author, Buenos Aires, November 1, 1994.

of wrongdoing, the police will then report their findings to a public prosecutor, where yet another assessment is made: whether or not to issue an indictment. The district attorney's office is within its powers to reject a case for any number of reasons. Thus, the citizen is at the mercy of the chain of legal command, where his plea for justice is heard but often denied.

In Argentina, however, a victim, relative, or any one citizen for that matter can walk right into a courtroom and file a complaint with a magistrate. No police report is necessary, nor is the presence of an attorney. The plaintiff can also provide investigatory leads and suggest lines of inquiry to the courts. Under this *querellante* (plaintiff-prosecutor) scheme, a victim or his representative is entitled not only to introduce incriminating evidence of a purported infraction directly to a judge but actually to join in the prosecution of a criminal offense.[38]

Even in military court a *querellante* may present evidence, although his rights are more restricted since the presiding judge can decide whether or not to admit the evidence or how much weight to place on it. Nonetheless, the plaintiff's due process rights are protected because he may request an appeal to civilian courts where all the facts can be entered.[39] Needless to say, such principles afford Argentine citizens a form of judicial entrée that is unheard of in our legal system. It is a legal opening that the human rights movement would exploit fully.

Once handed the charge and regardless of its seriousness, a magistrate is bound to investigate where there is some reasonable cause to believe a crime has been committed.[40] He has no power to reject or postpone an inquiry out of hand. In fact, formal proceedings are usually triggered immediately simply by virtue of an individual having filed a complaint. Having determined that a crime has been committed, the public prosecutor, who works on behalf of the courts and not the ministry of justice, must take the case.[41] Prosecution is compulsory; neither the attorney general nor anyone below him in rank

38. See Kathryn Lee Crawford, "Due Obedience and the Rights of Victims: Argentina's Transition to Democracy," *Human Rights Quarterly* 12 (1990): 39 and note 123.

39. Ibid., p. 41. Also see Article 9 of Law 23.049, which amends the Military Code of Justice; reprinted in Sancinetti, *Derechos humanos en la Argentina post-dictatorial*, p. 192.

40. The Argentine legal system is inquisitorial rather than adversarial in nature. Thus, a pretrial inquiry is conducted by an investigatory judge. It is the magistrate and not the attorneys who assembles and reviews the evidence and who calls witnesses in for cross-examination. There is no jury of peers. A panel of presiding judges hears the case. See Henry J. Abraham, *The Judicial Process*, 5th ed. (New York: Oxford University Press, 1986), pp. 98–103; Alejandro D. Carrió, *The Criminal Justice System of Argentina: An Overview for American Readers* (Baton Rouge: Paul M. Hebert Law Center, 1989), pp. 8–15.

41. Carrió, *The Criminal Justice System of Argentina*, p. 39.

has discretion where there is knowledge that the law has been violated.[42] Neither the nature of the infraction nor a work overload can ever justify case dismissal. This is known in Argentine jurisprudence as the *legality principle*.[43]

To the families of the disappeared, judicial attributes such as these were priceless vehicles with which to seek retribution. They could press their charges directly in court and thereby avoid the awkward and no doubt frightening prospects of having to confront the "face of terror" by reporting to police headquarters. It is well known that the police forces were inextricably embroiled in the *Dirty War* repression, having been pressed into "extralegal" missions by their military superiors. Police installations became favorite sights for clandestine detention centers, and police officials like Ramón Camps acquired notorious reputations for their brutality.[44] Moreover, human rights groups who represented the families were also relieved to know they did not have to square with law enforcement officials. During the *Proceso* many such organizations had been subjected to police raids during which personnel were arrested and valuable documents confiscated.[45]

Once within chambers, citizens could level charges against military and police officials and fully expect the presiding judge, under the restrictions of the *legality principle*, to pursue the investigation. An institutional channel of sizable proportions lay waiting for the victims' families and the human rights organizations that represented their interests. They wasted no time in utilizing this channel to their advantage.

From the opening moments of the democratic regime, human rights groups such as the *Asamblea Permanente de Derechos Humanos, Las Madres del Plaza del Mayo*, and, most important, the *Centro de Estudios Legales y Sociales* (CELS) began flooding the military and civilian courts with denunciations.[46]

42. The only exception to the rule being crimes where the "dignity or reputation of the victim is involved," such as rape. See ibid.

43. Omar Breglia Arias and Omar R. Gauna, *Código penal y leyes complementarias*, 2d ed. (Buenos Aires: Editorial Astrea, 1993), art. 274, p. 939.

44. The first army corps, centered in the Buenos Aires area, kept the majority of their prisoners in buildings operated by the federal and provincial police. See Argentine National Commission on the Disappeared, *Nunca Más: The Report of the Argentine National Commission on the Disappeared* (New York: Farrar, Straus & Giroux, 1986), p. 56.

45. The Center for Legal and Social Studies (CELS) was raided on February 27, 1981. A federal judge ordered the intervention and arrests, based on an allegation that CELS had military maps and documents that could adversely affect state security. All suspects were eventually released and the confiscated material, none of which revealed any state secrets, was returned. See ibid., pp. 424–25.

46. In addition, the Argentine National Commission on the Disappeared, appointed by President Alfonsín and chaired by famed novelist Ernesto Sábato, was mandated to "receive depositions and evidence concerning these events, and pass the information on to the courts where crimes had been committed." See ibid., p. 428. This they did at the end of 1984, turning over to the Federal Court

The number of charges filed against senior and junior officers grew geometrically in the span of just nine months, going from thirty in February 1984 to some two thousand by the end of August. Six hundred of those were filed by CELS alone. One-third of the six hundred and fifty alleged perpetrators tied to these reported crimes were on active duty.[47]

The sheer number of cases combined with the complexities of each posed a daunting problem for the government: How could justice be delivered in timely fashion? Overwhelmed with charges, testimony, and mounds of evidence, it was unlikely that either the undermotivated Military Supreme Council or the notoriously slow federal judicial system could render verdicts expeditiously.[48] The courts would be tied up for years. The human rights organizations were fully aware of that fact yet forged ahead with their denunciations, pushing the political envelope as far as they could.[49]

Commenting on the problem in 1985, then Defense Minister Roque Carranza, who had immediate authority over the military courts, estimated that some ten to fifteen testimonies, each one-half hour in length, would be recorded for each of the approximately fifteen hundred charges in front of the Supreme Council. With that caseload, and working seven days a week from

of Appeals 1,087 cases implicating some 1,500 individuals with human rights crimes. See Alison Brysk, *The Politics of Human Rights in Argentina: Protest, Change, and Democratization* (Stanford: Stanford University Press, 1994), p. 71.

47. Shortly thereafter the numbers grew again, as six of the leading human rights organizations presented to Congress a list of 896 military and police officers allegedly associated with repressive acts. Despite the passage of Law 23.049, which gave the military jurisdiction over cases involving uniformed men, individuals continued to bring forth charges in civilian courtrooms. While civil-military jurisdiction was being debated, civilian judges ordered the arrest of many junior officers as well as some of the most notorious human rights violators, including Generals Suaréz Mason, Ramón Camps, Luciano Benjamín Menéndez, and former president Reynaldo Bignone. See Americas Watch, *Truth and Partial Justice in Argentina*, pp. 27, 48, 56. Cases heard in civilian courts were eventually sent to the Military Supreme Council once the Supreme Court ruled that Law 23.049 was constitutional, giving the armed forces original jurisdiction. By the middle of 1986 the military court had been saddled with some three thousand cases. However, most of these cases returned once again to civilian courts by July of that year.

48. All those lawyers and judges interviewed agreed that the Argentine judiciary is notoriously slow—an age-old attribute of the court system. Interviews with Ricardo Entelman, legal advisor to Dr. Raúl Alfonsín, Buenos Aires, November 3, 1994; and Ricardo R. Gil Lavedra, Buenos Aires, November 3, 1994.

49. This tactic was admitted to me in a candid interview with Emilio Mignone, founder of the Centro de Estudios Legales y Sociales. I asked Mignone how justice could ever have been served in time to have averted military reprisals, given the extraordinary number of charges filed in courts by his organization and others like it. He replied that it would have taken ten years or more given the slowness of the justice system. However, as he stated, "his responsibility as the head of a human rights organization was to carry things to their extreme, without measuring the political consequences [for the government] of doing so." Interview with author, Buenos Aires, November 2, 1994.

dawn to dusk, it would have taken the military tribunal more than two years just to process the files![50]

From the vantage point of the accused, the judicial process was unnerving. Defendants were immediately summoned to court as soon as an investigating judge found "justifiable suspicion" that the accused had committed a crime.[51] In fact, even where the evidence fell short of justifiable suspicion, the justices were within their powers to depose officers for questioning simply because they had been identified by victims.[52] Those suspects and defendants who might flee or who refused to cooperate with court orders were placed under arrest. In the federal capital alone the appeals court detained about fifty army and naval officers,[53] all of whom remained in a state of suspended animation regarding their legal status and indeed their careers. They could not be as- sured of speedy trials and would have to wait indefinitely to learn their fate.

The Government Response: Double Speak

Both the probable prolongation of the judicial process along with its expand- ing scope had some administration officials worried by early 1985. It was then that Defense Minister Raúl Borrás and his secretary of defense, José Horacio Jaunarena, suggested to the president that a bill be sponsored to politically restrict the human rights trials by setting a time limit and by excluding from prosecution all those officers below a certain rank.[54] They argued that such a bill would be completely consistent with Alfonsín's cam- paign pledges to limit the scope of the trials and thus spare the government and the party any electoral losses.

In April of that year Borrás went public with his own position, stating that the trials could not go on indefinitely. "I deny talk of an amnesty, but the country cannot remain in 'aeternum' with an open wound. Democracy does not rest upon vengeance and persecution."[55] He added, "some day the

50. *La Nación Edición Internacional*, July 1, 1985, p. 1.
51. Carrió, *The Criminal Justice System of Argentina*, p. 50.
52. Ibid., pp. 50–51.
53. Andrés José D'Alessio, interview with author, Buenos Aires, November 1, 1994.
54. Dr. José Horacio Jaunarena, interview with author, Buenos Aires, July 27, 1993. In essence, that proposal presaged the *Punto Final* legislation of 1986 and the Law of Just Obedience of June 1987.
55. *La Razón*, April 3, 1985, p. 2.

book will have to be closed" on the *Dirty War*.[56] This was the first public allusion to a *punto final* or final stop—a measure that would begin the process of legal closure and give anxious officers some assurances about the future. But with Borrás's untimely death in May 1985, the proposal lost momentum and was shelved. At the time, neither Alfonsín nor his human rights advisors felt any great urgency about finding a means to curtail the steady advance of the judiciary.

Politically, Alfonsín reasoned correctly that this was not a propitious moment to initiate legislative curbs on the judicial process. Public support for prosecution was still fierce, and mid-term elections were coming up in September. A *punto final* was an electoral gamble that was not worth taking.[57] But by December of that year the elections had passed. The Radical Party had won, maintaining its plurality in the lower chamber, with the Peronists losing ten seats to minor third parties. The trials had proven successful, with the ex-junta members receiving long prison sentences. The conclusion of the trial itself acted as a decompression valve, releasing the enormous pent-up fury of an angry public in the form of a long-awaited punishment for the *Proceso* leaders. Thus, this could have been the time to phase out a policy of retribution and phase in a policy of reward by rebuilding military pride and professionalism. Yet Alfonsín could not do this so long as matters remained in the judicial branch. And it was by no means clear that the Congress was prepared to legislate an end to the trials.

In February 1986 the Argentine head of state said on U.S. television that the process must come to an end but that "it will be the justice system that has the final word."[58] Rather than vigorously contest the court's decision to pursue offenders at lower ranks, the president seemed willing to let things run their course, at least for a while.[59] When asked by this author why he

---

56. *Foreign Broadcast Information Service—Latin America* (*FBIS-LAT*), April 8, 1985, p. B3.

57. Much of Alfonsín's appeal up until then had rested with the public's perception of a leader unafraid to take on a powerful institution like the armed forces. To have backed down in his pursuit of justice could have cost his party votes. Moreover, he did not wish to detract from the strong expression of public interest in the trials of the junta leaders that were going on at the same time.

58. *La Nación Edición Internacional*, February 17, 1986, p. 5.

59. With his appointment of German López as the new defense minister on February 13, Alfonsín only reinforced his preference for a judicial solution. López (who replaced Roque Carranza who had died the week before after serving as defense minister for only eight months) had no defense experience whatsoever, having served as labor undersecretary in the Arturo Illia government. But he was a party loyalist, whose longtime membership in Alfonsín's *Renovación y Cambio* movement gave the president added assurance he would faithfully represent the government's interests before the armed forces, rather than the other way around. Jaunarena was the man with greater experience, but also one perceived to be more sympathetic to the military's point of view.

did not take a strong political initiative in December 1985 to bring the judicial proceedings to a close, Alfonsín responded: "I was hoping that the justices would establish the fact that the disposition [*obediencia debida*] had to be respected, . . . but they did not want to return to the initial idea [of *obediencia debida*] before [it was amended by] the Senate."[60]

When the trials continued against unit commanders charged with inflicting abuses of their own, the government unwittingly deepened military resentments against itself. It could no longer count on the loyalty of mid-ranking officers, who feared they would be the next victims of judicial action. In March of that year Alfonsín met with his ministers of defense and interior justice, along with the capital federal court judges, to review the options. Rejecting for the moment any political solution (including time or numerical limits), Alfonsín reportedly turned to the magistrates and said, "The country is indebted to you for what you have done. I will always consult with you first. I will never betray you."[61] But time was no longer on the president's side, and he was under concerted pressure to find some means of restricting the process. What emerged was a set of instructions to the military court that Defense Minister German López submitted to the military prosecutor, Brigadier Hector N. Canale, on April 24.[62] The orders were for the Military Supreme Council to consolidate outstanding cases by joining them together according to repressive agencies or territorial jurisdictions (as established under the *Proceso*), and then to drop all charges against those for whom the *obediencia debida* defense was justifiable (i.e., all those who followed orders) in order to spare them the ordeal of prolonged trials. Even those who had committed atrocities were to be exonerated so long as their actions had been carried out under strict orders.

The explanations accompanying the decree provide further insight into the thinking of part of the Alfonsín administration that had been growing increasingly concerned about judicial delays. The secretary of defense and soon-to-be minister, Horacio Jaunarena, who was in fact the principal author of the instructions, characterized the trials as "un desorden" that had harmed the military esprit de corps by appearing to render a collective judgment against the institution, which in turn could so demoralize the forces as to threaten their defensive readiness. The proceedings, according to him, had also endangered the constitutional rights of individuals to a speedy trial. The

60. Dr. Raúl R. Alfonsín, interview with author, Buenos Aires, July 20, 1993.
61. Verbitsky, *Civiles y militares*, p. 158.
62. *Clarín*, June 4, 1986, p. 2. The text of the instructions can be found in *La Nación Edición Internacional*, April 28, 1986, p. 5.

instructions would protect that right by freeing the defendant from a "state of suspicion of . . . having committed a crime through a sentence that establishes . . . in the most rapid means possible . . . his status with respect to the penal law."[63]

For Horacio Jaunarena *obediencia debida* was problematic since it provided no assurances to those accused or to others who could potentially face indictment. Despite repeated claims by Alfonsín that he had no intent of prosecuting those who had justly followed orders, who was to say what the final verdict of the judicial process would be or when it would be rendered? Reflecting back on this time, Jaunarena added:

> The problem was that limits could not be set in advance as to which individuals would be criminally pursued. Nearly everyone remained involved. It could not be determined beforehand that there were fifty to be indicted and the rest exculpated. Only the sentencing would distinguish clearly who followed the orders and who didn't. But meanwhile you had to go through [the entire process] which was going to take years. . . . That is to say, the result would be produced at the end of the trials and not at the beginning.[64]

According to one legal scholar, the instructions made it "virtually impossible to reject a plea of due obedience,"[65] and it would seem that the military court agreed. True to form and literally within hours of the government's directive, the *Consejo Supremo* acquitted one of the most notorious figures of the *Proceso*, Naval Lieutenant Alfredo Astiz, for the murder of Dagmar Hagelin. Soon after army General Luciano Menéndez was also acquitted for the murder of María Amelia Inzaurralde.[66]

Alfonsín admitted he was trying to walk a narrow path between two perilous rivers: on the one side an increasingly restless armed forces closing ranks around its accused, on the other a defensive judiciary anxious to protect its

---

63. *La Nación Edición Internacional*, April 28, 1986, p. 5.

64. Interview with Dr. José Horacio Jaunarena, Buenos Aires, July 27, 1993. In admitting that continuance of trials would generate the appearance of a wholesale indictment against the institution rather than a selective punishment against a few individuals, the administration was also acknowledging that the distinction upon which his entire human rights strategy rested, that of individual vs. collective guilt, was in danger of being lost on the armed forces. The defense minister made this point in *Clarín*, June 4, 1986. Also see *La Nación Weekly*, April 28, 1986, p. 1.

65. Crawford, "Due Obedience and the Rights of Victims," p. 25.

66. *La Nación Edición Internacional*, April 28, 1986, p. 1.

sovereignty against political encroachment.[67] But rather than walk the path steadily, the president would occasionally stumble into one current, lift himself out, only to stumble into the other.

For example, at first he appeared to fully back Jaunarena's instructions. But after vigorous judicial protest, he reinterpreted those instructions on June 11, claiming the rules would permit the trials to continue, were consistent with *item thirty* of the December 1985 sentence, and would not preemptively exonerate any of those accused of atrocious or aberrant acts. This was a double message that led one well-placed government source to candidly admit to *La Nación* that "we do not see clear signals from the executive branch."[68] These contradictory moves reflected the mind of a president wrestling with difficult choices. Looking back on his predicament, Alfonsín said: "I asked myself to what extent would paying attention to human rights in the past risk human rights in the future? This was a torture that I endured during my entire term, and one which limited action in other areas."[69]

The Court Retaliates

The Federal Court of Appeals was enraged not only over the instructions but also over Alfonsín's rationalization. Its anger was directed toward the president's claim that the instructions had been naturally derived from prior decisions of the federal court itself. This was simply not true, and it constituted an effort to disguise a political decision with legal garb, according to Andrés D'Alessio.[70] Citing unwarranted delays in the Supreme Council's deliberations, the federal court took over the military's caseload on June 20 of that year.[71] Unwittingly, Alfonsín had accelerated the delivery of cases to civilian judges who were now prepared to examine the charges against hundreds of defendants.

Once the civilian courts resumed jurisdiction, the human rights policy would again be molded by judicial norms. Lest he trespass on the judiciary (which he was not inclined to do), or switch policy arenas legislatively (which he eventually would have to do), the president was for now forced to

---

67. Dr. Raúl R. Alfonsín, interview with author, Buenos Aires, July 20, 1993.
68. *La Nación Weekly*, June 23, 1986, p. 5.
69. Dr. Raúl R. Alfonsín, interview with author, Buenos Aires, July 20, 1993.
70. Andrés José D'Alessio, interview with author, Buenos Aires, November 1, 1994.
71. *La Nación Edición Internacional*, June 23, 1986, p. 5.

watch the wheels of justice turn ever so slowly, grinding out more indict-ments that would implicate more officers and that made it ever more likely that trials would persist into the indefinite future. Human rights organiza-tions would be there to represent the families, provide testimony and investi-gatory leads if needed, and agitate for prosecutorial action.

The autonomy of the courts and the human rights movement, which con-formed to and resonated so well with Alfonsín's moral mission, were now clashing with his more politically pragmatic aspirations. As a member of the bar himself and one who had defended the victims of the *Dirty War*, the president always retained a tremendous respect for the integrity of the magis-trates. Yet to passively watch the legal process unfold by its own design was to assume a political risk: that the military would continue to be patient rather than retaliate.

Punto Final

By December 1986 the president could wait no more. The new judicial "of-fensive" carried out against the "instructions" had led many in the military to believe there were no limits to the number of soldiers who could be prose-cuted. The proceedings, now in their third year, had a corrosive effect on the military. Forced to absorb the unrelenting costs of prosecution and public humiliation at the hands of the media, some members of the armed forces became more adversarial in their dealings with the government. True, Al-fonsín continued to enjoy support from the top commanders of the three forces as well as from a core of career-minded officials. But the judicial "agony" suffered by servicemen widened a swath of resistance to official pol-icy within the middle and lower ranks.

Finally, the president sponsored a bill designed to bring all the proceedings to a rapid conclusion. Under intense lobbying by Alfonsín himself, the Ar-gentine Congress on December 24, 1986, passed the *Punto Final* or "Full Stop" bill. This piece of legislation allowed charges already filed against human rights offenders to remain, but placed a sixty-day time limit on new indictments. Those who were not accused within the sixty days would go free.[72]

Alfonsín reasoned that the *Punto Final* law would meet with military ap-

---

72. The text of *Punto Final* is found in *La Prensa*, December 27, 1986, pp. 1, 4.

proval on the one hand and public scorn—especially from the human rights lobby—on the other. To contain the political fallout to *Punto Final*, he tried to put the best face on the legislation that he could. Far from a surrender to military will, this law represented the culmination of a policy that had achieved a measure of justice, he contended. Because the political leaders of the *Proceso* had been punished, Argentina was now ready to turn the corner on its past and look toward a brighter future.[73]

Then, on the eve of congressional deliberation on the *Punto Final* bill, the president orchestrated a series of statements by his chiefs of staff designed to allay public fears that this legislation was both an exoneration of wrongdoing during the *Dirty War* and a form of impunity for future military offenders.[74] General Teodoro Waldner, head of the *Estado Mayor Conjunto*, said that the levels of violence used by the junta in its antisubversive campaign caused him to "doubt the legality of many repressive actions." And in a caution against future military intervention, he added, each time the military has assumed public office the result has been "a loss of prestige, estrangement from the Argentine public, and an inexorable breakdown in the morale and discipline of . . . the institution."[75] Ríos Ereñú, head of the army, pledged that the military would never again involve itself in politics.[76] The chiefs of staff for the navy and air force issued similar statements. The timing of this institutional mea culpa could not have been better, helping Alfonsín to win passage of his measure with a vote of 126 for to 16 against and 1 abstention in the Chamber of Deputies, and a 25 to 10 vote in favor in the Senate.[77]

The chief executive, however, had less success convincing the public that this was a just and lasting solution to the problem. The *Punto Final* solution was in fact anything but lasting. For one, it did not put an end to the trials but rather resulted in a kind of last-minute panic on the part of some federal courts to comply with the edict. This was especially true of courts in the interior provinces of Argentina, which had been reluctant to press charges against military offenders. Judges there tended to be more conservative than those in the nation's capital because of close family ties to military officers.[78] Federal courts in Córdoba, Rosano, and elsewhere that had for months postponed decisions on literally hundreds of cases now faced intense public and

---

73. Ibid., December 6, 1986, pp. 1, 4.
74. Ibid.
75. Ibid., December 7, 1986, p. 4.
76. Ibid., December 2, 1986, p. 1.
77. *La Nación Edición Internacional*, December 29, 1986, p. 1.
78. *New York Times*, March 29, 1984, p. 32.

governmental scrutiny that would not allow them to shirk from their obligations. Suddenly they were scrambling to indict as many officers as they could.

Unfortunately, the tremendous constraints of time forced the courts to act irrationally. When in doubt over the involvement of an officer in a human rights crime, the justices, lacking sufficient time to investigate further, erred on the side of punishing everyone.[79] The results were hardly what Alfonsín had desired or anticipated. Rather than still the prosecutorial waters, the measure only unleashed a torrent of indictments. By the February deadline some three hundred summons had been handed out to alleged perpetrators within the armed forces.

Alfonsín now had to allay military fears by arguing that few individuals were at risk of being convicted since human rights crimes were hard to prove. For example, to thirteen naval cadets brought up on charges of committing torture at the Naval Mechanics School (Escuela de Mecánica de la Armada, ESMA), the government pointed out that Navy Lieutenant Alfredo Astiz had already been acquitted of kidnapping.[80] But the president's appeal fell on deaf ears. Six of those cadets refused to appear in court when subpoenaed and were issued arrest warrants. The belief that convictions and more indictments would follow led to the organized rebellion of junior officers against their senior commanders during Holy Week in April of that year. This would be followed by two more uprisings that would rattle the Alfonsín government.

The Law of Due Obedience

A month after the *Semana Santa* rebellion was quieted, the president submitted a bill to Congress that would exonerate all officers at the rank of lieutenant colonel or lower charged with human rights offenses. This measure, which was similar to that which Jaunarena and Borrás had been urging upon Alfonsín two years before and which was amended by the Senate to exculpate superior officers who were not key decision makers, passed into law on June 5. Called the law of due obedience (Law 23.521), it instructed justices

---

79. In one rather amusing though telling case, the Federal Court of Appeals in La Plata investigated a murder that occurred at an artillery school in 1978. The justices requested the names of all the directors of the school, and ended up indicting General Dante Caridi for the murder, even though he became director in 1982, four years after the incident. The story was related to me by Andrés José D'Alessio, November 1, 1994, in Buenos Aires.

80. *Latin American Monitor*, March 1987, p. 389.

to presume the heretofore-mentioned officers innocent and prohibited them from considering evidence to the contrary, even where atrocious or aberrant acts had been committed.[81] While the great majority of those affected were below the rank of colonel, several senior officers would go free as well. Only those in charge of security areas or forces (military and police)—about thirty to forty in all—were vulnerable to continued prosecution. In introducing this bill to the Congress, Alfonsín admitted that his government had previously taken steps which "for one reason or another, were not sufficiently effective to bring about pacification." The Law of Due Obedience represented the "necessary and sufficient measure that will "allow us to be generous without capitulating."[82]

Alfonsín was essentially correct in stating that the law did not represent a capitulation. But sometimes in politics appearances are as important if not more important than reality. The timing of the due obedience legislation could not have been worse. Coming as it did on the heels of a major military rebellion that the government could not subdue by force, the law only strengthened the perception that the government had conceded under the duress of military recalcitrance.[83] And despite his contention that such legislation had been planned well in advance of the rebellion, Alfonsín could not escape from the public view that his proposal had been pressured into existence.

To date, Alfonsín denies that such a concession had arisen from negotiations between himself and rebel leader Aldo Rico. Indeed, eyewitness accounts of the session tend to confirm his version of the events that transpired at the Campo del Mayo garrison in April. Yet at the same time, and by Alfonsín's own admission, the law "took on the appearance of" a concession that fueled speculation about a negotiated end to the uprising.[84] That appearance lowered public confidence in the government and invited junior officers to rebel again.

81. The due obedience bill found in República Argentina, Diario de Sesiones (Buenos Aires: Camara de Diputados, May 15–16, 1987), p. 618. The defense would not be available for those who engaged in rape, theft, and the kidnapping of minors. See Crawford, "Due Obedience and the Rights of Victims," p. 28.

82. FBIS-LAT, May 14, 1987, p. B4.

83. Clarín Weekly, May 25, 1987, p. 1. Accounts of the military uprisings can be found in various issues of La Nación and Clarín between April 17–20, 1987. The speed with which Alfonsín made his concessions coupled with the fact that the new law went beyond earlier versions of obediencia debida by extending an amnesty to all junior officers—whether or not they had committed excesses (torture, executions, etc.)—and to more senior officers who were not key decision makers in the Dirty War reinforced the view that the government had emerged in a weaker position.

84. Dr. Raúl R. Alfonsín, interview with author, Buenos Aires, July 20, 1993.

The problem with the due obedience law lay not in its logic but in its delay.[85] Right up until the rebellion itself, Alfonsín, according to Carlos Nino, still held a lingering belief that "the Court would resolve the theme,"[86] and thus never spoke of the need for legislation until it was too late. Only when the justices refused to render a decision, citing this as a political problem and not a judicial one, did Alfonsín call in his advisors to contemplate the unsavory alternatives.[87]

Conclusion

President Alfonsín was aware that as a result of the thorough collapse of the *Proceso* government, the balance of forces had swung decisively in his favor. He enjoyed a window of opportunity that at another time or place would have been unthinkable. But despite his strengthened hand, the president was also fully cognizant of the potential risks to prosecuting officers charged with human rights abuses. He knew that the military had the capacity to resuscitate itself. In climbing back from the depths of its professional despair to discover a new resolve, soldiers would eventually seek retribution against the government if a sufficient number of them perceived that the military institution and not just a handful of officers was under attack. Thus he designed a strategy with these potential problems in mind: he permitted the military to "clean its own house," and he provided a legal escape hatch for subordinate officers who had done as they were told.

As well intended as these policies were, they were insufficient, not well received by the armed forces, and, most important, modified by an array of institutional actors. Thousands of charges were left in the hands of a few military judges who were neither able nor willing to render verdicts on any

85. The law of due obedience was a much more effective piece of legislation, since by quickly whittling down the number of human rights cases to a manageable few, it instantly eased the anxieties of most mid-level officers awaiting trial, and thereby helped to restore the chain of command. It was also to be the first major blow against the *carapintadas* themselves. But coming as it did after military frustrations had boiled over into open rebellion, it only hurt the UCR government politically.

86. Carlos Nino, interview with author, Buenos Aires, July 2, 1993.

87. Dr. José Horacio Jaunarena insists that ten days before the uprising in Córdoba, Alfonsín had already announced his intention to submit a bill of due obedience. Apparently, his announcement was not widely picked up by the press at the time. After the uprising the damage had been done since Rico insisted this was a result of concession to the *carapintadas*. José Horacio Jaunarena, interview with author, Buenos Aires, July 27, 1993.

of the accused. Once those cases were transferred to federal court, junior officers could have used the just obedience defense but chose not to.[88] But even if they had, this would not have freed them from the ordeal they were about to face: the agonizing and seemingly timeless uncertainty regarding their fates as they waited for the process to come to a close. The more time elapsed, the more anxious and defiant they would grow.

The government's unique window of opportunity would not stay open much longer. Timing was critical here. Alfonsín would have to bring to an end the phase of moral condemnation before his military foes revitalized themselves. Delays in the judicial process would only further complicate the sequencing of policy and prove potentially damaging to the government's human rights and civilian control objectives. Unfortunately, the human rights program did not remain in the hands of the chief executive. After designing the initial plan, he could no longer singularly control its fate. Other governmental and nongovernmental actors and institutions, with their own unique rules of behavior, perspectives, and interests, were entering the fray. Each of these institutions enjoyed a level of autonomy high enough to impede the administration's quest for complete policy success.

Judicial autonomy cut both ways. On the one hand, the judiciary's unwavering resistance to any form of intimidation, most especially from the military itself, made possible the completion of the trials against the ex-commanders and handed Alfonsín a major political victory. The judicial branch had done its work, unfettered by forces outside of it. The human rights organizations helped, providing some of the most critically damaging evidence needed to build a case against the nine defendants.

On the other hand, a similar spirit of judicial independence expressed toward the executive branch later meant a loss of presidential control once Alfonsín began to search for legal closure. The judges would not be moved. Once having unearthed evidence of criminality at lower levels of the military hierarchy, they were prepared to let justice run its course. Alfonsín left the courts alone and yet always retained an undiminished faith that they would

88. For the armed forces the *Dirty War* was a just war. As viewed through the lens of the National Security Doctrine (NSD), the war was the fulfillment of their highest obligations to the state: the elimination of "subversive terrorism" and the restoration of political "order." Because the *Dirty War* had become an object of pride for Argentina's soldiers, they could not accept the principle of due obedience since to do so would have been to implicitly endorse the concept of improper obedience. Having fought the just war and having won, the military deserved recognition rather than blame, so they claimed. The reluctance of all officers to be forthcoming—whether in civilian or military court—was so great that not one soldier of lower rank had ever availed himself of the legal defense as provided for by *obediencia debida*.

interpret the law to his liking. When they did not, he resorted to subterfuge (i.e., the instructions to military courts) to spare himself the ordeal of confronting the justices head-on.

The courts were miffed by the president's tactics and insisted on doing things their way, at their pace. But the normal business of the courts was now the preoccupation of the president. As the military grew increasingly restless about its legal status, something had to be done. The only thing left to do for a president who was unable or unwilling to tamper with judicial prerogatives was to shift the human rights issue to the legislative arena. This he did in preparing the *Punto Final* legislation in December 1986.

But shifting arenas was not easy, nor a guarantee of success. The idea of putting closure to the human rights proceedings was still politically unpopular with the public and its representatives. The Congress represented yet another institutional hurdle to clear. While the Radical Party held a majority of the 254 seats in the Chamber of Deputies at the time, the Peronists held the largest plurality in the 46-seat Senate. Moreover, thirty Radical Party congressmen, not to mention the entire Renovador wing of the Peronist Party, favored the prolongation of the trials. It was only through the president's last-minute personal appeals to Radical Party deputies, his rallying of orthodox Peronist and provincial party votes, and his pledge to absorb all the political costs for the decision that he was able to garner the necessary votes for *Punto Final*.[89]

Unfortunately, the legislative solution was insufficient and late in arrival. The delay was due to Alfonsín's unshakable though misguided trust in the justices' willingness and capacity to solve the crisis on their own legal terms. This meant that he would not marshal his forces to do political battle until the eleventh hour. By then the military rebels known as the *carapintadas* were already plotting their subversive activities.

The rebellion of April 1987 was not so much the cause of the decline of Alfonsín's human rights policy as it was the logical consequence of a policy already mired in the complexities of organized democratic life. It occurred because the democracy had performed the way it was supposed to. The application of and allegiance to normal institutional rules of procedure caused the trials to be prolonged and widened in scope, which in turn precipitated the military unrest. It is ironic that on this occasion a functioning democracy ended up generating its own nondemocratic resistance.

89. See Andrés Fontana, "La política militar del gobierno constitucional Argentino," Centro de Estudios de Estado y Sociedad *CEDES* (July 1987): 26–27.

The human rights story depicted here underscores how institutions mediate between leadership choices and policy outcomes. Once the chief executive designs a policy, its smooth implementation depends upon the cooperation of those along the policy path. Will it be a rather short, straight journey with few obstacles, or will it be a winding journey filled with detours and roadblocks? That depends upon the nature of the institutions it passes through along the way. What is certain is that from the moment it leaves the president's desk, it has escaped his control. As it passes through each institutional checkpoint, it is altered by the actors and processes that inhabit each site.

In the case of human rights those sites were innumerable and relatively autonomous. Aside from the executive branch itself, the Federal Court of Appeals and the Supreme Court, the human rights organizations and the Congress all played a role. Just the sheer number of protagonists ensured that policy clearance would be made more difficult by virtue of the fact that each agency brought with it its own perspective, interests, structures, and rules of procedure.

One might have fathomed that on so delicate and transcending a matter as human rights trials, with implications for the future of Argentine democracy, that some prior agreement would have been worked out between these disparate institutions. But none were. This was not a pacted democracy: there were no formal or informal accords to ensure procedural or substantive understandings. "Thus," as Carlos Nino pointed out, "the different parties involved acted independently, without significant coordination."[90] Decision-making authority was indeed decentralized among independent institutional actors. The particular combination of high institutional autonomy and dispersed authority created the essential conditions for a moderately successful human rights policy, as shown in Figure 4.1.

True, Alfonsín's human rights program met with only partial success. And some of the wounds that the Radical government suffered were self-inflicted. But another kind of question needs to be raised. Did the policies of this era have a more beneficial impact on civil-military relations in the longer term? Was there, in other words, a kind of sacrificial quality to the government's human rights program? The answer would seem to be yes. Even by the accounts of some of his foes, the Radical Party president had both inflicted

90. Carlos S. Nino, "The Duty to Punish Past Abuses of Human Rights Put into Context: The Case of Argentina," *Yale Law Journal* 100, no. 8 (June 1991): 2631.

Fig. 4.1. Explaining human rights policy outcomes: the role of institutional authority and autonomy

Institutional
Concentration of Authority

		High	Low
Decision-Making Autonomy	High	A. High Success	B. Moderate Success (human rights) 1983–87)
	Low	C. Moderate Success	D. No Success

costs on the armed forces and absorbed costs of his own that made civil-military tasks easier for his Peronist successor, Carlos Menem.[91]

Whatever else can be said about Alfonsín's human rights strategy, it is generally agreed that the decision to hold trials for the ex-comandantes was one that made political and moral sense. Though unprecedented and risky, the judicial proceedings were nonetheless beneficial to a government that had pledged to punish the perpetrators of the *Dirty War*, expected by a society eager to vent its anger and repulsion over state-sanctioned violence, and acceptable to many officers who were anxious to divorce themselves from disreputable figures of the past and earn their credentials as professionalized soldiers under democratic auspices. Perhaps most important, the trials served as a warning to future authoritarian governments who might contemplate reprisals against their citizens.

In punishing the *Proceso* leaders, Alfonsín defeated the principle of impunity and thereby raised the stakes for future acts of military defiance. Once the costs of defiance had been increased, Carlos Menem was free to increase the benefits of compliance, confident that such moves would not set in mo-

91. This admission was made to me in an interview by Dr. Virgilio Beltrán, who served the Menem government as undersecretary of defense for policy and strategy. Interview held in Buenos Aires on July 1, 1993.

tion predatory and praetorian forces that would undermine the democratic order as they had done in the past. That is to say, Alfonsín had made clear the democratic regime's refusal to allow military, political aggression to go unchecked. In setting new limits he had altered the parameters of the civil-military game and in doing so created opportunities for his successors to interact with the armed forces without the fear of a military coup. Menem could now more confidently reward good behavior knowing that to concede was not to capitulate; that one reward would not unleash a torrent of new and unreasonable military demands that if left unfulfilled could generate calls for regime change. Conversely, if need be, Menem could withhold rewards to the armed forces in order to husband scarce resources or redistribute them elsewhere, confident that when called upon to assume its share of the burden, the military would cooperate.

As the next chapter on military budgets will reveal, this is precisely what he did between the years 1989 and 1993. It has been argued here that Alfonsín must receive substantial credit for this new civil-military equilibrium. Regrettably for him, his efforts were more selfless than self-serving. Thus, he was unable to personally reap the political rewards of a human rights policy that may in the end have significantly furthered the Argentine cause of civilian control.

CHAPTER 5

Trimming the Fat
Military Budget-Cutting Successes Under Democratic Rule

When it comes to fiscal resources, all organizations want more.[1] The Argentine armed forces are no different. Despite the fact that they had enriched themselves unabashedly while in office, they were not about to remove themselves from the competition for budget shares once out of office. But under democratic conditions they would be just one other agency scrapping for scarce funds. Their struggle would lie with the misers who controlled the purse strings. Those misers reside in the economics ministry, where they jealously guard their coffers against plundering raids by the spenders—other ministries and the organized interests they represent. The task of the finance minister is neatly stated by Wildavsky: "His job is to guard the treasury. Emblazoned on its doors, engraved on its innermost consciousness, the Ministry of Finance subscribes to this creed: That there Shall be Money on Hand to Pay the Bills."[2]

The spenders' task is to procure the most resources they can for their agencies and the constituents they serve. Unless they can capture outside

---

1. See Aaron Wildavsky, *Budgeting: A Comparative Theory of Budgetary Processes* (Boston: Little, Brown and Co., 1975), p. 5.
2. Ibid., p. 143.

funds, they are forced to maneuver for position within the government to feed off what is often a diminished pie. This is a difficult and sometimes contradictory assignment. Take the defense ministry for example. On the one hand, it is part of the executive branch, and must dutifully serve its own administration. On the other hand, it serves military clients, who beseech the ministry to act on their behalf, to pry loose more funds from the accounts that the economists so vigilantly protect. The minister may feel torn between his clients and his loyalties to the president. Should he not act spiritedly on their behalf, the armed forces may be frustrated in their attempts to secure resources. But even when he comes to their defense, he can never be sure that he will prevail against the guardians of the purse. The thematic questions to be addressed in this chapter are as follows: How have the Argentine armed forces fared in this budgetary struggle since the return of democracy? And how do institutional arrangements account for their successes or failures?

A balance-of-power hypothesis would suggest that in the immediate post-authoritarian environment the Argentine armed forces would have been at a decided disadvantage. Its precipitous fall from grace certainly should have strengthened the hand of the Alfonsín and Menem administrations who were preoccupied with limiting military spending.[3] However, such a hypothesis fails to explain an important anomaly. The fact is, the scales of power had tipped back in favor of the armed forces during the latter part of the Alfonsín era. Time had allowed the military to recover, to heal its wounds, and to regain some measure of confidence and combativeness that had been lost after the Malvinas fiasco. That recovery seemed pronounced by the end of Alfonsín's term, when a string of military rebellions stunned the UCR government.[4]

Alfonsín's successor, Carlos Menem, who assumed power in July 1989, sought to avert the fate that had befallen his predecessor. He quickly pardoned the military mutineers, an act that only heightened the perception of civilian vulnerability to military provocation. Menem's reprieve capped off a successful drive by elements within the military to end what they saw as a campaign of judicial persecution waged against them. It also seemed to be an admission that civilian strategies of confrontation with the military would

---

3. For an elaboration on this point, see David Pion-Berlin, "Between Confrontation and Accommodation: Military and Government Policy in Democratic Argentina," *Journal of Latin American Studies* 23 (October 1991): 549–52.

4. Most observers concur that those uprisings left the administration in a weakened position vis-à-vis the military.

simply not work. The Menem government signaled its desire for a more amicable approach with the appointments of Italo Luder and then Humberto Romero as his first two ministers of defense. Both men enjoyed close ties with the armed forces.[5]

All this apparently indicates that the military had regained the momentum by 1989. Nonetheless, at this very moment the defense budget would begin its steepest descent, plummeting by 17 percent that year and by 23 percent the year after. Why couldn't the armed forces defend their budget? No simple, zero sum, tug of war between the armed forces and government could account for this remarkable and indeed paradoxical trend. What then could?

The armed forces had regained some institutional composure. They could more confidently voice demands as a unified actor rather than as one torn asunder by internecine conflict. But they were still subordinate actors whose overtures were largely restricted by institutional protocol. The vocalization of demands by some rebellious, mid-level, army officers outside the chain of command had produced no budgetary gains to speak of.[6] When soldiers stayed inside the chain of command, as most did most of the time, the limits to their influence were defined by institutional arrangements. It will be argued that those arrangements—at least as they pertained to budget formulation and implementation—favored civilian decision makers of both administrations who were determined to substantially reduce military expenditures. It will be shown that in large measure they succeeded at this task.

To better understand their success, it is important to first detail the specific objectives of the governments they served. The desire for budget cutting can be traced back to the military dictatorship of 1976 to 1983. The *Proceso* years marked a period of financial gluttony for the armed forces. The nature and consequences of this engorgement will be briefly recounted. Then we will turn to the democratic governments of Raúl Alfonsín and Carlos

5. When Italo Luder became interim president of Argentina in September 1975, taking over for Isabel Perón who was convalescing from an illness, he signed a decree that authorized the armed forces to annihilate subversion. The military frequently point to that decree as evidence of the legitimacy of their *Dirty War* since it had been endorsed by a constitutional regime. Dr. Humberto Romero described his defense ministry as "La Casa Militar." He hails from the province of Corrientes, where his home was well known as a place for reunions with military families.

6. Not withstanding the harmful impact that the *Semana Santa* rebellion had on Alfonsín's human rights policy, the fact is it had no impact on budgetary matters. In fact, five months after that uprising, economics minister Juan Sourroille met with the military chiefs of staff to tell them that (1) the military budget was correct, (2) any proceeds from the sale of military property would go toward modernization, not salaries, and (3) the real enemy was inflation. See *Clarín*, September 24, 1987, p. 14.

Menem who were left saddled with inflated military budgets. Although there was an unmistakable continuity in defense-related fiscal policies preserved across administrations, each one had its own agenda. Whereas Alfonsín slashed the defense budget out of a desire to politically weaken the armed forces, Menem's fiscal attacks were motivated largely out of economic priorities. Finally, a detailed accounting of defense budget making will be undertaken to reveal its structural and procedural dimensions and how these allowed civilian decision makers throughout the democratic period to achieve their ultimate objectives.

The *Proceso* Years and Military Extravagance

The years under military dictatorship were distinguished by extravagance. The *Dirty War* excesses committed by the officer corps against its victims were fully matched by the intemperance with which it seized and expended resources. The military enriched itself unabashedly and in doing so drove the state's deficits to unparalleled heights, thus undermining the core economic objectives of the regime itself. This was not the way it was supposed to be, according to the regime's economic czar and architect, José A. Martínez de Hoz. Upon assuming power, Martínez de Hoz had a vision of an economy free from the harmful effects of inflation brought on by the unrelenting expansion of the state. The state, with its myriad agencies, bureaucracies, and enterprises had become, in his view, a monument to the irrational allocation of public resources and the politicization of price, wage, and managerial policy.[7] This political behemoth would have to be tamed.

In his first address to the nation on April 2, 1976, the economics minister pointed to the state's deficit as the "motor" force behind the nation's inflation.[8] It was imperative, according to the minister, that the deficit be brought under control before price volatility would subside. But to his chagrin the deficit was never contained during the *Proceso* years, and public-sector spending continued to run amok. Expenditures that equaled 42.1 percent of GDP in 1979 swelled to 49.8 percent of GDP by the time Alfonsín took office in 1983. Meanwhile, the fiscal deficit that had declined moderately during the

7. David Pion-Berlin, *The Ideology of State Terror: Economic Doctrine and Political Repression in Argentina and Peru* (Boulder, Colo.: Lynne Rienner Publishers, 1989), p. 108.

8. República Argentina, *Memoria: Marzo 29, 1976–Marzo 29, 1979* (Buenos Aires: Ministerio de Economía, 1981) 3: 1–15.

first few years of the *Proceso*, climbed steadily to nearly 16 percent of GDP by the period's end, the highest figure in Argentine history. The public sector's share of that deficit was a sizable 72 percent.[9]

The minister who had been more zealously committed than anyone to shrinking the size of the state could not do so. Nowhere did the economic minister have greater difficulty than with the armed forces themselves. The military's penchant for spending and borrowing could not be subdued, despite his considerable efforts. And it was that proclivity that drove public-sector expansion during the *Proceso*. For example, in the year before the coup defense expenditures accounted for 13.5 percent of public-sector outlays. That jumped to 23.1 percent in the first year of the dictatorship, and then rose to 36.8 percent by 1981.[10]

These figures reveal just how disingenuous the military was. The generals would listen attentively to the minister when he spoke about the need to change old economic habits that had led the nation to the brink of ruin. They would nod their heads approvingly as he laid out the risks of failing to arrest inflationary trends, to reduce wages, to curtail spending, and to rationalize the state. And while they would lend their support to his overall economic plan, they would not submit themselves to the same kind of self-scrutiny and frugality that was demanded of everyone else.

Discipline, in the words of Adolfo Canitrot, was the central objective of this economic plan: to discipline those social groups who would not curb themselves and whose unrelenting demands upon the state had contributed to the gross distortion of the Argentine economy over so many years.[11] In the short run the minister had at least considerable success in restraining the influence of rent-seeking interest groups. Predictably, labor was well heeled under the neoliberal regime. More surprisingly, powerful, rural entrepreneurial groups who had lent their fervent support to the coup of 1976 were also adversely affected.[12] Only a ministry well insulated from and impervious to their calls for policy reversal and one rigidly committed to staying the course

9. For the 1979 data, see Aldo Ferrer, "The Argentine Economy, 1976–1979," *Journal of Interamerican Studies and World Affairs* 22 (May 1980): 149. For other data, see República Argentina, *Diario de Sesiones* (Buenos Aires: Cámara de Diputados, June 28 and 29, 1984), pp. 1632, 1634.

10. Figures provided to author by Thomas Scheetz, who in turn obtained raw data from the Argentine Central Bank.

11. Adolfo Canitrot, "Discipline as the Central Objective of Economic Policy: An Essay on the Economic Programme of the Argentine Government Since 1976," *World Development* 8 (1980): 913–28.

12. Pion-Berlin, *The Ideology of State Terror*, pp. 188–90; Canitrot, "Discipline as the Central Objective of Economic Policy," pp. 924–25.

could have resisted the pressures from this dominant class. Martínez de Hoz's ministry was that and more. But while it could be safely said that the economics ministry enjoyed an unprecedented degree of isolation and autonomy from civil society, the same could not be said of its relation to the armed forces. Military spending and borrowing continued to eat at the heart of the minister's program.

As can be seen in Table 5.1, the military's expenditures maintained a steady course upward during the first four years of the *Proceso*, with the greatest increase having taken place once the military assumed power in 1976. There was also a jump in spending in 1978 when Argentina feared that it might go to war with Chile over possession of islands in the Beagle Channel, and a slight increase in 1983 when the military paid for equipment purchased the year before that it used in the Malvinas War.

As a proportion of the output of the overall economy military spending reached unprecedented heights, the mean for those years of 4.2 percent far exceeding the average displayed over the previous seven years (1969–75) of 1.8 percent (four of which were under military rule) and twice that of the nation's historical average of 2 percent. Moreover, military spending was also associated with poor economic performance, as indicated below by the convergence between sharp increases in the defense budget and severe con-

Table 5.1. Military expenditures (MILEX) and economic growth during the Argentine *Proceso*, 1976–1983

Year	MILEX in 1986 Australes* (× 1000)	MILEX % Change from Previous Year	MILEX as % of GDP	GDP Annual Growth Rate
1976	3,597.1	57.1	3.9	0.0
1977	3,770.1	4.8	3.8	6.4
1978	4,826.0	28.0	5.1	−3.2
1979	4,913.5	1.8	4.8	7.0
1980	4,546.4	−7.5	4.4	1.5
1981	4,735.2	4.2	4.9	−6.7
1982	3,297.9	−30.3	3.5	−5.0
1983	2,679.6	5.0	3.5	2.9
1976–83 annual averages	4,045.7	7.9	4.2	.4

NOTE: "Australes" was the name of the Argentine currency at the time. Figures on defense spending include retirement disbursements, military health and educational institutions, and arms purchases. Excluded are expenditures on Argentina's internal security forces like the Naval Prefecture and the *Gendarmería*, which beginning in 1984 were disassociated from the navy and army respectively.

SOURCE: Figures provided to author by Thomas Scheetz. Raw data from the Argentine Ministry of Economics, Secretary of Finance, 1994.

tractions in economic growth. Martínez de Hoz could not have been pleased with these developments. But the military's widening girth in the face of general economic emaciation is proof enough that the minister lacked the kind of enforcement powers he needed to bring the armed forces into line.[13]

The State of the Armed Forces on the Eve of Transition

For the military, power certainly had its privileges. With institutional control over their own budgets, the services' opportunity for unlimited self-aggrandizement was fully exploited. The armed forces pressed up against the outer limits of the federal budget. When they could squeeze nothing more out of it, they turned to borrowing. Military-owned enterprises participated in a borrowing frenzy, feeding at the trough of foreign banks and multinational lenders.[14] Between 1978 and 1983 alone, $1.8 billion dollars in foreign credit became available for arms procurement, as arms imports increased from forty million in 1977 to three hundred and sixty million in 1978—an 800 percent increase.[15]

The military feared being saddled with foreign currency repayment obligations, but the economics minister made its task easier in 1978 by progressively reducing the rate of devaluation for the Argentine peso, thereby cheapening the dollar. Even so, the poorly run, heavily subsidized military industrial complex never came close to meeting its debt obligations, and the armed forces simply bequeathed the burdens of repayment to their democratic successors.

Unrelenting spending and borrowing during the *Proceso* had allowed the Argentine armed forces to grow geometrically. On the eve of Alfonsín's inauguration the military was overfunded and oversized by most reasonable measures or comparisons. The dimensions to this problem can be visualized

13. Authority over defense budgets resided neither in the economics ministry nor in the ministry of defense, nor in the cabinet itself, but rather with each of the service branches. In this feudalized dictatorship each branch of the armed forces exerted autonomy over its budget. See Andrés Fontana, "Political Decision Making by a Military Corporation: Argentina, 1976–83," Ph.D. diss., University of Texas at Austin, 1987.

14. The economics minister encouraged this behavior as a means of shifting the terrible burden of deficit defense financing from the Central Bank (whose remissions to the depleted treasury were inflationary) to external lenders.

15. Mario Esteban Carranza, "The Role of Military Expenditure in the Development Process: The Argentina Case, 1946–1980," *Nordic Journal of Latin American Studies* 12 (1983): 146.

from several angles. First, the number of men under arms was large in proportion to the country's population. In 1982 the country had 6.7 men in uniform for every thousand inhabitants. Not surprisingly, Chile and Uruguay, with vastly smaller populations, had a greater proportion of soldiers to citizens: 8.2 and 9.5 per thousand, respectively. No one else in Latin America did, however. Colombia, whose population of 27.5 million was nearly identical to that of Argentina at the time, had 72,500 men in the services, or 2.6 per thousand, and the average for Latin America as a whole was 3.2 per thousand.[16]

Second, the number of men under arms was sizable in proportion to the nation's territory. When compared to several other very large states in and outside of Latin America, only Mexico had deployed more troops per square kilometer. Argentina's ratio of soldiers to land was twice that of Brazil's and seven times greater than that of Australia and Canada, two nations that it is often compared to in terms of size, natural endowments, and economic structure. However, when compared to Chile, Argentina's soldier/land ratio was less (see Table 5.2). Since Chile was Argentina's perennial military rival next door, and since the two countries had stood on the brink of war in 1978, force levels might have found some justification, at least at the time.

Finally, let us return to the budget for the moment in order to make some cross-national comparisons. Argentina's military commanded a 36.8 percent share of all public-sector outlays in 1981, the year before the Malvinas con-

Table 5.2. Country size and military force levels in comparison, 1984

Country	Territory (× 1000 sq. km.)	Military Personnel	Military Personnel (× 1000 sq. km.)
Argentina	2,767	175,000	63.24
Australia	7,687	71,642	9.32
Brazil	8,512	277,300	32.57
Canada	9,205	83,000	9.01
Mexico	1,958	130,000	66.39
Venezuela	916	40,500	43.76
Chile[a]	740	93,000	125.55

SOURCE: Fundación Arturo Illia para la Democracia y la Paz, *Lineamientos para una reforma militar* (Buenos Aires: Fundación Illia, 1988), p. 22.
[a]For Chile data, see Adrian J. English, *Armed Forces of Latin America* (London and New York: Jane's Publishing Co., 1984), p. 132.

16. Adrian J. English, *Armed Forces of Latin America: Their Histories, Development, Present Strength, and Military Potential* (London and New York: Jane's Publishing, 1984).

flict. This compared to a 16.6 percent share in Pinochet's Chile and a 17.6 percent share in Peru. By 1983, the year after its resounding defeat, the Argentine armed forces still retained a 21.4 percent share, compared to 17.9 and 19.1 percent for Chile and Peru, respectively.[17] The contrast is even greater when examining Brazil. Argentina's military share of Central Government expenditures averaged five to six times that of its northern neighbor during the early 1980s.[18]

Whether it be compared to other nations in the region, or to itself at other times in history, Argentina's military did not have sufficient cause to enlarge its defense shares. Despite this reality, two powerful forces conspired against the prospects of fiscal restraint. The first was the weight of civil-military history itself. Whether it be prompted by corporate self-interests, collective or individual greed, or the perceived loss of status that may accompany declines in salaries, the armed forces of Latin America in general and Argentina in particular have not hesitated to use their power when necessary to preserve budget shares. Military demands were not always placed in proportion to defensive needs but rather in proportion to corporate desires. Politically powerful armies in the region would play the card of threatened intervention as a lever with which to force up defense spending—regardless of economic consequences. In the past, leaders in the region had little choice but to satisfy the insatiable military thirst for more. Those who did not often paid the ultimate price.

By way of illustration Eric Nordlinger cites a study of Peru that linked every coup in that country between 1912 and 1964 to declines in the relative budgetary shares going to defense.[19] Barry Ames notes that of twelve elected Latin American chief executives who failed to pay off the military, eight were victims of coups. Conversely, of six who attended to military demands, five survived their full terms of office.[20] It follows that leaders in countries such as Argentina that suffered from repeated bouts of military intervention would find it especially difficult to deprive the armed forces of resources.

The second force conspiring against fiscal constraint is the weight of prior decisions. Despite its institutional girth, the Argentine military would be expected to build upon its financial base. This behavior is not unique to

17. Data provided to author by Thomas Scheetz.

18. David Pion-Berlin, "Between Confrontation and Accommodation," p. 554.

19. Eric Nordlinger, *Soldiers in Politics: Military Coups and Governments* (Englewood Cliffs, N.J.: Prentice-Hall, 1977), p. 67.

20. Barry Ames, *Political Survival: Politicians and Public Policy in Latin America* (Berkeley and Los Angeles: University of California Press, 1987), p. 77.

military institutions. "Every agency wants more money; the urge to survive and expand is built in," writes Aaron Wildavsky.[21] The best predictor of this year's budget is last year's. The prior commitment of funds means that programs have been set into motion, individuals have been hired, contracts have been signed. These are sunken costs that limit the budget maker's flexibility.[22] Hence, the expenditure patterns established during the *Proceso* years set an expectation that the budget curve would continue to move in an upward direction, remain unchanged, or at the very worst taper off ever so slightly. The powers of budgetary inertia worked to the advantage of the armed services. But despite these realities, the Alfonsín and Menem administrations were determined to reverse course by trimming the defense budget substantially. Why and how they did it are the subjects that we now address.

The Alfonsín Years and the Primacy of Politics over Defense

President Raúl Alfonsín used his newfound strength to weaken the armed forces politically. Under Radical Party rule soldiers would no longer be exempt from the obligations they had as citizens to conform to the realities of the new political order *and* to share the burdens of austerity imposed by the new economic order. Therefore, the president added: "We really want to provide the nation with the Armed Forces that each situation requires; forces whose size and preparation will be in accordance with our own possibilities."[23]

Toward the goal of creating an "appropriate" defense for the nation, the government supported a series of budgetary measures aimed at paring down the institution's size, power, and prerogatives. Its plan was foreshadowed in the campaign of 1983. Speaking shortly before his selection as Radical Party candidate for president, Alfonsín pledged that if elected, he would trim the military's budget back to its historic level of 2 percent of GDP, a move that he insisted would "not affect the political health of the [Argentine] democ-

21. Wildavsky, *Budgeting*, p. 7.

22. Ibid., pp. 13–16. Moreover, claims Wildavsky, governments usually cannot afford to spend the time and energy needed to annually review the entire budget and so only modest changes at the margins are ever debated.

23. Dr. Raúl R. Alfonsín, "Discurso del Señor Presidente de la nación Argentina en la cena de camaradería de las fuerzas armadas" (Buenos Aires: Secretaría de Información Pública, July 5, 1985), p. 7.

racy."[24] But he was then asked whether such a drastic cut might trigger a coup. His response revealed the lower priority he had already assigned to the armed forces: "I believe that the best way to invest in national defense is by safeguarding the education and health budgets of the nation, and by achieving development, since anyway it is best to have a small professional and well-equipped army rather than a large army that lacks all the necessary elements."[25]

Once in office, the president wasted no time setting his plans in motion. Budget cuts were being prepared in general allotments, salaries, and materials, while investment funding was being restricted to only those military projects with export components. Defense expenditures plummeted by 21 percent between 1983 and 1985, representing one of the world's largest reductions in military spending for any country whose total defense budget exceeded one hundred million dollars. Although on average the deepest cuts were made in operations and equipment, army salaries were also down considerably as well.[26] Overall, defense spending declined by 37.6 percent during the Alfonsín years, and the military's share of the public-sector pie diminished considerably as well, from its height of 36.8 percent in 1981 to 13.2 percent in 1987.

These trends were certainly disconcerting to the military, but more so when viewed regionally. Argentina's neighbors and perennial military rivals, Chile and Brazil, were now doing better. Though in absolute terms Argentina still spent more on defense than Brazil, by 1985 the gap had narrowed considerably. Moreover, once adjusted for the production of goods and services and population levels, Argentina's advantage dissipates. Argentine defense spending as a proportion of GNP declined steadily from 1983 to 1985, while Brazil and Chile's military budgets remained more or less constant. Argentina's defense share of the government budget also declined, as did Chile's, while Brazil's portion increased. Finally, military spending per capita improved somewhat in Brazil and Chile while dropping sharply in Argentina.[27]

24. The UCR platform promised that the military budget will be cut "drastically" and in no case shall it exceed 2 percent of GDP while the nation remains at peace. The reductions will be "progressive with the reform and reorganization of the forces." Union Cívica Radical, *Plataforma electoral nacional de la Union Cívica Radical, 1983* (Buenos Aires: UCR, 1983), pt. 3, pp. 8–9.

25. *Foreign Broadcast Information Service—Latin America (FBIS-LAT)*, July 19, 1983, p. B2.

26. General defense expenditure data provided by Thomas Scheetz. Governmental source is Economics Ministry, Secretariat of Defense, 1994. On service breakdown, see *Clarín*, November 4, 1984, pp. 6–7.

27. David Pion-Berlin, "Between Confrontation and Accommodation," p. 554.

Table 5.3.   Military expenditures (MILEX) under Alfonsín, 1984–1989

Year	MILEX in 1986 Australes (× 1000)	MILEX % Change from Previous Year	MILEX as % of GDP	MILEX as % of Public Sector Expenditure
1984	2,304.8	−14.0	2.3	17.0
1985	2,135.2	−7.4	2.3	13.3
1986	2,306.1	8.0	2.3	14.2
1987	2,340.0	1.5	2.3	13.2
1988	2,135.2	−8.8	2.1	19.8
1989	1,775.1	−16.9	1.9	18.2
1984–89 annual averages	2,166.1	−6.3	2.2	16.7

SOURCE: Figures from Thomas Scheetz. Compiled from data provided by the Argentine Ministry of Economics, Secretary of Finance, 1994.
NOTE: The figures on military expenditures contain same line items as those in Table 5.1.

The civilians would point out that external threats to national security had receded thanks to persistent, peaceful diplomatic initiatives pursued with the neighboring states. Since defensive needs are assessed in proportion to risk, and since the risks of regional conflict had subsided, some spending reductions were warranted. Nonetheless, there was a growing uneasiness within the ranks over the allocation of resources. The military chiefs of staff were generally respectful of civilian authority and therefore unwilling to publicly challenge the president on his budget proposals. Brigadier General Ernesto Crespo, the air force chief of staff, expressed the sentiments of the other chiefs of staff when he said that his force would manage with budgetary restrictions that were "in accord with the country's situation."[28] But the commanders approved of Alfonsín's budget with trepidation, fearing that without a thorough restructuring, severe budget cuts could further harm military preparedness already impaired due to losses suffered in the Malvinas War.

Unfortunately for the armed forces they were not to find a particularly helpful voice within the ministry of defense (MOD). Unlike other South American democracies that had no defense ministry (Brazil), or whose defense ministry was periodically headed up by active or retired military men (Uruguay, Peru), Argentina's MOD was always under civilian control. Furthermore, during his first two years in office, Alfonsín had placed his closest political confidants in charge of the ministry: Raúl Borrás and Roque Carranza. Both were friends and Radical Party loyalists whom the president

28. *FBIS-LAT*, April 16, 1985, p. B2.

could trust implicitly to faithfully administer his military policy.[29] The president knew that his military program would be controversial and needed political officials he could confide in. In Borrás and then Carranza he had such men.

It is not that either minister was necessarily antagonistic toward the armed forces. It is just that neither would permit ministerial policy to be "captured" by military interests, as it had been in the past. As stated at the outset, there are tensions and contradictions inherent to the management of defense affairs. A minister must represent and enforce administration policy. But at the same time, his position puts him in closer proximity to the officers and soldiers who are the subjects of that enforcement. Familiarity often breeds respect, as the minister comes to appreciate the challenges and difficulties of military life, as well as the contributions made by its profession. Thus he may be moved to advocate on their behalf. And yet neither Borrás nor Carranza ever manifested divided allegiances. Both were bound and determined to see the president's military programs through to completion—however unpopular they were with the men of arms.

In March 1984 Borrás said that the military budget will be "reduced to the maximum" and "to the benefit of other crestfallen sectors."[30] Dismissing any possibility of retaliation, he confidently boasted that such cuts would be accepted by the armed forces "without irritation because they are subordinate to civilian power."[31] Though often the bearer of bad news, his self-described role was to "soften the blow" by opening up channels of communication between his government and the armed forces, which he would use to defuse tensions before they got out of hand.

The defense minister's style was firm but nonconfrontational. He kept up a hectic schedule of meetings with military personnel at all ranks, often visiting installations in the evening after work. As one of his first acts of duty, he flew south to Patagonia, accompanied by the head of the joint command, Julio Fernández Torres, to present the government's case to military units there "frankly and clearly . . . so that no one could have any doubts."[32] Defense cuts, he said, would not be made across the board, but selectively, aimed at preserving the operational capacity of the armed forces while eliminating activities that did not serve territorial defense needs.[33] He

29. *Ambito Financiero*, May 31, 1985, p. 2.
30. *Clarín*, March 16, 1984, p. 2.
31. Ibid.
32. *FBIS-LAT*, February 8, 1984, p. B7.
33. Ibid., March 16, 1984, p. B7.

also took time out to calm fears about the projected scope of the human rights investigations.

Still, the armed forces remained jittery about the prospect of trials looming on the horizon and the deterioration of the defense budget. In December of that year General Fernández Torres took the government by surprise when he publicly decried the loss of budget shares and what he called a campaign of "psychological aggression" being waged against the armed forces, especially by elements in the media, which had contributed to a growing deterioration in military morale and readiness.[34] This culminated in crisis in March 1985 when Torres handed in his resignation. The designated successor to Torres, General Ricardo Pianta, then suddenly withdrew in apparent opposition to Alfonsín's budget and human rights policies.

Although immediately stunned by these developments, Borrás and Alfonsín quickly resolved the crisis, refusing to be intimidated into backing down from their budgetary mission. In fact less than a month later the defense minister was in rare form, stating that while military salaries were low, "there is no possibility of increasing the budget. Things are not as they were before."[35]

Indeed they were not. Roque Carranza, who took over the top defense post after the untimely death of Borrás in May 1985, continued to hold the line against military spending. Defending current levels that he termed "not especially low" in light of historic averages, Carranza contended that the military had itself to blame for its misfortunes. He traced current difficulties to lavish expenditures on arms imports, unprofitable military-industrial investments, and huge debt obligations incurred by the armed forces during the 1970s.[36] Substantial damage had been done, but the Alfonsín administration was resolved to, if nothing else, loosen the military's grip on the federal budget.

Borrás and Carranza were sentinels at the gate, discouraging military hopes that the procurement of years past could be restored. But they and their ministry constituted only the first wall of defense. Further inside the state lay the much insulated economics ministry and its technocratic staff of financial experts and accountants. Chief among the *técnicos* was Alfonsín's trusted, Harvard-trained minister of economics, Juan Sourrouille. Sourroville insisted that for his heterodox stabilization program called *Plan Austral* to succeed, a tight rein must be kept on central government spending, with few if any

---

34. *La Razón*, March 5, 1985, p. 12.
35. Ibid., April 3, 1985, p. 11.
36. *La Prensa*, October 17, 1985, p. 3.

concessions granted to the armed forces.[37] Alfonsín and his team at MOD could not agree more. By the time he left office in July 1989, the president had achieved his budgetary goals, bringing military expenditures down to less than 2 percent of the GDP.

These cuts hit the army particularly hard, having suffered comparatively greater losses in budget shares than the navy or air force.[38] This gives credence to the idea that the UCR government had followed a deliberate strategy of weakening the army vis-à-vis the other two forces. Alfonsín's logic was primarily political. In his eyes the army had come to symbolize all that was wrong with the Argentine armed forces: oversized, overfunded, wrongly committed to fighting internal wars, and ominously deployed in and around major cities. As the nation's land force it dominated the offensive against the guerrillas and all those who had opposed the military regime. It assumed an occupational role, establishing zones of military operation and hundreds of clandestine detention centers in and around populated areas. The senseless killings that took place in these centers could not go unanswered. Although Alfonsín's form of retribution was primarily judicial, the budget represented another weapon in his arsenal. He deprived the military, and especially the army, of resources they had come to rely upon for decades, sending a clear signal of disapproval.

The message was received and the impact felt. The army reported basic provisions such as fuel, food, and clothing in short supply. Equipment lay in a state of serious disrepair, with many units suspending daily activities and training exercises. Because military salaries were no longer sufficient to support officers and their families, many had to leave the service at midday to take on secondary forms of employment. They became part-time professionals, a trend that would persist into the Menem years and foster an erosion of military morale. Others simply abandoned the service altogether—even before meeting the minimum number of years to qualify for a pension. The increasingly restless and defiant junior officer corps within the army published a statement saying that budget cuts will lead to "a clinical death [of

---

37. At the beginning of 1988 the economics minister agreed only to minor increases (in the range of 4 to 12 percent) in military salaries, which were then quickly wiped out by inflation. See *Clarín*, January 26, 1988, p. 4. The overall economic plan was modified to help civilian, wage-earning employees. See William C. Smith, "Hyperinflation, Macroeconomic Instability, and Neoliberal Restructuring in Democratic Argentina," in *The New Argentine Democracy: The Search for a Successful Formula*, ed. Edward C. Epstein (Westport: Praeger Publishers, 1992), pp. 20–60.

38. Rosendo Fraga, *La cuestión militar: 1987–89* (Buenos Aires: Editorial Centro de Estudios Unión para la Nueva Mayoría, 1989), p. 167.

the military] within a relatively short period of time," and belittled the defense ministry, calling it a "Ministry for Disarmament."[39]

This bitterness reflected an unmistakable deterioration in defense readiness (a trend that began with the Malvinas War, not with Alfonsín). However, the plight of the armed forces was less critical than was advertised.[40] Like any institution facing cutbacks, the military tended to accentuate the negative, venting its displeasure in the hope that a sufficient amount of grumbling would evoke sympathy from the administration. The strategy hardly paid off. By the time Alfonsín turned the presidency over to his successor, Carlos Menem, in July 1989, the armed services were still anxiously wondering whether any real fiscal relief was in store for them.

The Menem Years and the Primacy of Economics over Defense

With the coming to power of Carlos Menem the emphasis shifted from political retribution to economic readjustment. Macroeconomic stability became the defining imperative for an administration coping with huge deficits, hyperinflation, and loss of productive growth. Upon Menem's assumption of office the state had become virtually insolvent. There were no means to pay its bills, and with inflation hovering at about 5,000 percent, printing money was the furthest thing from the government's mind. Public spending had grown unabated, "driven by powerful interest groups with minimal accountability to the electorate."[41] State enterprises, had, according to the World Bank, evolved into "nonaccountable fiefdoms," which had pushed their deficits back on the Treasury and Central Bank.[42] Foreign liabilities continued to hang over the government like a sword of Damocles, diverting precious resources away from capital investment and toward the repayment of accumulated debt. Combined, spending and indebtedness were vastly out-

---

39. *FBIS-LAT*, April 16, 1985, p. B2; ibid., December 31, 1984, p. B4.

40. For example, many officers at the time charged that Argentina had been rendered "indefensible" by the cuts. These claims are still heard today. But in conversations with this author, officials from the army and navy admitted that the country is not defenseless, and never has been, although its state of readiness leaves something to be desired.

41. World Bank, *Argentina: From Insolvency to Growth* (Washington, D.C.: World Bank, 1993), p. 8.

42. Ibid., p. 4.

stripping the state's revenue-generating capacities while producing huge fiscal deficits that kept upward pressure on the consumer price index.

Menem knew that for inflation to come under control he would have to put the public-sector house in order. He called upon his economics ministers to undertake an ambitious program of state shrinking and restructuring. In August 1989 he signed into law a measure that declared the public sector in a "state of emergency," preparing the most disabled of firms for liquidation or privatization.[43] Then in March 1990 he prohibited the Central Bank from financing the operating deficit of the Treasury, or from engaging in any monetary expansion without prior authorization from the economics ministry.[44] The ministry received a further boost in August 1991, when it was given new and broad powers to exercise control over all federal government finances.

But the ministry really came into its own with the arrival of Domingo Cavallo as minister of economics in February 1991. Cavallo was described by one close aide as someone who "has been preparing for this job all his life."[45] A Ph.D. in economics from Harvard University, he had been undersecretary for development in Córdoba and then vice president of that city's central bank. Since the opening moments of the Menem candidacy, Cavallo had been angling for the top economic position but had to settle initially for appointment as foreign affairs minister until his time came. Once minister, he became a virtual premier among fellow cabinet members. Aside from the duties normally assigned to an economics minister, he was also authorized to advise on assignments within ministries other than his own, to coordinate all government policies, and to manage all relations between the executive branch and the Congress.[46]

His central objective was to lower inflation, and toward that end he moved on several fronts simultaneously. First, he "dollarized" the economy, meaning that the peso was made fully convertible with and equivalent to the U.S. currency. To bolster the freely convertible peso, he developed a program to eliminate the federal deficit by widening the revenue base while drastically curtailing public expenditures. He improved tax-collecting measures, reorganized public finances, accelerated the privatization of state enterprises, and

---

43. República Argentina, "Reforma del Estado," Ley 23.696, in *Boletín oficial de la República Argentina*, January 29, 1992, p. 2.

44. República Argentina, Decreto 435, March 4, 1990, in *Anales de legislación Argentina* (Buenos Aires: Editorial La Ley, 1991), pp. 170–71.

45. *Latin American Regional Report: Southern Cone*, March 14, 1991, p. 2.

46. Ibid.

eliminated special (nonbudgeted) accounts outside the purview of the minis-try.[47] He trimmed public payrolls by freezing wages and dismissing some sev-enty-one thousand employees from Central Administration and public firms. By the end of 1992 total employment in government had declined by 15.4 percent from levels in 1990.

Described by Menem himself as a form of "surgery without anesthesia," Cavallo's conceptually bold adjustment plan was one that would certainly inflict considerable short-term pain on a society that for decades had become dependent on the state as the economic employer of first resort. The plan's endurance would of course ultimately hinge on the "patient's" capacity to absorb the pain and respond favorably to the treatment. Fortunately for Ca-vallo and the Menem administration the response was quite dramatic.

Public spending as a percentage of GDP declined from 49.8 percent in 1989 to 40.1 percent in 1992. As a result, the government's account balance moved from a deficit of 6.1 percent in 1990 to a surplus of 1.5 percent in 1992.[48] Retail and wholesale prices adjusted accordingly. Inflation, which had dangerously hovered at 27 percent in the month of February 1991 just prior to Cavallo's arrival, dropped to single digits by August of that year—the lowest rate in a quarter of a century. At year's end, with inflation now below single digits, growth in the economy stood at an impressive 8.5 percent. The synergistic effects of the plan now took hold. As the economy continued to expand, so too did the tax base, which combined with greater tax compli-ance and lower government spending led to greater revenues and an even larger fiscal surplus.[49]

In an address to the nation in April 1992 Cavallo said that the fiscal balance achieved "has allowed us to recover credibility in three essential economic areas: our currency, the government budget, and public credit."[50] "The peso," he added, "has a basic constant value, it is worth a dollar": watching over it means maintaining fiscal discipline.[51] Argentina's perennial nemesis—inflation—had been subdued, but the surgery would continue to sustain the economic recovery. The minister went on: "We have reorganized our economy; we have adopted rules which will allow our economy to pro-gress. . . . What we have to do is to act in keeping with these rules firmly

47. World Bank, *Argentina: From Insolvency to Growth*, pp. 12–13.
48. Ibid., Table 2.1, p. 291.
49. *Latin American Regional Report: Southern Cone*, November 21, 1991, p. 6.
50. *FBIS-LAT*, April 23, 1992, p. 11.
51. Ibid.

and responsibly. We have to act with austerity, efficiency, openness, and sensibility."[52]

This was good news for the economy but bad news for the armed forces, whose budgetary needs were no longer of transcending importance to the nation. In December 1991 the Congress passed an executive bill that placed thirty military-industrial firms up for sale to the private sector.[53] State shrinking continued to be the order of the day, and the government's economic team was not about to let the military get in its way, nor was Menem. The president had hitched his political fortunes to Cavallo's rising star, believing that the minister's plan was good medicine not only for the nation but for his own career. After listening to military officers complain about their earnings, Menem responded tersely: "The military cannot discuss salaries, because they are not a union, and if their incomes are low, so too are those of other sectors of the community."[54]

During the first four years of the Menem presidency defense expenditures either declined or remained stagnant, as shown in column one of Table 5.4. Of great significance is column three, which demonstrates how once the recovery took hold in 1991, defense spending lagged behind the general growth in the nation's goods and services. Additionally, defense requests lost out to other claims on public-sector finances, as noted in column four.

Shortly after Cavallo's adjustment plan was set in motion, voices within the armed forces sounded alarms once again about the harmful impact of fiscal austerity. The budget cuts, they said, have "direct repercussions on the

Table 5.4.   Military expenditures (MILEX) under Menem, 1989–1993

Year	MILEX in 1986 Australes (× 1000)	MILEX % Change from Previous Year	MILEX as a % of GDP	MILEX as % of Public Sector Expenditure
1989	1,775.1	− 16.9	1.9	18.2
1990	1,368.9	− 22.9	1.5	18.4
1991	1,547.8	13.1	1.5	18.3
1992	1,587.5	2.6	1.4	16.2
1993	1,559.2	− 1.8	1.3	10.6
1989–93 annual averages	1,567.7	− 5.2	1.5	16.3

SOURCE: Figures from Thomas Scheetz. Compiled from raw data from the Argentine Ministry of Economics, Secretary of Finance, 1994.

52. Ibid., p. 16.
53. *Latin American Weekly Report,* December 19, 1991, p. 11.
54. *El Financiero Internacional de México,* May 17, 1991, p. 33.

military's operating capacity and place the country in a state of indefensiveness."[55] Symptomatic of the military's frustration over economic changes that seemed beyond their control were the expressions of Vice Admiral Antonio Mozarelli in May 1991. Mozarelli had a reputation as a strict careerist—not one prone to exhortations. Nonetheless, in what was clearly a public rebuke of his government's policy, he said that with the current defense budget, the Argentine military could do little more than "adopt a strategy of containment, with no capacity to project offensive power." The president quickly relieved him of his duties.[56]

Unlike Alfonsín, Menem's objective was not to punish the armed forces politically but rather to insist they not interfere with larger macroeconomic objectives. The armed forces must try to make do with less because the rest of Argentine society had been called on to do exactly the same, the president argued. The watchwords under Menem were "shared sacrifice," a phrase repeatedly mentioned to me in interviews with soldiers and civilians alike. In spreading the costs of austerity the government hoped to diffuse political opposition to the painful adjustment program. And it is that program, Cavallo argued, which would restore stability and growth to an economy that had seen neither in decades. In the end, argued the minister, a fortified economy would mean a more secure nation.

This was a difficult pill for the military to swallow. They had already suffered through a period of retrenchment under Alfonsín; now they were in for more of the same. The protests that had begun under Alfonsín would continue, but these were for the most part orderly, restrained, and without much effectiveness. By the end of Menem's first term there had been no substantial increases in the military budget, either for salaries, operations, or investments.

Asked to comment about this state of affairs, those interviewed within and outside of the armed forces and across party lines converged on at least one point: defense is simply not a priority any more. Admiral Emilio Osses, head of the joint chiefs of staff from 1989 to 1992, responded: "The president has many other problems to resolve and at this moment defense is not a priority."[57] Deputy Antonio Berhongaray, a member of the Radical Party and a specialist on defense, regarded the military as "just one more sector in society, and as such they have to accept the rules of the game."[58] And Juan

55. *Clarín*, May 11, 1991, p. 3.
56. Ibid., May 14, 1991, p. 3.
57. Almirante Emilio Osses, interview with author, Buenos Aires, July 19, 1993.
58. Diputado Antonio Berhongaray, interview with author, Buenos Aires, June 23, 1993.

Carlos Costa, a Peronist and former undersecretary for budgeting in the ministry of defense under Menem, said that "from the point of view of public expenditures, military spending is no longer important."[59]

Salience quite naturally is in the eye of the beholder. To the military, there are no satisfying cuts; each one is more painful than the next. To the misers in the Ministry of Economics (MOE), each cut is desirable, another step toward fiscal solvency. Understandably, then, the Menem budget reflected its own priorities, which were economic, not defensive, in nature. But this begs a significant question: *Why* did the military continue to lose the "fiscal wars?" Put differently, what enabled the civilians in the Radical and Peronist administrations to pursue budgetary policy at the expense of the military purse, and over military objections? For an answer we turn to a discussion of state institutions.

Institutional Dimensions to Defense Budgeting

The budget process was essentially the same under Presidents Alfonsín and Menem. Although there has undoubtedly been a further concentration of power in the hands of the economics ministry since 1991, this is a matter of degree only. The centrality of that ministry and its officials, the sequencing of decisions, and the criteria and mechanisms for producing budgets remained unchanged across Radical and Peronist administrations.[60] Those realities placed the armed forces at a decided disadvantage.

In democratic Argentina the budgetary decision-making hub resides deep within the chambers of MOE. It is here, not over in the defense ministry or at army, navy, or air force headquarters, that the process of allocating resources begins and ends. It is here that the ceilings for defense are established and where officers are told what they can and cannot purchase. And it is here that all of the real fiscal military planning and control resides.

Within the ministry is the secretariat of finance, the agency that collects the tax revenue and controls its disbursement. And within that secretariat lies the national budgeting office. The office (first called the Department of Programming and Budgetary Control) was created by the UCR government

59. Juan Carlos Costa, interview with author, Buenos Aires, July 6, 1993.

60. A point confirmed for me by an official within the national budget office who served under both administrations. Carlos Deambrosio, interview with author, Buenos Aires, October 27, 1994.

in September 1984 as part of its overall reorganization of MOE aimed at strengthening that ministry's administrative and fiscal powers.[61] It is charged with drawing up the federal budget that will ultimately be presented to Congress. It evaluates and revises the budget submissions from each ministry, seeing to it that these conform strictly to MOE guidelines and objectives, sending nonconforming documents back for revision. And it dictates the technical accounting procedures that each agency of state must adhere to in both formulating and executing its budget.[62]

The defense budgeting process can be visualized as a movement from the fiscal "center" to its "periphery" and back. At the center of the center lies the secretary of finance, with his budget office and coterie of fiscal experts. The secretary gathers round him a budget formulation support group that includes government officials involved in revenue collection, investment, and privatization. Together they estimate the amount of revenues likely to be collected for the next fiscal year from taxes and the proceeds of sales of public property. From this estimation they derive preliminary budget ceilings for each ministry, conforming to the rule that no amount of expenditure approved can exceed what is taken in. In addition, they compile a budget formulation manual and set up courses to advise ministry officials on how to prepare their own accounts. Then the finance secretary, with the concurrence of the economics minister himself, passes on his recommendations in May to the full cabinet.[63]

The first steps are often the most important because the preliminary fiscal limits that are set are likely to be closely observed in the end. Yet on a decision as critical as this, one that will affect the state of the nation's security, no one in the defense orbit—military or civilian—is consulted: not the services, not the chiefs of staff, not the joint chiefs, not the defense minister,

61. The reorganization of MOE began in December 1983 with the creation of an undersecretary for budgeting who would go on to direct the national budgeting office. See República Argentina, Decreto 15, in *Legislación Argentina, Tomo 1983-B* (Buenos Aires: Edición de Jurisprudencia Argentina, 1984), p. 1921. On the creation of the budgeting office, see Gerardo R. Gargiulo, "Gasto militar y política de defensa," *Desarrollo Económico* 28 (April–June 1988): 97.

62. See República de Argentina, Ley de Administración Pública (Ley 24.156), in *Legislación Argentina, Tomo 1992-C* (Buenos Aires: Edición de Jurisprudencia Argentina, 1993), pp. 3355–56.

63. The details of the budgeting process were revealed to me through interviews with those involved. Confirmatory observations were made by José Manuel Ugarte in a communication with the author and by Rut Diamint, adviser to the subsecretary for policy and strategy, ministry of defense, in an interview with the author, Washington, D.C., July 19, 1994. Also see Rut Diamint, "Gasto militar y ajuste económico en Argentina," in *Gasto militar en América Latina: Procesos de decisiones y actores claves*, ed. Francisco Rojas Aravena (Santiago, Chile: Centro Internacional para el Desarrollo Económico, 1994), pp. 146–57.

nor the national defense council. No one in a position to inform the econo-mists and accountants within the MOE about the strategic repercussions of their budget decisions is ever conferred with. An initial decision is made solely to conform with general fiscal and monetary objectives, not with na-tional security needs.

As ill-advised as this process may seem on security grounds, politically speaking it has its enormous advantages. It insulates civilian policymakers from military influences that in the past had narrowly served corporate—not national—interests. In a country that had been so militarized as Argentina, where the armed forces would regularly and easily exert their will upon hap-less politicians, budget meddling usually produced undesirable results. Far from utilizing their influence to see to it that pesos would be spent wisely to ensure the development of their defense forces, the military would usually push its weight around to assure unlimited perks and privileges for them-selves. Their entrée into policymaking circles did not inform the budgetary process so much as to subvert it for their own self-serving ends.

Looking back on that era, a senior member of the army's general staff now admits that the military had failed to achieve an understanding with the political class about the larger purposes behind defense spending. In not defining more clearly what fundamental national interests were at stake, while relentlessly pursuing their shortsighted objectives, the military instilled within government a lingering suspicion about their intentions.[64] Those sus-picions were and continue to be fully justified. Thus, although contemporary budget makers deprive themselves of military input, they simultaneously in-sulate themselves from pressures that could prove debilitating to the govern-ment.

Budget allocations are received and discussed by the full cabinet. Little in the way of bargaining can take place here, since any appeal for greater allot-ments by one minister will quickly be matched and anted up by all others. The meeting is a mere formality at which time the ministers receive their distressing news and then report back to their respective agencies. They must now fashion budget proposals that will be compatible with the limits, norms, orientations, and technical guidelines established by the economics ministry. Defense is no exception. All those interviewed, whether they be civilians in the ministry or military officers in each service, concurred that under Radical and Peronist administrations alike, budget proposals were profoundly shaped

---

64. General Aníbal Laíño, general secretary of the army, interview with author, Buenos Aires, July 8, 1993.

and constrained by the macroeconomic objectives as enunciated by the economics ministry.

As candidly admitted by Secretary of Planning for Defense Dr. Guillermo Etchechoury, the preliminary ceilings set by the secretary of finance are "always insufficient with respect to the needs of each force."[65] Certainly the armed forces are within their means to propose budgets that exceed the preliminary limit in order to hedge against losses once the final budgetary stone is set. In fact, it is quite rational for state agencies to embellish their requests since not doing so would only place them at a decided disadvantage with respect to those agencies that did. But the military's powers are not what they used to be. In the past there was a self-reinforcing and self-perpetuating mechanism at work: the military was intemperate in its demands because this usually produced results. If not through inflationary means then through indebtedness, the finance secretary would oblige the armed forces with larger budgets, which in turn would spur even more exorbitant requests the next time around.

Now it is not simply that the economics ministry refuses to honor military requests, which it regularly does. It is that by legal procedure it cannot do so. As mentioned previously, the Central Bank is prohibited from financing Treasury deficits and cannot engage in any operations that would expand the money supply without the prior authorization of the economics ministry.[66] Domestic or foreign borrowing is sparingly permitted but confined to debt repayment, restructuring, and investment. Loans cannot be secured to sustain current expenditures. These are pieces of legislation originally drafted by the economics ministry itself to enforce an unparalleled fiscal discipline upon the Argentine state.[67] As members of that state, the armed forces are principal targets for these frugally minded economists. Theoretically, the only other recourse would be either to raise taxes, something the Congress is reticent to do, or to pry resources away from another account, something the administration is reluctant to do.

The changed rules of the game thus establish new expectations and behaviors. Knowing that their rapacious appetite will no longer be satiated, the military restrain themselves. Purposeful budgetary padding is resented by the

65. Dr. Guillermo Federico Etchechoury, secretary of planning, ministry of defense, interview with author, Buenos Aires, October 26, 1994.

66. See Articles 1 and 7 of Decreto 435 of March 4, 1990, in República Argentina, *Anales de Legislación Argentina*, Tomo L-A (Buenos Aires: Edición de Jurisprudencia Argentina, 1990), pp. 170–71.

67. On the use of credit, see Ley de Administración Pública (Ley 24.156), pp. 3361–63.

economics ministry, is certain to be counterproductive, and is thereby avoided. On the other hand, rarely do service requests come in under budget, since there is no incentive to do so. Any savings achieved by the armed forces via more cost-effective procurement and programming does not first revert back to them but instead goes to the general accounts. Only some proportion of this surplus will ever return to the defense sector, and it is not clear how much or when.[68]

The general rule is that the armed forces not propose extravagant ventures lest they be financially penalized next year for doing so. They must devise operations that can be completed efficiently and within budget. The difficulties are twofold. First, funds are released triannually, not in one lump sum. Economics will not guarantee beforehand that the disbursements will be steady or of equal size, thus generating problems of cash flow. The military must continually realign its annual, programmatic agenda to conform to an unstable flow of resources in the short term.

Second, and in the longer term, the armed forces cannot be sure that the plans they hatch now can be fulfilled with the budget they receive later. If they initiate projects that cannot be subsequently financed, they may be accused of having squandered resources on undoable missions. But if they don't plan for the future, they lay themselves open to the charge that they had consumed funds myopically to gratify immediate corporate needs.[69] Consequently, the services have begun to develop malleable contingency plans that can respond more adequately to an unstable economic environment. The army and navy, for example, have prepared various defense alternatives within a unified plan. If they receive less funding than expected, they will revert to more modest options. Should more money be made available, they have more ambitious strategies ready to be launched.[70]

The military must also see to it that real, not imaginary, costs are figured into their budgets. All programs must be cost appraised, unit by unit, weapon by weapon. Established accounting procedures have to be used so that the central auditors can easily review, interpret, and critique how budgets are formulated and executed. The armed forces are by law compelled to adhere to an "efficient and efficacious" system of management, finance, and control,

---

68. Rut Diamint, interview with author, Washington, D.C., July 19, 1994.

69. Ibid.

70. General Aníbal Laíño, interview with author, Buenos Aires, November 4, 1994; Contraalmirante Horacio F. Reyser and Capitán Leonardo Arnoldo Steyerthal, interviews with author, Buenos Aires, November 3, 1994.

as are all other state agencies.[71] This too is a painful adjustment for an institution that had never employed any trained accountants nor deployed any reasonable accounting procedures. It will, claims the military, take time for them to fully organize their accounts, and programs already phased in cannot be warehoused until the budgets are in order.[72] It may be difficult to redeem a shelved operation, three to five years hence, with equipment lying in disrepair due to lack of maintenance and soldiers who had been denied training now inadequately prepared to resume duties. Again, it is not clear how empathic the economics ministry is toward these arguments, but the new rules make it painfully evident to the armed forces that the days of fiscal heedlessness are a thing of the past.

With its margin reduced the military's task is now simplified to one of prioritization. Which operations does it believe are most expendable? Which ones can it not do without? A hierarchy of needs is established so that anticipated cuts can be absorbed rationally while inflicting the least damage possible on force structure and personnel. These proposals get returned to the undersecretary for budgeting and administration within MOD, whose job it is to make additional cuts where necessary and to meld these three separate documents (one each from the army, navy, and air force) into one.[73]

That defense proposal now meanders back to the "center." Its first stop is at the defense ministry's own cabinet session, where the military's joint chiefs of staff are invited in to assess the overall impact of a tightened budget and to undoubtedly make a plea for more. The minister will pass on the request along with the budget to the MOE's secretary of finance. The secretary's budgeting officer will then revise the defense accounts, along with all other ministerial accounts, where necessary, and combine these into a single federal budget.

Beforehand, the defense minister may also request a private session with the president where he makes the case for higher authorizations. The minister is specific, only pleading for programs that would directly serve the highest political priorities as set by the president himself. For example, under

---

71. Ley de Administración Pública (Ley 24.156), art. 4, p. 3354.

72. It is only since 1993 that the army has taken up the task of cost estimation, something they had never practiced before. This admission was made to me by General Aníbal Laíño, general secretary of the army, in interviews conducted in Buenos Aires on July 8, 1993, and November 4, 1994.

73. These and other duties of the subsecretary were detailed for the author by Dr. José Alberto Torzillo, subsecretary for budgeting and administration of the ministry of defense, in an interview in Buenos Aires on November 3, 1994.

Menem the defense minister argued for increased funding to enable Argentina to participate more effectively in international peace missions, something the president had attached great importance to.[74] The minister also pointed out how the president's own plan to transform the military into a volunteer force would not succeed without more defense funding. These sessions bore fruit for him only on occasion. More commonly, the president was persuaded by his economics minister that extra defense spending, regardless of the mission, yields inconsiderable political returns; that ultimately the political viability of the administration is ensured through continued economic stability, which is made possible by holding the line on expenditures.

And so the economics ministry has the final word. An immutable ceiling is now set, and all that remains is the president's signature before the budget bill is sent on to the Congress.[75] Once it is signed, what little executive branch leverage the armed forces had to begin with is now fully exhausted. What recourse then is left for them? Can they rely on the legislative branch itself for restitution?

The Congressional Option

According to the Argentine constitution, the Congress enjoys the power of the purse. Only it may levy taxes, borrow money on the nation's credit, arrange for the payment of debt, and set the annual expenditures for the nation.[76] But as is often the case in Argentina, the law only conveys a partial truth. In reality the Congress exerts very little control over the budgetary process.

Some comparisons are in order. In the United States the president's February budget presentation to the Congress is merely a proposal, one that will undergo countless modifications by assorted committees before it sees the light of day. The Congress is in every sense of the word a coequal player, unafraid to flex its muscles when it comes to fiscal matters of state. In Argen-

74. This ministerial strategy was revealed to me by the Argentine ambassador to the OAS, Hernan Patiño Mayer, in an interview with the author, Washington, D.C., July 5, 1994. Also Rut Diamint, interview with author, Washington, D.C., July 19, 1994.

75. Once signed, the budget is sent back to the armed forces for final programmatic adjustments. Here program officers for each service make final realignments in light of the ceiling.

76. See Amos J. Peaslee, *Constitutions of Nations*, Constitution of the Argentine Nation, art. 67, items 2,3,6, 7 (The Hague: Martinus Nijhoff, 1984), p. 36.

tina the president's budget submission is a virtual fait accompli. What he submits is more or less what he will eventually sign into law. Congress may tinker around the edges but cannot undo what the executive has done.

The U.S. Congress marks up its own defense budget. No less than twenty committees and subcommittees staffed with specialists on defense take a pen to the president's bill, adding to or subtracting from specific programs as they see fit. The process unfolds within the House and Senate Congressional Budget Committees (not the Office of Management and Budget), which determine ceilings on budget outlays for the coming fiscal year as well as spending and revenue targets for two additional years, three in all. Through their annual Concurrent Budget Resolution they not only define the fiscal boundaries within which the other committees must work but make defense expenditure recommendations as well.[77]

But as has been said, the job of setting financial limits in Argentina goes to the secretary of finance within the economics ministry. Congressional weakness in Argentina has two fundamental causes. The first is informational in nature. Historically, the budgets always arrived to Congress late, meaning that legislative deliberation was superfluous.[78] But even though the budget is now delivered in timely fashion, there is another problem. Data on federal revenue resides in the executive, not legislative, branch. There is no congressional budget office as in the United States. Only the secretary of finance is privy to the most current tax receipt information. Without this key data, legislators who might wish to raise budget ceilings are at an enormous disadvantage. How can they argue persuasively for budget enlargement when the economics ministry is telling them that the revenues are just not there to support it?

The second problem is that the Congress of Argentina lacks the institutional infrastructure necessary to translate its constitutional prerogatives into real power. Only one legislative body convenes on the budget and that is

77. Congressional Research Service, Report for Congress, A *Defense Budget Primer* by Keith Berner and Stephen Daggett (Washington, D.C.: Congressional Research Service, March 9, 1993), pp. 29–31. Also see the Department of Defense, Joint DOD/GAO Working Group on PPBS, "Planning, Programming, and Budgeting System" (Washington, D.C.: Government Accounting Office, September 1983), GAO-OACG-845, pp. 142–44.

78. Commonly, Argentine national accounts would not be settled until mid-year or year's end. For instance, the Alfonsín government apologetically submitted its 1985 budget to the Congress on July 19 of that year, admitting that the delay was caused both by reformulation of short-term economic policy *and* by fluctuations in prices, salaries, and exchange rates. At the end of 1990 the Menem government deliberated upon no less than three budgets simultaneously: for the two years that had already transpired without budgets and for the year ahead. Starting in 1992, however, budget proposals have made their way to Congress on schedule.

the Committee on Budgeting and Finance. Its powers of authorization are a formality: it largely discusses but seldom amends; it requests ministerial testimony, but this is for purposes of clarification only. The most that can be said for the committee is that it serves a watchdog function, holding the administration's feet to the fire for inconsistencies between its programmatic objectives on the one hand and its budget on the other.[79] In the end, however, the committee will usually sign off on the president's bill.

In the United States, after the budget committees have finished with their work, the authorization committees then sanction and define the scope of defense-related programs. Then the all-powerful appropriations committees take over, determining the actual amount of funds to be made available for each defense program. Their jurisdiction spans seventy-three Department of Defense (DOD) accounts, within the areas of personnel, operations and maintenance, procurement, research and development, construction, and housing.[80] Within the limits set by the budget resolution, these committees may raise or lower the president's request at will. By contrast, in Argentina there is no appropriations committee or process. The Congress is without the wherewithal to reopen, examine, or rewrite the packaged budget. There is no item-by-item review, no markup, and thus no real capacity to assign resources to defense accounts.

U.S. military officials understand what the separation of powers is all about. They are able to exploit the division of budgetary authority between the executive and congressional branches to their advantage. In principle, the services are supposed to fall in line behind the DOD's recommendations once the president signs off on them. In practice, they have been making end runs around the executive branch for decades. For example, the navy may desire two hundred Tomahawk missiles annually whereas the Office of the Secretary of Defense (OSD) prefers that they purchase only one hundred. A naval procurement officer will then contact the chief lobbyist for McDonnell Douglas, the company that supplies the weapon, and ask him to make a direct appeal to Congress. Typically, the lobbyist will target a key representative or senator who sits on or chairs an authorization or appropriation committee and whose district depends heavily on defense contracts for employment. With a little bit of persuasion it is probable that the congress-

---

79. An example would be with the proposal for an all-volunteer force. Some congressmen were wary, believing that the funds committed in the budget were grossly insufficient to support such a force—a sentiment shared by the military. They brought administration officials in for questioning. Dr. José Horacio Jaunarena, Diputado, interview with author, Buenos Aires, November 2, 1994.

80. See Congressional Research Service, *A Defense Budget Primer*, pp. 32, 53–54.

men in question will soon see the Tomahawk issue from the military's point of view (if he hadn't already) and have the power to do something about it.[81]

With fiscal powers so centralized in the executive branch it is little wonder that the Argentine armed forces cannot make the same end run. They have no institutional means to circumvent the economic authorities. The Argentine Congress has neither the institutional resources nor the will to provide the military with an effective counterweight. This is not to say, however, that military-congressional relations are nonexistent. To the contrary, they exist and are well routinized. But the limits to military influence within congressional chambers is eloquently disclosed by the Spanish title for those officers assigned to legislative duty. They are "enlaces," which means liaisons; they are not "cabilderos," or lobbyists. By their own account their primary purpose is to establish fluid relations by opening up a permanent line of communication between the legislature and army, naval, and air force headquarters.[82]

The military fully recognize the limitations of the exchange. This is evinced by the fact that senior officials, including the chiefs of staff, hardly ever make personal appearances before Congress. They neither request a hearing, nor are they invited. The indifference is mutual. The Congress prefers that the military retain their legislative ties but yet restrain their collective voice. And the armed forces realize that when it comes to so vital an issue as the defense budget, the Congress can never effectively champion their cause.

Conclusion

The institutional processes heretofore described define the boundaries to military influence in the contemporary democratic period. Budgetary power during the Alfonsín and Menem years resided exclusively in the executive branch, and more precisely within the economics ministry. During the dem-

81. The details of this process were revealed to me by a navy captain and former procurement officer in the Chief of Naval Operations Office in a telephone interview in October 1994.

82. The military *enlaces* will provide legislative aides with useful information when requested and on occasion suggest modifications in statutory language. But their influence is at best modest and largely confined to nonbudgetary themes. Their contacts are mainly with the congressional defense commissions in each chamber. Those commissions have written important pieces of legislation on defense and security missions but have no authority over financial matters. The author interviewed several military liaison officers in their congressional chambers on November 2, 1994.

ocratic period, policy success was measured in political and economic terms. The reduction of military power and the adroit management of fiscal affairs were of transcending importance; the management of the nation's defenses was not. These substantive priorities naturally placed the economics ministry at the hub of governance. And the ministry was unquestionably up to the task. The pros and cons of the economic plan can be debated, but the qualifications of those on the economic team could not. These were trained economists with years of experience. Their expertise and confidence translated directly into greater ministerial capacity.

But institutional capacity goes well beyond the issue of skills to that of structures and procedures. Economic policymaking is concentrated in a sole agency. Budgetary technocrats in the ministry of economics do not have to negotiate endlessly with other state functionaries, although they do communicate with them. They execute the will of their minister, who in turn single-handedly shapes the president's economic agenda.

Those technocrats are also distant from military reach. The armed forces have no official presence within the economics ministry or its secretariat of finance, and certainly very little clout. Bureaucratically speaking, the military is twice removed from economics, separated by the defense ministry and the presidency itself, and even further distanced from the budgeting office that resides within the finance secretariat. It must appeal through MOD and simply hope that the civilian functionaries there will adequately and fairly represent its interests. While, for example, the minister and his secretaries and undersecretaries communicate regularly and directly with the MOE, military figures do not. Military commanders must beseech the minister or his subordinates to negotiate on their behalf. Sometimes their pleas are heard, other times not.

After all, the MOD is not simply a conduit; it is a player, a part of the administration itself. All those MOD officials interviewed spoke essentially the same language: it is the language of economic stability, fiscal restraint, sacrifice, and national priorities. It is the official language of their chief executive.[83] Defensive needs could not be ignored, they said, but should be guided by the current economic realities. MOD's official charge is to formulate and execute defense policies in conformance with the president's wishes.[84] The chain of command dictates that the defense minister will be subservient to

---

83. Author interviews with Dr. Guillermo Federico Etchechoury, Dr. José Alberto Torzillo, Rut Diamint, Juan Carlos Costa, Juan Ferreira Pinho, 1993 and 1994.

84. See Decreto 15 of December 10, 1983, in República Argentina, *Legislación Argentina, Tomo 1983-B*, pp. 1926–27.

the will of the commander in chief. The armed forces chiefs of staff, in turn, are subordinate to the defense minister. That hierarchical structure privileges top-down flows of influence, ensuring that the military will have its work cut out for it when the president and the economics minister are of one mind regarding the fiscal affairs of state. With budget decisions so centralized, and with no competing centers of power to turn to, the armed forces must attempt to negotiate influence within that hierarchy or not at all.

Certainly, a similar kind of hierarchical structure exists in advanced democracies such as the United States. The difference resides in the rules governing budget formation. In the U.S. executive branch, early budget decisions are made inside the Department of Defense. Although the Office of Management and Budget (OMB) will prepare its own evaluation, it weighs in during the final phase of the process, not before.

Moreover, there is a close intermingling of military and civilian personnel and functions within the DOD. If there is a division of labor, it is essentially one between strategic assignments (dominated by civilians) and operational duties (dominated by officers). But procedures dictate that both strategic and operational inputs come together to inform the budget process and that they be delivered to the OSD *before* any financial decisions are made. This rule brings into the decision stream such military figures as the chairman of the joint chiefs of staff, who is the principal military advisor to the president and the Secretary of Defense (SECDEF), and who is asked to contribute a report that assesses threats to the nation and possible military responses. Only with that report in hand can the services prepare their program memorandum, and only then can budgets be devised.[85]

In the Argentine system, national security considerations and fiscal considerations are largely divorced from one another, with the latter taking precedence. That means that the military is left "out of the loop." The flow of

85. This is called the Planning, Programming, and Budgeting System (PPBS), first introduced by Secretary of Defense Robert McNamara in 1961. The system acts as a bridge between security and finance that "allows officials to make decisions in the budget process based more upon the explicit criteria of the national interest." Decisions are sequenced through three phases: planning, programming, and budgeting. See Lawrence Korb, "The Budget Process in the Department of Defense, 1947–1977: The Strengths and Weaknesses of Three Systems," *Public Administration Review* (July/August 1977): 340; see also the Department of Defense Joint DOD/GAO Working Group on PPBS, "Planning, Programming, and Budgeting System" (Washington, D.C.: Government Accounting Office, September 1993), GAO-OACG-845, p. 33. PPBS is not completely foreign to the Argentines. During the Alfonsín administration, an effort was made by then MOD Secretary for Programming and Budgeting Dr. Adalberto Rodríguez Giovanini to import and apply PPBS. Unfortunately, the program in its entirety never got beyond the pilot phase. But bits and pieces of the system do remain, and the ideas embedded within it get bantered about from time to time.

budgetary decisions does not involve a constant mix of defense and fiscal strategists. It is only after the budget is assembled and approved that the military moves to center stage, with planners and programmers figuring out how to spend the scant funds delivered to them. Economists within the secretariat of finance are not obligated to consult with defense experts on how the size of the budget would impact national security objectives. Although the civilian defense "establishment" has grown in size in recent years, defense expertise still resides mainly within the armed forces. Consequently, it is military officers who are denied access to budget-making quarters. While their exclusion may leave the economists bereft of defense wisdom, it also shields them from harmful, predatory influences as well.

In short, the rules of the game afford civilian budget makers an unusually high degree of autonomy and centralized authority. That combination translates into a high degree of policy success, as shown in Figure 5.1.

The findings recounted here are especially significant since they hold across two markedly different administrations: one Radical, the other Peronist; one preoccupied with human rights injustices, the other worried primarily about economic recovery. Although their priorities differed, together they profited from the same built-in, institutional arrangements that allowed them to greatly reduce the military purse. Neither chief executive had to intervene personally to shepherd his budget through or bargain with his

Fig. 5.1. Explaining budget policy outcomes: the role of institutional authority and autonomy

		Concentration of Authority	
		High	Low
Decision-Making Autonomy	High	A. High Success (mil. budgets) 1984–93)	B. Moderate Success
	Low	C. Moderate Success	D. No Success

military commanders. To win, each simply had to establish political priorities and then utilize the governmental instruments at his disposal. In democratic Argentina budget making is institutionalized, not individualized.

This chapter's portrayal of policy success now needs to be tempered by situating the budget theme in a slightly larger context. As civilian policy-makers trimmed away the fat from the military budget, they faced another challenge: how to reform the armed services so that they could adequately adapt to new fiscal restraints while facing the security challenges that lay ahead. In many ways the military still resembled the outdated, occupational force that held a grip over Argentina during the late 1970s. Perhaps its bud-get was no longer bloated, but its structure surely was: too many officers, too many units, too much redundancy and inefficiency. That structure, under-nourished as it was by the depleted budget, could not simply be left intact. If it were, the military could collapse under its own weight. But as the next chapter will make clear, propping up the behemoth by reforming it was far easier said than done.

CHAPTER 6

Forgoing Change
The Failure of Defense Reform Under
Democratic Rule

The same [military] structure is sustained on a budget
that is appreciably lower. . . . that is the paradox of the
famished elephant.

              —Ernesto López

The image of a famished elephant is captivating. The military beast finds its
food supply dwindling. It desperately scrounges around for every morsel it
can lay its trunk on, but only with diminishing returns for its effort. It knows
it must rein in its huge appetite but somehow seems incapable of doing so.
Drawing weary of its search for nourishment, it comes to rest in the shade,
unable to lift its huge body off the ground any longer. Sitting still now feels
more comforting than advancing forward.

In a real sense the famished elephant serves as a metaphor for the Argentine armed forces. Necessity is usually the mother of invention. The military's devastating defeat on the Malvinas battlefield in 1982 should have
been the proper stimuli for a creative recovery. But not so. Like the slumber-
ing mammal, the Argentine military has not moved substantially forward. It
has not as yet been motivated to engage in a profound, critical reexamina-
tion of itself—the kind that serves as a prelude to fundamental reform. And
reform it must if the Argentine soldier is to ever again fight effectively against
his foreign foes. The tasks are numerous, but one stands above the rest:
the reorganization of force structures and operations of the services along
collaborative lines.

Reform eludes the armed forces not only for lack of self-motivation but for lack of external direction. They have not received the kind of firm mandate they need from the political authorities. Reform must first be authorized from above. The broad strokes of institutional reorganization must be painted by the president and his defense staff. Only then can the detail be filled in by the military.[1] Even if it was intended to, the deprivation of military "fiscal nourishment" as recounted in the last chapter was never enough to stimulate a profound reorganization of the institution. It resulted in some limited downsizing, but nothing more. Both Alfonsín and Menem expressed desire for real, structural reform and took some initial steps in that direction. But the reform effort floundered, and a comprehensive, strategic plan was never implemented. Why not? And who or what is to blame? These are the central questions to be addressed in this chapter.

The Illusion of Military Preparedness

Though the Argentines did not expect to easily defeat the British in the 1982 Malvinas War, still their decisive loss came as a surprise for two reasons. The first was the armed forces' belief that they had achieved an adequate if not superior level of force modernization. The second was the belief that their victory over leftist insurgents had confirmed their status as able warriors. Neither view was well founded. Having had its attention diverted for so long toward counterinsurgency and away from conventional warfare, the military had left itself vulnerable to defeat from foreign military powers: weapons were not carefully procured for use in modern warfare, technical training lagged behind, and separate service branches were strategically and tactically uncoordinated. However, with its impressive victory over guerrilla forces during the mid-1970s, the military was not exceedingly preoccupied with such deficiencies.

Argentina has always been one of the region's most militarily self-reliant nations.[2] At the opening of the twentieth century the "Reforma Ricchieri"

1. This was the view of former defense minister Raúl Borrás who said that government can only set general contours to reform, whereas the specification and execution rests squarely with the military itself. See *Foreign Broadcast Information Service—Latin America* (FBIS-LAT), March 16, 1984, p. B7.

2. It was General San Martín who founded Latin America's first factory for army weapons. Situated in the Buenos Aires area, the factory produced guns and artillery for his soldiers in the wars of liberation in Chile and Peru. This installation survived through most of the nineteenth century, turning out light Krupp field guns in the 1880s.

(named after the general who directed it) made significant advances in the professionalization and modernization of the armed forces.[3] Beginning in the 1930s defense-related industries grew and flourished. Argentina's arms industry experienced its greatest expansion in 1941 with the founding of its own state-funded and supervised military industrial complex, the *Dirección General de Fabricaciones Militares* (DGFM). The DGFM became a sprawling conglomerate of thirteen separate industrial complexes employing more than 14,000 individuals with production lines in military transport, armored vehicles, tanks, antiaircraft missiles, and the region's finest aerospace and shipbuilding industries.[4]

As a result of technological advances in the post–World War II era, much of Argentina's hardware had been rendered obsolete. Improvement was difficult in the 1950s and 1960s owing to the reluctance of the United States to supply Latin America with conventional weaponry. Washington was convinced that its neighbors to the south could not contribute effectively to hemispheric defense and therefore were not in need of state-of-the-art munitions. According to the United States, the Latin forces could be counted on only to enforce internal security. With the victory of Castro's forces in Cuba, and the reconfiguration of military strategies and doctrines to prepare for internal warfare, Washington became an eager supplier of small arms, riot gear, and transport vehicles to armies and especially police forces who were to be in the front line of defense against leftist insurgency.[5] Even though the strategic shift in military supply and procurement was welcomed by the Argentine army, it eventually contributed to its own uneven development, a fact that became fully apparent only with the Malvinas defeat.

Argentina closed some of the technological gap in the early 1970s with its *Plan Europa*, a series of agreements with European suppliers to either coproduce or import a variety of more sophisticated weapons, including light tanks, antiaircraft missiles, and even submarines.[6] The impressive develop-

3. Robert Potash, *The Army and Politics in Argentina, 1928–1945: Yrigoyen to Perón* (Stanford: Stanford University Press, 1969), pp. 2–3.

4. John Keegan, *World Armies*, 2d ed. (London: Macmillan Publishers, 1983), p. 24.

5. Michael T. Klare and Cynthia Arnson, *Supplying Repression: U.S. Support for Authoritarian Regimes Abroad* (Washington, D.C.: Institute for Policy Studies, 1987).

6. Edward S. Milenky, "Argentina," in *Security Policies of Developing Countries*, ed. Edward A. Kolodziej and Robert E. Harkavy (Lexington, Mass.: Lexington Books, 1982), p. 40. As a result of the *Plan Europa* the Argentines also discovered the advantages of technological reversal, where they dismantled imported items and then reconstructed these using their own resources and know-how. More recently, the nuclear industry, which is well established by Latin American standards, was serving as a springboard for further modernization with plans to refit diesel-powered electric submarines with nuclear propulsion, especially in the wake of the Malvinas disaster. I do not know what

ment of its own arms industry and the upgrading of its defensive systems through cooperative ventures with the Europeans all contributed to an image of military preparedness, if not superiority within the region. This image in turn fostered a high degree of professional self-confidence and pride.[7] That image was reinforced during the military's antiguerrilla campaigns of the 1970s.

During that time the Argentine military believed itself to be at the pinnacle of its professional powers. It had undertaken counterinsurgency operations against native guerrilla forces and had emerged victorious. "Operation Independence," fought in 1975 in the mountainous Tucumán province against the ERP (*Ejército Revolucionario del Pueblo*) guerrillas was an unmitigated success. In what appeared to have been a textbook-perfect display of counterguerrilla strategy, the armed forces destroyed the ERP's rural "foco" while absorbing few casualties of its own—all in the span of just eleven months.[8] The Tucumán operation was of course followed by the *Dirty War* itself, which dealt the final blow to the Peronist-affiliated *Montonero* guerrillas. Combined, these wars represented the fulfillment of the Argentine national security mission to pursue and defeat domestic agents of international communism, a mission that had its genesis with the introduction to Argentina of French counterinsurgency doctrine in the late 1950s and that received further impetus from the North Americans in the 1960s.[9]

Other national security–minded armies were marching to the same tune. Pinochet's forces had crushed the left in Chile, and the Uruguayan armed forces had launched their final offensive against its *Tupamaro* guerrilla opponents. To be a military professional in Latin America in the 1970s was to

---

kind of success the navy has recently had in this endeavor. See Lt. Keith E. Wixler, "Argentina's Geopolitics and Her Revolutionary Diesel-Electric Submarines," *Naval War College Review* 42 (Winter 1989): 86–107.

7. Of course, military professional reform is not directly dependent upon force modernization. Technological deficiencies aside, an army can still produce able soldiers and maintain high levels of internal cohesion. Conversely, modernized armies have often fallen prey to unprofessional modes of conduct. With that said, there are still important links between modernization and professionalism. In a broad sense, modernization refers not only to material improvements but to advances in leadership, strategy, organization, and coordination, all of which fall under the professional rubric of coercive management. The ultimate test of any army is its ability to weld all of these components together and deploy them effectively under battlefield conditions. It is that test which the Argentines failed miserably during the Malvinas War.

8. FAMUS (Familiares y Amigos de los Muertos por la Subversión), *Operación independencia* (Buenos Aires: FAMUS, 1988), pp. 217–20.

9. Ernesto López, *Seguridad nacional y sedición militar* (Buenos Aires: Legasa, 1987), pp. 137–44. Also see David Pion-Berlin and George Lopez, "Of Victims and Executioners: Argentine State Terror, 1975–79," *International Studies Quarterly* 35 (March 1991): 63–86.

show expertise in the management of counterinsurgent violence. The Argentines had done just that.

But their victory in the internal war helped to mask underlying deficiencies that would spell defeat in the external war. First of all, the internal war allowed the army to operate without dependence on air or sea support. This was essentially a land-based operation situated first in the rural mountains and then in the cities. For example, all of those soldiers reported killed in Tucumán were from the army.[10] When the war moved to the cities after 1975, each service conducted its own operations independently of the other, with the bulk of the repression still inflicted by terrestrial forces. Consequently, at no time did any branch of the military have to concern itself with interservice coordination.[11]

Second, the Argentine military was mistaken in its belief that it was up against an enemy equal to the Vietcong. The *Montoneros* and ERP were poorly trained, poorly equipped, and greatly outnumbered. Most accurate estimates placed the armed combatants at no more than five thousand men and women, compared to the two hundred thousand strong Argentine armed forces, a proportion that far exceeded the 10:1 parity thought necessary to win a guerrilla war.[12] Unlike their Vietnamese counterparts, the Argentine revolutionaries exhausted their forces quickly. These insurgents were like "fish out of water," never having built a secure base of mass support from which to recruit new personnel. They crumbled easily under the weight of the army's offensive, never putting the military to a full test.

These comparisons were lost on an Argentine military whose operations in Tucumán and in the urban centers of Buenos Aires, Rosario, and Córdoba were receiving widespread regional praise. The military largely succeeded in preserving for itself the image of competence right up until the Malvinas invasion of April 1, 1982.

The Malvinas Debacle and Shattered Illusions

In all likelihood the illusion of military preparedness would have persisted for years had not the Malvinas War so dramatically intervened. The War of

10. There were sixty reported army deaths, forty-five in combat and fifteen in an airplane crash. See FAMUS, *Operación independencia*, pp. 217–20.

11. The army could rely entirely on light armaments, easily matching and surpassing the weaponry of the insurgents. Careful procurement of and training in the most technologically sophisticated hardware was nonessential for the fulfillment of this mission.

12. Richard Gillespie, *Soldiers of Perón: Argentina's Montoneros* (London: Clarendon Press, 1982), p. 178.

the South Atlantic exposed the wide disparity between the image of Argentina's professional skills and its reality.[13] There was no unified planning nor any operable, unified command. Each branch operated unto its own, as if it were fighting a separate war. A multiservice command hierarchy was established but never exercised the authority invested in it. A military committee (Comité Militar, COMIL) was ostensibly in charge of the Malvinas operations, and was to have delegated tasks to the Commander of the South Atlantic Theater of Operations (Comandante del Teatro de Operationes Atlántico del sur, CTOAS), who in turn would guide the activities of the Malvinas Garrison. But the COMIL never enforced a comprehensive, strategic plan for fighting the war, while the CTOAS did not elaborate an integrated, strategic plan for the Malvinas Garrison, but instead instructed the forces separately.[14] And the Garrison never assembled a joint military operational plan that would have "established with clarity and precision the missions that each of its components would undertake."[15]

The unwillingness to sufficiently concentrate power and authority at the very top fueled centrifugal tendencies below. Thus, for example, the air force, navy, and army normally have their own aircraft. But the CTOAS allowed each to control decisions about their use rather than deferring to a single air command, which would have deployed these planes according to principles of unified action.[16] What scant military intelligence that was gathered was done so by the separate branches. No effort was made to share in the collection, analysis, or dissemination of intelligence, each component circulated and recirculated its own data, which was often poor in quality not to mention incompatible with information picked up by other services. Logistically, no coordinated action was ever seen at either a national, strategic, or operational level. The result: no infrastructure was ever erected to deposit and then efficiently transport materials to all the units.[17] A joint

13. Defense specialists agree that while the nation has accumulated a large stockpile of weapons, these have not always been carefully selected for deployment in a modern war. Problems in procurement were evidenced during the Malvinas engagement by the navy, which remained reliant on surface attack ships while the British (and virtually all other advanced Western powers) had moved to nuclear-powered submarines and aircraft-carrier warfare long before. The sinking of the Argentine destroyer *General Belgrano* by undetected British nuclear submarines, with the resultant loss of nearly four hundred lives, underscored just how far behind Argentina had lagged in naval readiness. But the procurement problem was just symptomatic of a more profound, underlying malady: the lack of proper planning, training, and coordination.

14. Rattenbach Commission, *Informe Rattenbach: El drama de Malvinas* (Buenos Aires: Ediciones Espartaco, 1988), pp. 206, 250.

15. Ibid., p. 213.

16. Ibid., p. 207.

17. Ibid., p. 235.

operations center that would have centralized intelligence and logistical activities was never conceived. Generally speaking, the duplication of efforts
and the lack of coordinated action on the ground seriously hampered Argentine efforts there.[18]

Disrespect for the unified command was rampant. Service commanders
seldom took heed of the orders handed down by the multiservice committees. For example, immediately after the Argentines invaded the Malvinas
and planted their flag, the junta assigned army General Menéndez to be
governor of the island as well as head of strategic operations there. Joining
him on the ground in Port Stanley were senior air force and naval officials.
But rather than collaborate with Menéndez, the senior officers instead com-
municated directly and only with their superiors, Brigadier General Ernesto
Crespo and Vice Admiral Lombardo, respectively, who were stationed hundreds of miles away on the mainland at Comodor Rivadavia.[19]

General Menéndez followed suit, deciding that he would report directly to
his army superiors, bypassing the CTOAS. He uncritically accepted plans
hatched at army headquarters that were poorly conceived and that only complicated matters on the ground. The army leadership encouraged this disrespect since it too had little regard for the unified command. After a brief
visit to the islands on April 22, 1982, General Leopoldo Galtieri, then head
of the junta and commander in chief of the army, suddenly decided to dis-
patch the Third Infantry Brigade to the Malvinas. This he did without con-
sulting either with the COMIL or CTOAS, nor did he consider the Malvinas
Garrisons' own plea that nothing greater than a regiment-sized force be sent.
The brigade had its headquarters in Corrientes province, where its troops
had trained under semitropical, climatic conditions. They arrived in the
Malvinas scantily clothed and completely unprepared for the frigid tempera-
tures of the South Atlantic. General Menéndez had no idea of how to deploy
the brigade, which not surprisingly went on to perform quite poorly, while
straining beyond limits the provisions available to troops already on the

---

18. Ibid., p. 214. It should be added that many of the military commanders exposed their ignorance regarding basic tenets of warfare by hatching plots that could not be realistically executed
while discarding others that could have turned the war around. Most notably, they failed to launch
ground attacks against the British beachhead landing force; and they deployed a force of only two
hundred men to defend the critical high ground around Port Stanley—an area that was quickly
overtaken by the British and that positioned them for their final descent on the coastal town. See
Lawrence Freedman and Virginia Gamba-Stonehouse, *Signals of War: The Falklands Conflict of 1982*
(Princeton: Princeton University Press, 1991), pp. 377–78; Frederick Turner, "The Aftermath of
Defeat in Argentina," *Current History* 2 (1983): 60.

19. Freedman and Gamba-Stonehouse, *Signals of War*, pp. 178–79.

ground.[20] This fiasco all derived from Galtieri's personal obsession to occupy the islands by landing as many troops there as quickly as possible.[21]

The Rattenbach Commission's scathing report left no room for misinterpretation. Of all its charges of malfeasance and incompetence, one stood above the rest: the failure to prosecute the war according to a doctrine, strategy, and program of unified action. This constituted a "decisive weakness for our armed forces," said the commission.[22] More than an indictment of past behavior, this reflection would remain an acid test for future reform efforts. To know whether fundamental military reform has taken place, we would need to find evidence that (a) the government had a presidentially authorized defense plan guided by principles of unified action, and (b) such a document was then made operational by the armed forces.

Did these lessons seep into the consciousness of military and political leaders? Institutional inertia is a powerful force. Most well-established organizations tend to resist change unless absolutely compelled to do so by adversity. If as some theorists claim it takes a crisis to sufficiently jog an institution out of its lethargy, then the Malvinas War should have been the Argentine armed forces' wake-up call. Never in its history had it suffered such a crisis. But oddly enough, the observance of poor combat and the shock of devastating defeat did not jolt the military into a new readiness to transform. Instead of trying to extract lessons through a genuine examination of the conflict, military leaders outside of the Rattenbach Commission reviewed the facts superficially. And rather than propose profound changes in military structure and behavior, their solutions were cosmetic, designed to protect the institution's image or, perhaps more tellingly, their own.[23]

Commanders, who could no longer endure the embarrassing revelations of deficient, improvisational, and error-ridden military conduct as critically recounted by young combatants who fought in the Malvinas, had no incentive to examine their own failures. Any serious reform would have to be preceded by a trenchant, sobering critique of military performance that would no doubt look unfavorably upon them. Hence those directly responsible for the war preferred to conceal rather than reveal. But if the problem was simply one of poor performance by a handful of individual Malvinas

---

20. Rattenbach Commission, *Informe Rattenbach*, pp. 201–2.

21. Testimony of Colonel Carlos A. Landaburu recounted in Lic. Marcela R. Donadio, *El papel del Estado Mayor Conjunto de las fuerzas armadas en el sistema de defensa nacional* (Buenos Aires: Centro de Estudios para el Proyecto Nacional, 1993), p. 73.

22. Rattenbach Commission, *Informe Rattenbach*, pp. 248, 249.

23. Ernesto López, *El último levantamiento* (Buenos Aires: Legasa, 1988), pp. 23–24.

commanders, then their retirement from the service should have set in motion a process of reform. It did not, and to this day military leaders—many of whom had nothing to do with the Malvinas War—continue to resist the notion of fundamental change. Others are more reform-minded, yet the burden cannot be placed solely on their shoulders. As will be shown, reform cannot proceed apace without able institutions and strong political leadership—things that have been lacking in the Argentine government.

Democratic Government and Reformist Intentions

If the military seemed complacent about reform, then at least initially the UCR seemed equally unsettled about the status quo, and intent on doing something about it. The goal of military reform was not only enshrined in the UCR platform but enunciated in countless addresses by the president and his defense ministers throughout the period. The Radical Party called for "drastic" defense budget cuts that will be "progressive," meaning in step with the reform and reorganization process. It hoped "to mend its [the military's] deficiencies through a modernization [program] that would augment its capacity while simultaneously reducing funds assigned to defense."[24] In a policy-defining speech to the armed forces in July 1985, the president said that defense problems will not be resolved through "conceptually narrow ideas" but through "true military reform."[25] While the president only hinted vaguely at what this would entail, he seemed to be suggesting that fundamental restructuring of the institution was in order.

Alfonsín's first defense minister was more specific. Raúl Borrás cited the disastrous showing in the Malvinas War, where each branch operated as if the others did not exist. The tripartite military would have to learn to behave as one. The unification and coordination of military operations was a precondition for the modernization of Argentina's fighting forces, he said. Conceivably, modernization could be facilitated by purchasing technologically advanced weaponry, but only after reorganization since these sophisticated systems depended upon force integration. That is why in October 1985 Al-

24. Unión Cívica Radical (UCR), *Platform electoral nacional de la Unión Cívica Radical, 1983* (Buenos Aires: UCR, 1983), pt. 3, pp. 8–9.

25. See Dr. Raúl R. Alfonsín, "Discurso del Señor Presidente de la nación Argentina en la cena de camaradería de las fuerzas armadas," (Buenos Aires: Secretaría de Información Pública, July 5, 1985), p. 7.

fonsín's army chief of staff, Ríos Ereñú, urged that separate branch schools be dissolved and that cavalry and infantry artillery divisions be eliminated and replaced with interservice units that would correspond more closely to advanced technologies. Shortly thereafter the newly appointed minister of defense, Roque Carranza, repeated these themes, advocating the rapid integration of the services' separate research and decision-making units as well.[26]

President Menem, too, took up the banner of military unification in an important address to the armed forces on July 5, 1991. He said the objective of reorganization is this: "to merge the armed forces into a single bloc bonded by the principle of unity and solidarity."[27] Among other things, merger meant shrinkage, and both leaders sounded the call for size reduction more than once. In borrowing a metaphor, Alfonsín said he wanted to convert "the military elephant into a spirited horse."[28] And Menem would repeatedly emphasize how current economic realities could not sustain a military of massive proportions. Like other state agencies, the military would have to place its head on the chopping block.

As recounted in the previous chapter, the armed forces had simply become too big: too many armed and administrative units, too many officers, too much bureaucracy. Certainly size had served the nefarious goals of the *Proceso*. Its ubiquitous military became a leviathan of control, intimidation, terror, and extermination. The armed forces stretched itself from the tropical province of Misiones to the windswept expanse of Patagonia, partitioning the territory into a set of security zones, subzones, and areas that displaced normal political units.[29] The system's vast network of government offices, physical installations, communication systems, and personnel throughout the nation's major cities made easier the gathering of intelligence, the rounding up of suspects, the coordinated action with police departments to cordon off neighborhoods in search of "subversives," and the conversion of army, navy, air force, and police headquarters into some three hundred clandestine detention centers to which prisoners were transferred. While the Radical Party government quickly stripped the military of all its political control and put an end to its terrorist practices, one outstanding feature of the leviathan survived: its girth.

26. *FBIS-LAT*, October 2, 1985, pp. B2–B3; *Latin American Weekly Report*, October 25, 1985, p. 1.

27. Carlos Menem, President of the Argentine Republic, speech delivered at the Cena de Camaradería de las Fuerzas Armadas, July 5, 1991, p. 8.

28. Dr. Raúl R. Alfonsín, interview with author, Buenos Aires, July 20, 1993.

29. For further detail on the terrorist structure, see Centro de Estudios Legales y Sociales (CELS), *692: Responsables del terrorismo de estado* (Buenos Aires: CELS, 1986).

What served the cause of internal warfare was now counterproductive to the goal of national defense at a time when economic resources were scarce.[30] As recounted earlier, the nation is huge. It stretches 3,550 kilometers from north to south. It has 14,450 kilometers of frontier—more than one-third of which is shared with its perennial nemesis to the west—Chile. The nation cannot sustain an armed forces capable of spreading out in all directions across this vast expanse of land to guard against external attacks, where and whenever they might arise. Naturally, neither president wanted to sacrifice defensive readiness in their pursuit of force contraction, nor did they have to. Each generally subscribed to the view, widely shared by defense experts, that size reduction could go hand in hand with, and might even stimulate, military rapidity, flexibility, and firepower. They wanted leaner but meaner fighting machines. The goal seemed reasonable and commendable given Argentina's territorial dimensions.

Since military installations cannot be placed everywhere, strategic choices have to be made. Units would be stationed at certain key locations and not at others. Locations would be determined in part by hypotheses of conflict and war that would indicate areas of strategic vulnerability. Other units would be stationed in the geographical center of the country, positioned to respond rapidly and efficiently to conflicts as they developed elsewhere. Still other forces would be held in reserve.[31] What would guide all these selections? A national defense plan inspired by principles of unified action that would identify potential threats and design strategies capable of confronting them. Such a plan would then generate programmatic implementation, including the selection of appropriate force structures, the procurement of arms, and the redeployment of units and troops.

These then constituted the goals of military reform as enunciated by Argentina's democratic governments and defense planners. But despite the

30. Retired Colonel Gustavo Cáceres, author of a proposal for army reform, says that the *Proceso* military was "an enormous skeleton that served well to control the population but [had] little value in conventional warfare operations." In anticipation of a confrontation with Chile, the army added a new army corps with its seat in Santa Rosa, and in addition formed two new infantry brigades. According to Cáceres, however, none of these were prepared to fight a conventional war and served only police functions. See Gustavo Cáceres, "La crisis militar argentina," paper delivered at the International Conference on Nonprovocative Defense, Buenos Aires, October 24 and 25, 1994, p. 31.

31. These ideas were expressed by both active and retired officers. General Carlos M. Zabala, Argentine military attaché, interview with author, Washington, D.C., June 29, 1994; Colonel (ret.) Gustavo Jose Cáceres and Colonel (ret.) Carlos Mariano Gazcón, "Visión de la fuerza terrestre argentina," paper presented at the International Conference on Nonprovocative Defense, Buenos Aires, October 24–25, 1994, annexes 1 and 2, pp. 39–42.

good intentions, structural reform was never implemented.[32] To be sure, some superficial changes were made. On October 20, 1984, the president banished the First Army Corps from the nation's capital, its property sold to the University of Buenos Aires. But he did so by transfer, not dissolution. Elements associated with the first corps were relocated elsewhere. The first cavalry brigade was moved to Bahia Blanca, the seat of the Fifth Army Corps. The tenth motorized infantry brigade was placed under the control of the army general staff. Meanwhile the Patricio Infantry regiment and the *Campo de Mayo* infantry school remained untouched.[33]

Insofar as these transfers removed symbols of military control from the nation's largest city and center of political life, they were important. But these were isolated moves that did not reduce the massive girth of the institution nor respond to any strategic plan.[34] Absent during the democratic years has been an underlying political commitment to see reform initiatives through to completion. Inside the defense ministry, studies on force reorganization were commissioned, but formal plans were never drawn up nor executed. The government, the joint military staff, and all three services agreed in principle on the need for force integration, joint planning and procurement, the elimination of unnecessary support structures, and the collapsing and merging of other military units. But for years it remained just that—an agreement. By 1986 these ideas were still in the planning stage. Even minimal cost-saving reforms had not been achieved by Alfonsín's midterm. By 1988 independent scholars stated that the military force structure remained

32. When asked why he did not initiate structural reform, President Alfonsín replied, "I could not; I lacked funds. . . . modernization requires an initial outlay and later as you downsize, the expenditure declines, but initially we didn't have it." However, he could have raised money by selling off military property and investing the earnings in defense. This he did not do. Dr. Raúl R. Alfonsín, interview with author, Buenos Aires, July 20, 1993.

33. *FBIS-LAT*, October 22, 1984, p. B5; Ernesto López, *Ni la ceniza ni la gloria: Actores, sistema político, y cuestión militar en los años de Alfonsín* (Buenos Aires: Universidad Nacional de Quilmes, 1994), pp. 86–87; *Latin American Regional Report: Southern Cone*, November 16, 1984, p. 5.

34. At the same time, Alfonsín ordered administrative changes in the nation's two security forces. The coast guard, or *Prefectura Naval*, and the frontier patrol, or *Gendarmería*, were taken out of the hands of the navy and army respectively and placed under the auspices of the defense ministry. This was done to further distance the armed forces from internal security missions while placing these functions under civilian control. The Radical Party also began to divest the armed forces of its industrial holdings by placing the management of these firms under defense ministry auspices. The Peronist administration would take this one step further by placing these firms up for sale in the private marketplace. See República Argentina, Ley de Privatizaciones (Ley 24.045) *Legislación Argentina, Tomo 1991-C* (Buenos Aires: Edición Jurisprudencia Argentina, 1991), pp. 2930–31. Again, none of these measures struck at the heart of the matter: the need to completely overhaul a fossilized institution to fulfill carefully defined strategic objectives.

essentially unchanged, yet still under study.[35] In July 1993 the MOD undersecretary for policy and strategy informed me that designs for a new Argentine system of defense had yet to be written, although he insisted that they soon would be.[36] To my knowledge and to date no such plan has ever been delivered to the armed forces.

In striving toward the goal of creating a compatible defense for the nation, the most serious and far-reaching reforms that were ever carried out were solely of a budgetary nature. Alfonsín and Menem proceeded apace with their budget-cutting endeavors that for reasons outlined in the preceding chapter could be enacted with remarkable celerity and effectiveness. Although these presidents had ample support to trim the fat off this bureaucratic leviathan, there were those who worried that without a thorough restructuring, severe budget contraction could harm military alertness. During Alfonsín's time the defense ministry itself posted warnings that reorganization would have to occur in time to avert the debilitating effect of rapidly declining military budgets. If reorganization lagged too far behind, then budget cuts would simply impair defensive operations. And if structural changes were slow in coming, then, logically, budgetary targets would have to be readjusted. An April 1985 defense ministry report acknowledged that the "current budget only allows for a minimal operation for a short time" and moreover that "if the same amount of funds is allocated without changing the structure, the decline is bound to continue inflicting growing damage on defense capabilities."[37]

Outside of the defense ministry most government officials seemed generally unruffled by these complexities. Some were cautiously optimistic that economic constraints would themselves compel the necessary reforms. They reasoned that as the availability of financial resources dwindled, the interest in cost savings would increase naturally, making transparent the need for reorganization and restructuring. In other words, when faced with scarcity, the armed forces would react rationally by realizing that the shared use of resources and interservice cooperation were necessary to their own survival.

However, such a restructuring—which would have depended heavily on civilian initiative and expertise—never took place. The expectation that harsh economic realities would automatically invite inventive solutions was completely unrealistic. The willingness of the three forces to adopt new pat-

35. López, *El último levantamiento*, pp. 36–39.
36. Dr. Virgilio Beltrán, interview with author, Buenos Aires, July 1, 1993.
37. *FBIS-LAT*, April 16, 1985, p. B3.

terns of interaction lagged far behind the budget cuts, something that neither Alfonsín nor Menem had fully anticipated. With the prospects of a speedy, military reorganization appearing dimmer by the moment, the governments should have readjusted their budgetary targets in order to avert operational decay. But rather than recalibrate, Radicals and Peronists alike continued to slash away at defense. By the end of 1986 military spending had plummeted to 2.3 percent of GDP. By 1993 it stood at 1.3 percent, the lowest level in decades.[38] And so the still huge, unwieldy, military beast had to scrounge around for morsels of food.

The history of reform efforts in democratic Argentina has been one of initiation followed by avoidance, postponement, and finally, abdication. The political class has passed up numerous opportunities to take a forceful lead on reform. And take the lead it must if systemic changes are to occur. As argued in Chapter 2, institutions (like defense ministries) are not always goal-oriented and self-motivated. Even if they are legally, structurally, and procedurally equipped to perform, they may languish if not given direction from above. That direction has historically been wanting in Argentina.

The Failure of Reform: Defense Institutions

The Ministry of Defense

Institutions are among other things buildings. A building's size, appearance, and state of disrepair may be, if nothing more, suggestive of the priorities attached to the activities taking place within it. As one rounds the corner from the elegant and recently refurbished Argentine executive mansion (La Casa Rosada), and walks eastward down Avenida Leandro Alem, two defense-related structures appear. The first, which is on the left-hand side of the avenue, cannot be missed. A massive, concrete edifice that stretches one city block and rises sixteen stories off the ground, it is the headquarters for the nation's army. *Edificio Libertador* is shaded by trees and set back a bit from the street. To reach its imposing entranceway, one must climb twenty-four steps, passing by soldiers armed with submachine guns on either side.

The second building, on the other side of the avenue, can be easily overlooked. Nothing except the small guard station on the ground level and the

---

38. Figures from Thomas Scheetz, compiled from raw data from the Argentine Ministry of Economics, Secretary of Finance, 1994.

frayed, green awnings over its windows distinguish it from the row of offices that sandwich it on either side. It stands nine stories tall and appears not to have been painted or resurfaced for many years. This is the Ministry of Defense.

The ministry's unseemly appearance contrasted with the more stately countenance of army headquarters reveals much about its undistinguished past. The defense ministry was born in 1949 as part of Juan Perón's ambitious effort to overhaul Argentina's defense system. The year before, the president's "Organization of the Nation for Times of War" became the first ever defense law in Argentina.[39] It created an entirely new doctrine and structure of command that included a national defense council, an external security cabinet, and a military staff of coordination—the precursor to today's joint military staff.[40] Uppermost in Perón's mind were the lessons of World War II: the victorious allied forces had overcome the German fighting machine by merging land, naval, and air force powers under a unified command. Historic rivalries and tensions between services were temporarily put aside as the commanders drew upon the distinct strengths of each in a highly centralized and well-coordinated assault on the Third Reich. This, thought Perón, would be the military model of the future, where army, air force, and naval forces would work in a disciplined, subordinate, and cooperative fashion under guidance from a strong, central authority.[41]

Argentina had devoted the better part of half a century to building up its separate service branches, having added an air force in 1945. Each had made substantial, professional strides but had done so in isolation from one another. It was now time to build an integrated system of defense, with the central government at its hub. The defense ministry was to be a permanent fixture in this new system, an organizational link between the president and the commanders in chief of each force. Unfortunately, the agency did not quite live up to expectations, through no fault of its own. The president never endowed the MOD with enough administrative or decision-making powers to give it greater prominence. In fact, governmental defense organizations as a whole were relegated to secondary importance. Rather than achieve subordination through the strengthening of the institutional hierarchy, Perón resorted to subjective techniques of civilian control that relied on ideological indoctrination and tests of political loyalty. This was unfortu-

---

39. República Argentina, La Organización de la Nación en Tiempo de Guerra (Ley 13.234) in *Leyes Nacionales* (Buenos Aires, 1948), pp. 72–79.

40. See Donadio, *El papel del Estado Mayor Conjunto*, pp. 17–21.

41. Ibid., p. 6.

nate and probably unnecessary, since the armed forces were by and large pleased with Perón's presidency and his ambitious programs of industrialization and modernization that were to benefit them directly.

But for Perón the future was uncertain: Argentina could be dragged into another world war; economic dividends from trade surpluses could dwindle; popular support for his movement could be withdrawn should he not continue to deliver on his promises. He worried about his future and wanted an armed forces with allegiances not just to the constitution but to himself and the movement that bore his name.[42] He ordered his subordinates to disseminate Justicialist (Peronist) doctrine throughout the ranks; he "Peronized" the curriculum at the Military Academy and at the Superior War School; he assigned six of twenty-one ministerial and secretarial posts to military men and he then rewarded the most obsequious of his generals by allowing them to purchase autos at cost from the Ministry of Industry and Commerce, reselling them at great profit.[43] His effort to cement military loyalties through political means eventually backfired, and in the interim, defense organizations suffered as a result.

And so the Ministry of Defense receded into the background. Its weakness became evident with the appointment of War Minister General Sosa Molina to head the newly created agency in 1949. Molina had fallen out of grace after an unsuccessful bid to have Evita Perón retired from public life. Evita wanted him cashiered but instead Juan Perón designated him as MOD head—a clear demotion since it removed him from any "direct authority over troop commanders . . . whose support was necessary to influence events."[44] Meanwhile Perón designated his close friend General Franklin Lucero as Molina's replacement—an appointment that typified the political manner in which Perón increasingly approached the armed forces.

Once cast aside, the MOD would not recover for decades. It disappeared from the scene entirely during the *Revolución Libertadora* of 1955–58. Although it was resuscitated by President Arturo Frondizi (1958–62) in 1958, this was in name only. Real power resided with the secretaries of war, navy, and the air force—all of whom were active-duty officers of the highest rank. Although all enjoyed cabinet-level status, these officers were first spokesmen for their respective services and only secondarily representatives of govern-

42. Alain Rouquié, *Poder militar y sociedad política en la Argentina* (Buenos Aires: Emecé Editores, 1982), 2: 83–93.

43. See ibid., p. 78; Robert Potash, *The Army and Politics in Argentina, 1945–1962: Perón to Frondizi* (Stanford: Stanford University Press, 1980), pp. 109, 113.

44. Potash, *The Army and Politics in Argentina, 1945–1962*, pp. 94–95, 99.

ment. Any attempt by either Frondizi or his successor, Arturo Illia (1963–66), to shift their loyalties were decisively rebuffed by the armed forces.

The military government of General Juan Carlos Onganía (1966–70) re-created a defense ministry with very limited powers.[45] It could only advise the president on administrative affairs, was never placed in the chain of command, and was vastly overshadowed by the National Security Council (Consejo Nacional de Seguridad, CONASE), which was charged with de-signing all security and defense-related policies. In fact, the MOD sat in fourth position in the governing hierarchy, below the president, the CO-NASE, and the *Comité Militar*.[46] The reason was simple. At the time, the concept of national defense of territorial borders was quickly giving way to the broader principle of security. Security-minded regimes were licensing Latin American military involvement in external *and* internal affairs to arrest hostilities of all kinds.[47] In an inversion of long-standing definitions, national defense was now subsumed within the rubric of national security. This new idea became enshrined into law in 1966, and with it the demotion of all defense-related institutions soon followed.

With the return to civilian rule in 1973, the defense ministry was only partially reinvigorated. Its responsibilities were broadened, allowing it to as-sist the president on all defense-related matters, not just administrative ones. Nonetheless, it still resided outside of the chain of command while the armed service branches continued to act "with absolute autonomy."[48] As Argentina plunged into crisis in 1974, and as the disabled and unqualified Isabel Perón government ceded more and more authority to the armed forces, the MOD receded into the background once again, only to be supplanted by a newly created security committee whose members included the three mili-tary chiefs.[49]

By the time the armed forces took control in March 1976, the role of the ministry was all but forgotten. The ministry served neither as a key link in the chain of command nor as an effective transmission belt for military preferences. The supremacy of the armed forces over government during this time meant that all state bureaucracies—the defense ministry included—

45. See the military's organic law of ministries, Orgánica de los Ministerios Nacionales (Ley 16.956), September 23, 1966, art. 28, cited in Donadio, *El papel del Estado Mayor Conjunto*, p. 28.

46. The defense minister's power was greatly diluted since, although a member of CONASE, he was one of many, serving alongside all other cabinet members and the military commanders in chief.

47. Pion-Berlin and Lopez, "Of Victims and Executioners," pp. 63–86.

48. Donadio, *El papel del Estado Mayor Conjunto*, p. 44.

49. Ibid., p. 45.

were rendered subordinate to the will of soldiers who in turn were answerable to a service commander. The state was partitioned into thirds, one for each force. This tripartite arrangement feudalized power, with each branch exerting autonomy over its share. Powers that might normally be delegated to the ministry instead resided with one service or another.[50]

With the commencement of democratic rule in December 1983, the Ministry of Defense was suddenly awakened from its dormant state. President Alfonsín knew full well that without an empowered ministry there could be no institutionalized civilian control. Shortly after assuming office, the president inserted the MOD into the chain of command, between the president and the armed forces. The heads of each service were downgraded from commanders to chiefs of staff and had to answer directly to a civilian defense minister.[51] These organizational reforms immediately reduced the decision-making autonomy enjoyed by each branch, while erecting a strong, hierarchical backbone from the president to his defense minister to his military subordinates.

The powers of the defense minister and ministry were subsequently clarified and enlarged. According to the 1988 Law of Defense, the minister "directs, regulates, and coordinates *all* defense activities not already reserved for the president" (emphasis mine).[52] As second in command he has the direct authority to (1) make, terminate, or change assignments of high-ranking officers, (2) arrange for the obligatory retirement or discharge of superior officers of the military and security forces, (3) take disciplinary action against uniformed men, and (4) call back into active duty retired officers to take on special duties.[53] With these measures came a corresponding reduction of military authority. From here on the chiefs of staff could appoint, reassign, or discharge only soldiers of lower rank.[54]

The defense ministry was invested with new responsibilities as well. The agency's mission was to "assist the President in all that adheres to national

50. Andrés Fontana, "Political Decision Making by a Military Corporation: Argentina, 1976–83," Ph.D. diss., University of Texas at Austin, 1987.

51. On December 7 the military expressed to General Bignone, then head of the outgoing military government, its displeasure over the proposed law since it would relegate the chiefs of staff to administrative functions, stripping them of their autonomy. *FBIS-LAT*, December 8, 1983, p. B5.

52. República de Argentina, Ley de Defensa Nacional (Ley 23.554), in *Diario Sesiones* (Buenos Aires: Cámara de Senadores de la Nación, April 7, 1988), art. 11, p. 2992.

53. República Argentina, Decreto 436, January 31, 1984, cited in *FBIS-LAT*, February 7, 1984, p. B4.

54. República Argentina, Decreto 436, *Legislación Argentina, Tomo 1984-A* (Buenos Aires: Ediciones Jurisprudencia, 1984), pp. 32–33.

defense and relations with the armed forces within the prevailing institutional framework."[55] It would formulate and execute defense policies in conformance with the objectives set out by the chief executive; coordinate all interservice military exercises and operations; plan, direct, and execute all state-sector, defense-related production—tasks formerly assumed by the separate services—and would formulate the military budget, while overseeing the distribution of allocated funds.[56] As the ministry assumed more and more tasks hitherto reserved for the armed services, the bureaucracy expanded as well, reflecting a need to delegate more duties to subordinates. In December 1983 four undersecretariats were created: defense, production, programming and budgeting, and military affairs. In September 1984 all of these offices except military affairs were upgraded to secretarial rank under the direction of civilian appointees. These changes built additional layers of authority between the civilian officials and military subordinates.[57]

None of these organizational reforms should be underestimated as they were responsible for an institutional foundation for civilian control. However, not all is well with the Ministry of Defense. In fact, MOD could be described as a weak link in the chain of command. Despite legal transformations that have given it a new lease on life, the agency still suffers from some fundamental maladies that prevent it from implementing structural defense reform as heretofore described. The first is itself legal in nature. Although the new defense law relieves the service chiefs of their powers to command their forces (delegating this authority back to the president as constitutionally mandated), it retains for them the power to "govern and administer"

55. República Argentina Ley de Ministerios (Decreto 438/92) Buenos Aires: Cámara de Diputados, Secretaría Parliamentario, Dirección de Información Parlamentaria, 1992), art. 18, p. 5. On all other ministerial powers, see art. 18, nos. 1–22, p. 5.

56. Decreto 15 of December 10, 1983, in República Argentina, *Legislación Argentina, Tomo 1983-B* (Buenos Aires: Ediciones Jurisprudencia, 1984), pp. 1926–27. For example, the secretary of defense for production assumed great importance with the transfer to MOD of administrative control over the military industrial complex. Suddenly, he had under his wing a sprawling conglomerate comprising dozens of companies. Owned (wholly or partially) and operated by the armed forces themselves, these firms were involved in everything from petrochemical production and refinement to shipbuilding to housing construction. They employed some thirty thousand workers of whom 68 percent were armed service personnel. The secretary was responsible for these employees and their firms, approving budgets and operational plans, naming directors, and finally presiding over the amalgamation, liquidation, or creation of defense-related industries. See *Latin American Weekly Report*, December 16, 1983, p. 6. Also see Ministry of Defense, Report on Privatization Plans, Undersecretary for Production for Defense, Carlos Carballo, July 1991.

57. The importance of the upgraded budget office in particular is underscored by the fact that at the time, no other ministry save economics had such a bureau either at the secretarial or undersecretarial level.

their respective services.[58] Governance and administration covers a great deal of ground. It includes decisions on hiring, personnel, deployment of troops, organization of units and materials, etc.

While the laws assign the ministry assorted powers in the general area of defense, they seem to reserve for each branch of the armed services the prerogative to organize itself. Thus the same law that instructs the defense minister to involve himself in all that inheres to national defense also tells him to defer to the armed services when it comes to their own administrative, legal, logistical, and organizational affairs. He may weigh in on these issues only insofar as they relate to interservice coordination. In other words, he may help to organize the national system of defense but not its components.[59] This contradictory assignment prevents him from directing the armed forces to engage in unifying reform, since the whole cannot be reassembled without its parts.

Thus, although the service chiefs are directly subordinate to the defense minister within the chain of command, they retain substantial powers nonetheless. Senior defense ministry officials realize this is a problem. The ministry's secretary for planning was asked what single structural change he would enact if he could. He replied that he would transfer substantial powers of administration from each force to the defense ministry.[60]

The second and rather vexing problem is the dearth of knowledge about defense-related issues among those in positions of authority. Without expertise there can be no civilian empowerment, and without empowerment the MOD will always be at a decided disadvantage with respect to the armed services. Lacking the confidence to lead, it will be unable to flex its organizational muscles when given a new lease on life, as it was granted by Alfonsín in 1983. Civilian defense officials are victims of their nation's past. For longer than anyone would care to remember, defense was a subject off limits to civil society. The military held on tight to its monopoly on the "management of violence." Doctrinal, strategic, tactical, and operational subjects were analyzed at military headquarters or debated in the pages of military journals. But these were not issues that found their way into the offices of government or into the classrooms of public universities.

There was a fundamental lack of intellectual cross-fertilization between military and civilian sectors. Officers were neither required nor encouraged

58. República de Argentina, Ley Defensa Nacional (Ley 23.544), art. 24, p. 24.

59. República Argentina, Ley de Ministerios (Decreto 438/92), art. 18, nos. 5 and 9, p. 5.

60. Dr. Guillermo Federico Etchechoury, MOD Secretary of Planning, interview with author, Buenos Aires, October 26, 1994.

to seek out educational experiences beyond the confines of the military institution. The armed forces have long sought exclusive control over the indoctrination of their recruits.[61] They would rather cloister their soldiers than expose them to the unpredictable and divisive influences of civil society and its universities.[62] Occasionally, civilians have taken and offered courses at the nation's Superior War School. But the intellectual content of these courses has been carefully controlled by the armed forces, and the screening process ensures that those professors who are selected are often as conservative as their military counterparts, if not more.

Similarly, the armed forces simply had no interest in either sharing or parting with knowledge about the nation's defenses, nor did they have confidence that governing officials could ever make informed decisions about military affairs. Their doubts created a self-fulfilling prophecy. The longer the rules of exclusion pertained, the more unknowing politicians became.[63] Yet in all fairness to the military, the political class must shoulder some of the burden as well. It never actively sought to educate itself on security issues and thus failed to become involved during critical junctures. For example, when during the late 1950s the armed forces decided to forsake its doctrine of national defense for the national security doctrine, politicians remained completely aloof from it all, never questioning the wisdom of such a forbidding move.[64]

Although a nascent, defense establishment is now active in Argentina, to this day most civilians remain in the dark about security themes. Officials with no pertinent experiences are called in to staff the defense ministry. Often assigned for political rather than defense-related purposes, these men are unfamiliar with the terrain. They are unable to design policy or even set general guidelines for others to follow. Their staff does its best to advise, but they too are not particularly well qualified.

The lack of defense-related proficiency within the ministry is highlighted in Table 6.1. As the table reveals, none of the defense ministers in the demo-

---

61. See López, *Ni la ceniza ni la gloria*, pp. 119–22.

62. The one exception to this rule is an arrangement between the University of La Plata and a naval school that allows cadets to take international relations courses alongside of civilians at the university. The link was forged by a former MOD undersecretary for policy and strategy, Angel Tello, who was interviewed by the author in Buenos Aires on July 1, 1993.

63. Carlos M. Zabala, Argentine military attaché to the United States in 1994, believes that civilian ministerial officials are not fully prepared because for so many years defense was an issue that was off limits to them. Interview with author, Washington, D.C., June 29, 1994.

64. See Ernesto López and David Pion-Berlin, *Democracia y cuestión militar* (Buenos Aires: Universidad Nacional de Quilmes, 1996), p. 160.

Table 6.1. Military expertise among Argentina's defense minsters, 1983–1996

Minister of Defense	Education	Career Experience in Defense	Military Background
Alfonsín government (1983–89)			
R. Borrás (1983–85)	Economics	None	None
R. Carranza (1985)	Industrial engineering	None	None
G. Lopez (1986)	Chemistry	None	None
H. Jaunarena (1986–89)	Law	Some: 1984–86	None
Menem government (1989–95)			
I. Luder (1989)	Law	None	None
H. Romero (1989–90)	Medicine	None	None
A. Gonzalez (1991–93)	Accounting	None	None
O. Camilión (1993–96)	Law	None	None

cratic period have come to the job adequately prepared. Horacio Jaunarena had the advantage of having previously served as secretary of defense under Borrás and Carranza and thus had gathered some on-the-job training.[65] None of the others had the kind of career or educational experiences that would have equipped them with the knowledge and strength of conviction to pursue vigorous defense reforms.

Then there is the related problem of discontinuity. Defense has experienced an unusually high turnover rate, with the average life span of its ministers being just over sixteen months. Under Alfonsín discontinuity was unavoidable, with the sudden deaths of Borrás and Carranza. Under Menem it was intentional. Officials were posted there temporarily for expediency, only to be withdrawn when convenient. Interruptions such as these breed unfamiliarity and institutional memory failure. Those who leave do so hurriedly, emptying their offices of important documents, hardly giving a thought to the transition. New officials come in bringing with them their own teams of advisors who must frantically familiarize themselves with the issues and the agency. Ministers and their staffs have had difficulty getting up to speed on defense issues with so little experience and time at their disposal.

The lack of ministerial competence and continuity translates into a deficiency of will. Being less confident in the area of defense, ministers are more reticent to demonstrate leadership and more willing to defer to more in-

---

65. Dr. José Horacio Jaunarena, interview with author, Buenos Aires, July 27, 1993.

formed military officers. Thus, they generate their own dependence on the armed forces. Unless and until the ministerial appointees step up to the plate to establish clear defense and security goals for the nation, further progress is unlikely. In short, the ministry has failed to establish its autonomy or exercise its authority on reform-related matters.

The Estado Mayor Conjunto

Ministerial frailties inevitably infect the institutions associated with them. One such victim is the Military Joint Staff, or *Estado Mayor Conjunto* (EMC). Although staffed by active-duty officers, the EMC is an advisory unit within the MOD with no independent authority. Its function is to counsel the defense minister on joint military strategy, operations, and training.[66] Each of the three services are functionally—not operationally—accountable to the EMC when considering joint action. They each send up mid-level officers to serve on the EMC staff.

The EMC has never been able to overcome the historic autonomy enjoyed by the services and their heads. Even under the military government of the Argentine Revolution (1967–73), when strategic planning was preeminent, the EMC remained largely ineffectual. As a working group for the *Comité Militar*, it was called on to devise joint military doctrine and strategies, and then assign relevant operational and logistical duties to each force.[67] But the EMC could never make obligatory any of its recommendations because the military leadership would not back it up. After all, the military command was never greater than the sum of its parts. The president, the junta, and the CONASE members were all products of their respective institutions, and averse to weakening service autonomy by ceding enforcement powers to the EMC. Thus, with the army, air force, and navy claiming sole jurisdiction over their affairs, while feuding with one another, the agency could not demand that they put their sectarian interests aside to engage in collaborative endeavors.[68]

Under democratic rule the *Estado Mayor Conjunto* has not fared much better. If the EMC finds any strength at all, it does so indirectly and only on paper. The very concept of national defense is now defined as the "*integrated and coordinated action* of all the nation's forces for the resolution of those conflicts that require the employment of the armed forces, in a dissuasive

66. República Argentina, Ley de Defensa Nacional (Ley 23.554), arts. 16, 17, 18, p. 2993.
67. Donadio, *El papel de Estado Mayor Conjunto*, p. 31.
68. Ibid., pp. 36–39.

posture, to confront aggressions of external origin" (emphasis mine).[69] Each service must organize and deploy its forces according to principles of joint action.[70] That would seem, in theory, to reserve for the EMC a special role as the principal agent of military collaboration. No single arm of the military can do it alone because each can only visualize defense from its own parochial perspective. It is the EMC and the defense ministry it is part of that must provide the more comprehensive view.

Like the defense ministry in which it is contained, the EMC is essentially much weaker in practice than in theory. It is not able to compel the services to comply with its proposals. Its advisory status earns it precious little advantage since each of the service chiefs still enjoy equal access to the defense minister. The head of the EMC cannot speak on their behalf. Rather than being the *principal* advisor to the defense minister on military matters, he is only one among equals.[71]

The EMC's fate is inextricably entwined with the fate of the defense ministry and, ultimately, the presidency itself. Where the ministry goes, so goes the EMC. If defense becomes a key player within the current political environment, it is sure to elevate the status of the EMC as well. To the extent that the president assigns priority to the development of the nation's defenses and to the professionalization, modernization, and integration of the armed services, the ministry and its advisory agencies are sure to benefit. The problem has been that to date, neither the subject of defense nor its correlative institutions have received the attention they merit from the commander in chief.

Presidential Weakness

Argentine democratic presidents have not had the intestinal fortitude to put "servicism" to rest in favor of collaborative defense. The problem is not one of general goals, or even initiative. As stated earlier, both the Alfonsín and Menem governments proclaimed the importance of interservice coordination and unified action. And both authorized subordinates to study and then

69. República Argentina, Ley de Defensa Nacional (Ley 23.554), art. 2, p. 1.
70. Ibid., art. 21., p. 4.
71. This is one of the central weaknesses of the EMC, according to its former chief, Almirante Emilio Osses; interview with author, Buenos Aires, November 1, 1994. Osses wanted the EMC chief granted greater powers, but President Menem would not go along.

report on the problems of defense reform. What they failed to do was to bring their full presidential authority to bear on the problem: to give enough urgency to it, to sustain interest in it, and to push for its implementation. Without the commander in chief fully behind them, civilians within the defense ministry who lacked sufficient knowledge about defense seemed incapable of spearheading the cause. They urged their president to turn to military personnel inside the ministry's EMC for advice, which is what happened. But Argentina's chief executives were reluctant to sign off on purely military recommendations, fearing that doing so would cede too much power to the armed forces.

The pattern first developed under Alfonsín. As previously recalled, the government seemed initially enthusiastic about the prospects of military reform. In 1984 the president is reported to have held a number of amiable discussions with key military personnel at his residence in Olivos regarding new directions for defense.[72] Out of those discussions arose a decision to authorize the *Estado Mayor Conjunto*, under the leadership of General Julio Fernández Torres, to devise a new strategic plan for the armed forces. The director of the EMC's Policy and Strategy Department, General Heriberto Auel, took up the challenge with vigor and issued a recommendation by midyear that would have redefined military strategic doctrine and functioning. In particular, it restated the urgency of joint military action and the creation of multiservice, operational commands answerable to the president in times of war. The proposal went further by suggesting that those commands be liberated from the administrative control of service headquarters to make their own operational decisions.[73] These ideas were then presented to the commander in chief.

The proposals came as no surprise to either Minister Borrás or to President Alfonsín because they largely conformed to the general wishes of their administration, or so it seemed. With EMC's recommendations in hand, Alfonsín issued an unpublished decree that authorized the creation of the joint strategic operative commands along the lines suggested by Auel. At about the same time, the president also authored and secretly delivered to the armed forces a strategic-military directive that detailed Argentina's hypotheses of conflict with potential foes, including Chile.[74] This, too, was an impor-

72. See López, *Ni la ceniza ni la gloria*, p. 79, n. 7.

73. Ibid., pp. 77–79.

74. The claim that Alfonsín sent such a directive was made by Dr. José Horacio Jaunarena, in an interview with the author, Buenos Aires, July 27, 1993. The minister's assertions about the hypotheses of conflict were seconded by Angel Tello, former undersecretary of defense for policy and strategy in an interview with the author on July 1, 1993. Also see López, *Ni la ceniza ni la gloria*, p. 80.

tant step taken by the commander in chief, since such hypotheses help guide the services in their elaboration of joint contingency strategies, if and when political disputes spill over into violent confrontations.

What happened next is not entirely clear, but it appears that the reform initiative was shelved, only to resurface later in the guise of military self-reform (to be explained below). The military was awaiting the president's final signature on additional documents that would have solidified the plans and set them into motion. But those documents never earned Alfonsín's official endorsement.[75] Why the president demurred is not known for sure, but one can speculate.

Alfonsín probably had second thoughts about placing so much faith in plans drawn up by officers whose views on other issues he did not share. For example, at the time, Fernández and Auel were still avid proponents of the national security doctrine. They rejected any distinctions between internal and external wars or any limitations placed on the military's right to conduct search-and-destroy missions against alleged subversives.[76] The president must have been perturbed, since he was resolutely opposed to these ideas and since his Radical Party supporters in the Congress were already at work drafting a new defense law that would prohibit domestic military action. He would not have felt comfortable leaving implementation in the hands of military personnel he did not completely trust. And who would supervise their work? Again, there were no civilians within MOD who knew enough to be able to perform such duties.

Alfonsín was also undoubtedly apprehensive about any military plans to actually begin training exercises based on war scenarios contained in his secret decree. While on one level the president understood the military need, on another he worried that maneuvers of this sort might interfere with his vigorous diplomatic efforts to amicably settle age-old disputes with his nation's perennial rival to the west. Moreover, the president's foreign relations minister had publicly asserted that Argentina would *never* contemplate offensive engagements against its neighbors. These mixed signals probably sowed doubts in the mind of many armed forces officials who suspected that the Alfonsín government did not take strategic planning seriously.

A similar trend continued under Carlos Menem. EMC officials have re-

---

75. Author's interview with General Heriberto Auel, Buenos Aires, July 31, 1989; also see López, *Ni la ceniza ni la gloria*, pp. 77–81.

76. This was made clear to me in interviews I held in Buenos Aires with both individuals. I met with General Heriberto Auel on July 31 and August 15 of 1989 and with General Julio Fernández Torres on August 11, 1989.

counted to this author their frustrations at repeatedly seeing their recommendations go unattended by the Peronist political leadership.[77] For example, in 1990 Menem's second defense minister, Humberto Romero, signed off on a resolution written largely by Admiral Emilio Osses, then chief of the EMC. Known as the *Libro Blanco*, or *White Book*, the proposal was an effort to link national political goals with military reorganization. Many of its provisions were rather vague, unnoteworthy reflections on the current regional and international state of affairs and how Argentina's armed forces might adapt to this environment.[78] However, some of its provisions were more specific at both operational and administrative levels. The *White Book* called for: (1) the constitution of rapid deployment forces based on reduced size, high mobility, and firepower. These interservice units would be swift and agile, able to respond to emergency situations at a moment's notice. (2) The formation of regional centers, common to the three forces, for maintenance, repair, and resupply. These units would eliminate logistical duplications while encouraging interservice collaboration. (3) The joining of training centers to provide for more uniform, multiservice orientations. (4) The organization of common accounting systems for the ministry and all three services.[79]

The resolution was then distributed throughout the armed forces to generate discussion and to decide how each armed service might fulfill the *White Book's* objectives. The proposals were returned to the EMC, now with more flesh added to the skeleton. Finally in 1991 the document was sent forward to the president for his consideration. Unfortunately, the resolution never acquired the force of law because the ministry of defense would not promote it and the president would then not sign off on it.[80]

Why not? There are several reasons. First was the problem of professional continuity. Minister Romero left office in January 1991, before the now-revised *White Book* had made its way back to the president's desk. Upon his departure the enthusiasm for the plan seemed to dissipate. His replacement, Antonio Erman González, brought with him a new staff, agenda, and priorities.

Second, Romero's associations and ideological proclivities were troubling.

77. Capitán José Maria Horton, chief of planning, *Estado Mayor Conjunto*, interview with author, Buenos Aires, November 1, 1994.

78. República Argentina, Resolución No. 1144/90 (Buenos Aires: Ministerio de Defensa, September 10, 1990), pp. 1–8.

79. Ibid., pp. 9–10.

80. Almirante Emilio Osses, interview with author, Buenos Aires, November 1, 1994.

Most objectionable was his sympathies toward dissenting, fundamentalist elements within the armed forces. When asked about his liaisons with the
carapintadas, the ex–defense minister replied that he "always maintains contact with those who represent the institution."[81] The folly of this policy of
benevolence toward defiant officers was finally exposed in December 1990
when several hundred troops, under the leadership of Colonel Mohamed Alí
Seineldín, staged a troubling but ultimately unsuccessful uprising against the
Menem government. With the defeat of the rebels came the ouster of Romero as well.

Third was the problem of civilian competence and control. Romero consistently deferred to the authority and judgment of the armed forces rather
than proclaiming his own. This is a man who once described his ministry as
"the house of the armed forces."[82] To the president, Romero had seemed a
bit too anxious to sign off on a reform package that was unquestionably the
exclusive work of military officers, bearing no stamp of civilian initiative or
input. Thus, to endorse the *White Book* was to cede undue authority and
influence to the EMC and the armed services.

And finally, there was Menem's preoccupation with the EMC itself. At
the persuasion of Admiral Osses, the president formed a Chiefs of Staff Committee that would preside over the EMC. Modeled somewhat after the U.S.
Joint Chiefs of Staff, the committee would formalize a more collegial relation
between the leaders of each service and the EMC staff by bringing them
under one roof. This would create a physical centrality that should make
difficult the accustomed avoidance of the EMC by the army, air force, and
navy.[83] Acting as president of this committee would be the head of the EMC,
who would be the most senior-ranking officer among active servicemen.[84]
His seniority would, in theory, invoke greater deference among the service
chiefs and invest the word of the EMC with commanding authority.

While the idea seemed worthy on paper, Menem and members of his
defense ministry had second thoughts, worried as they were about its effect
on civilian control once implemented. In interviews with this author, several
defense officials admitted they were concerned that the committee of chiefs
had a hidden agenda: to fashion themselves as a military general staff. Perhaps the committee would go too far by informally inserting itself into the

81. *Página Doce*, January 26, 1990, pp. 1, 3.

82. Ibid., April 7, 1990, p. 1.

83. Poder Ejecutivo Nacional, Decreto 1739/92, September 21, 1992, art. 3, pp. 4–5. Document
provided to me by a defense ministry official.

84. Ibid., art. 2, p. 2.

chain of command and seizing powers properly delegated to the president and his civilian defense minister.[85] Implementation of the *White Book*'s strategic plan could very well serve as the first test of their newfound powers.

The central difficulties described above are twofold and inextricably intertwined. The first is ministerial frailty. The defense ministry has not as yet built up a sufficiently large staff of well-trained civilian defense specialists. There are very few civilians at MOD—the minister included—who feel confident enough to participate in, let alone direct the formulation of, defense plans. Consequently, they leave these duties solely in the hands of military personnel within the EMC who haven't the power to demand that the services fulfill their wishes.

This situation is unfortunate since there is a small but viable "defense establishment" that has emerged within Argentine civil society that has not only fostered a new culture of openness between soldiers and citizens but that has yielded defense-related knowledge as well.[86] The government could do a much better job of drawing from this cadre of specialists in order to empower the civilian side of its ministry. But empowerment will take executive leadership, which brings us to the second problem.

Ultimately, it is the president that must make defense reform a priority. It is he who must instruct his minister to demand from the services full compliance with national defense policy. And it is he who must instill in the defense ministry a real sense of purpose and direction. As suggested in Chapter 2, organizations in general and certainly state agencies in particular are not necessarily oriented toward the fulfillment of goals unless they receive a clear mandate from above. In the absence of such a mandate, civilian appointees within the agency feel less motivated to bring themselves up to speed on issues of national security or to hire outsiders with the expertise necessary to confidently push through controversial programs. And so while a few studies have been commissioned, reports written, and decrees signed, no comprehensive defense reorganization has yet to commence, and will not likely commence until the president deems it vital.

When asked in May 1991 why the restructuring proposals that had been

---

85. The fear was that the EMC would be transformed from an advisory to a decision-making body and moved from outside to within the chain of command. The chief of the committee would command authority over service chiefs *who themselves had governing control over their forces and were in the chain of command*, thereby weakening civilian control. Eduardo M. Stafforini, senior advisor to the MOD's Secretary for Military Affairs, 1990–93, interview with author, Buenos Aires, July 27, 1993.

86. Many of these defense specialists advise members of Congress or consult with the foreign affairs ministry.

bantered about had not as yet been executed, Romero's successor, Antonio Erman González replied: "It is not the armed forces that have to present a plan. It is rather the political authorities who have to establish the ultimate objectives of restructuring."[87] Unfortunately, neither Menem nor Alfonsín have adequately heeded the call.

The Limits of Self-Reform

What both leaders did do was to toss the ball back to the service branches. In effect they said, "We and our ministry cannot or will not provide the direction. Why don't you give it a try?" This strategy has been a mistake because military organizations are fundamentally incapable of reforming themselves to any significant degree. Many officers within the Argentine military readily admit this fact. While some very limited, service-oriented changes are under way, none of these constitute the kind of adjustments urged upon them by the Rattenbach Commission.

One senior naval officer described with brutal honesty the so-called Argentine military self-reform as "changing so that nothing changes."[88] The military, and the army in particular, is out front in its revelations of reforms.[89] But this is largely a public relations stunt that veils just how inadequate the reforms have been.

For example, it is well known that two of the five command corps, which essentially perform administrative duties, have been abolished.[90] But it has also been reported that a number of other military units have either dissolved, transferred, or merged with others. All artillery groups associated with the three remaining corps have been eliminated, as have a number of logistical and intelligence groups, their functions shifted downward to specific combat units. Meanwhile various infantry, cavalry, engineering, and communications units have been relocated or consolidated. Combined, the army reports a 43 percent reduction in its organizational infrastructure be-

---

87. *Ambito Financiero*, May 31, 1991, p. 42.

88. Almirante Emilio Osses, interview with author, Buenos Aires, November 1, 1994.

89. In April 1993 Colonel Ricardo Brinzoni, then second in command of operations at army headquarters, issued a report entitled "Military Restructuring: When More Is Done Than What Is Said," *Agora, Centro de Estudios Internacionales* (April 1993): 1–5.

90. The First Army Corps was abolished by Alfonsín early in his term. The Fourth Corps, seated in Santa Rosa, was formed during Argentina's 1978 Beagle islands conflict with Chile. It was then disbanded largely because of budgetary reasons in July 1991. See *FBIS-LAT*, July 15, 1991, p. 34.

tween 1989 and 1994.[91] One senior army official described these transformations as ones that are turning the army into an organization that is "agile, versatile, flexible, and courageous."[92]

I have yet to see any independent confirmation of these changes. Supposing for the moment that they are real, one needs to ask several questions. First, what larger design do they fulfill? Are these moves in a strategic game plan or simply compensatory measures taken to survive in an economically austere environment? Second, to what extent are these measures synchronized with efforts under way in the air force and navy? Third, just how far do these changes go in reducing the army's girth?

It is best that we let the military speak for itself. Colonel Ricardo Guillermo Brinzoni, who has personally promoted army accomplishments, nonetheless admits that military restructuring cannot be adequately defined because "we have not as yet defined a model for the future Argentina."[93] Others suggest that the army's accomplishments are quite modest. In essence, the service is engaged in downsizing in response to diminished budgetary shares. An army colonel involved in operational details said that his service is "in a phase of rationalization not restructuring."[94] By this he means that the army is discovering incremental ways to make due with less rather than radically overhauling its structure to fulfill strategic objectives. To rationalize is to economize; to restructure is to reform.

Rationalization subscribes to principles of organizational efficiency and cost-effectiveness. The primary objective is to save money while salvaging priority programs and units. Unwieldy and unnecessary bureaucratic entities are the first victims under this schema. The adroit management of an army across so huge a territory cannot be undertaken at the highest level; authority and functions must devolve from administrative entities at the top to armed combat units lower down where field grade officers intimately familiar with the needs of their troops can make more informed decisions.[95] In large measure this explains the decision to scrap two of the army's five corps. Brinzone stated, "We began to sift through the nation's economic possibilities, but always taking defensive needs into mind. And we said, for those needs given these possibilities, what can we do?"[96]

91. Figures provided by the Army General Staff, June 1994.
92. Brinzoni, "Military Restructuring," p. 1.
93. Ibid.
94. Colonel Villalba, army general staff, interview with author, Buenos Aires, November 4, 1994.
95. Colonel Ricardo Brinzone and Colonel Evergisto de Vergara, army headquarters, interview with author, Buenos Aires, July 12, 1993.
96. Ibid.

Naval reforms have been likewise economically, not strategically, driven. In response to questions, senior officers tend to confound the verbs to ratio- nalize and to restructure. But when asked to explain what is actually transpir- ing within the service, they left no doubt. Said the director of the navy's general staff, Rear Admiral Horacio F. Reyser: "The sole objective of this rationalization and restructuring reform is to increase our efficiency, that is to assign priorities to resources to develop the operational capacity of the navy, and to lower the administrative and bureaucratic costs."[97]

By way of illustration Reyser explains that a current priority is to modern- ize the navy's information system, replacing old computer technologies with new ones. The goal is to accelerate information flows, maximize personnel utilization, reduce costs, and increase efficiency. The proposed changes are in response to a 30 percent reduction in military and civilian personnel over the last ten years, not in step with a forward-looking strategic plan.[98] Added Captain Leonardo Steyerthal, director of naval programming and budgeting, "It has been a 'situational plan' because it is necessary to face head-on budg- etary realities."[99]

Meanwhile, the air force still remains shell-shocked from the Malvinas War. Since that time it has been consumed with a struggle to replace the vast numbers of aircraft loss in the conflict, having little time to reflect on anything else. In this endeavor the air force has been stymied first by the British- and U.S.-led blockades on military exports to Argentina and then by the reluctance of two economically strapped democratic governments to finance the purchase of expensive aircraft.[100] Deficiencies continue to persist in the areas of radar, transport, combat and trainer aircraft.[101] Budgetary contraction has hit the air force hardest, fundamentally because it is so costly to keep military aircraft in flight. Technologically sophisticated planes count on well-trained pilots and large maintenance crews. Air force salaries have not been sufficiently high to keep technicians from entering the private sec-

97. Rear Admiral Horacio F. Reyser, interview with author, Buenos Aires, November 3, 1994.
98. Ibid.
99. Capitán Leonardo Arnoldo Steyerthal, navy general staff headquarters, interview with au- thor, November 3, 1994.
100. By 1993, thirteen years after the war, the air force had managed to only recover one-half of the seventy planes lost thanks mainly to the purchase of thirty-six U.S. Skyhawk A-4M training planes in December 1993. Even there the news was bittersweet, since the skyhawks were outmoded and would have to be refitted with more modern radar and electronics to be of any real value. See *Clarín Edición Internacional*, December 7, 1993, p. 7; February 1, 1994, p. 3.
101. Commander (ret.) Alfredo R. Cabeza, "Visión de la Fuerza Aerea Argentina," manuscript presented at the International Conference on Nonprovocative Defense, Buenos Aires, October 24–25, 1994, pp. 30–32.

tor, where they are quickly plucked up by commercial aeronautical companies. The result has been, according to one estimate, a 76 percent decline in aviators between 1983 and 1993.[102] So here, too, the air force has been singularly preoccupied with scales of efficiency: how to maintain some degree of operational capacity in the face of unprecedented scarcity.

Such calculus is useful but doesn't go far enough. The armed forces must contemplate how each move to cut costs simultaneously fulfills national defense and security plans while coinciding with like moves within the other service branches. Neither of these additional calculations can be made in the current environment. A national defense plan has yet to be handed down to the military from the political authorities, and the walls that traditionally segregate one armed services branch from another have yet to be torn down.

Retired senior naval officer Almirante Osses believes Argentina's forces are admirably endowed: they have the talent, the training, and the troops. What they are lacking are marching orders to commence with serious reform. According to Osses, "the political class does not provide us direction because they have not clarified in their own minds what it is they want from us."[103] Retired air force Brigadier Major Alberto Alegría concurs, putting it this way: "The military is accustomed to receiving orders. These orders serve to orient military action and reorganize our structure. We need to know what the political authorities want from us" in the form of a strategic directive. He adds, "The government talks about restructuring—that the military ought to be more powerful, more modern—but it has not formulated a written document stating what role the air force shall play."[104] These statements indicate that despite the inherent difficulties of breaking with old habits, there *is* a will to change, at least in some military quarters. But even the most future-oriented soldiers need to await commands from above before they can act.

And what about interservice coordination? None of those army officers interviewed were able to relate their reform efforts to those under way in the other two services. In fact, no one from the army had the faintest notion of what the air force and navy were up to, nor did they seem to care. The indifference was shared. Air force and naval officers were equally uninformed about and uninterested in developments within the army, and regarding each other. One senior official summed up the problem of excessive servicism with

102. Brigadier Major (ret.) Alberto Alegría, interview with author, Buenos Aires, July 12, 1993.
103. Almirante Emilio Osses, interview with author, Buenos Aires, November 1, 1994.
104. Brigadier Major (ret.) Alberto Alegría, interview with author, Buenos Aires, July 12, 1993.

this scenario: "The air force says we want four hundred combat planes. But perhaps the logic of joint defense dictates that at this time what is really needed is only two hundred and fifty plus one hundred and fifty transport planes to carry ground troops."[105] A collective decision of that sort should be made by "the joint chiefs of staff who devise an annual armament plan, but it is not. Each branch pursues its own procurement," he added.[106]

Said the Rattenbach Commission, "It is of no value for a force to acquire a potential or determined capacity if it is not accompanied by a similar development in the other forces."[107] It relates how during the Malvinas War, Great Britain never dispatched more ships to the South Atlantic than could be accompanied by the requisite number of aircraft. That kind of coordination never existed on the Argentine side, and is likely to elude the nation in the next war unless interservice planning is undertaken in times of peace.

Barring civilian leadership, military self-reform will not occur. Restructuring is hard because it calls upon the armed forces to abandon ingrained patterns of behavior that for decades had served its members well on an individual level regardless of how irrational they may have been on an institutional level. Each officer must look out for himself; each unit must attempt to ensure its own survival—even when its role has become strategically obsolete. Weapons systems, intelligence agencies, and research centers were assets to be jealously guarded and preserved in their historic forms, not to be handed over to the defense ministry to be abolished for the good of the whole.[108] Personal, unit (cavalry vs. infantry), and service (army vs. navy) rivalries over scarce resources complicated the quest for unification and rationalization of military functions.

Restructuring is also a painful ordeal because it results in losses that cannot be distributed equitably. If the weight of adjustment fell equally on all military shoulders, that would be one thing. But in fact it does not, as some units lose out while others gain and as some officers retain their powerful commands while others are forced to resign. These are choices that no single

---

105. Almirante Emilio Osses, interview with author, Buenos Aires, November 1, 1994.
106. Ibid.
107. See Rattenbach Commission, *Informe Rattenbach*, p. 306. The same report adds: "Modern warfare does not allow for the possibility of triumph by one force exclusively. To the contrary, defeat is insured if they [services] act in watertight compartments" (pp. 306–7).
108. The difficulties in acclimating officers to new and cooperative, multiservice patterns of behavior were revealed to me by Julio Alberto De'Orué, director of logistical affairs in the defense ministry, Buenos Aires, October 31, 1994. In 1984 Defense Minister Raúl Borrás stated that there was little assurance that the military would ever undergo thorough reform during the Alfonsín term because to do so would demand revised military thinking. And changing the military mind-set, said Borrás, would be a "formidable task." The armed forces, he added, "do not have the necessary equanimity and ability to judge their own actions." See *FBIS-LAT*, March 5, 1984, p. B2.

commander of any force, no matter how senior he may be, wants to ever make. So instead of cutting the card deck, the commander reshuffles it, reassigning rather than retiring, transferring rather than dissolving. Or more commonly, he just leaves the deck as is.

For example, as a result of budgetary reductions, the army's conscript population was reduced by 72 percent, from sixty thousand in 1985 to seventeen thousand in 1994. But the number of officers declined by only 24 percent, from sixty-six hundred to five thousand.[109] As a result, an infantry battalion that should have six hundred soldiers now retains only one hundred and fifty. Some combat units have no soldiers at all, but officers remain assigned to them nonetheless! When asked why the army doesn't just eliminate those units, a senior official replied, "because we are in a period of rationalization, not restructuring."[110] Would the armed services then ever graduate to real reform? Members of the military have their doubts, because as one put it, "reform is tied to resources, and no one wants to lose power. If we try to reform ourselves we are going to have problems."[111] The same officer added: "In the absence of any political direction, we are left to our own devices. But the remedies are superficial, since all that is done outside of this process of [politically mandated] restructuring is nothing more than an internal accommodation to the downsizing of the force."[112]

The problem can only be overcome by shifting the decision upward to a political level. Most officers agreed that it ought to be the government's policymakers who act as arbiters, setting the guidelines that they will then work within. This is not only because the government stands above the sectarian interests of each service but also because only the government can define the national interests that render any reform effort truly significant or that delineate the risks to the country should that effort fail. Military adjustments of any kind are only imbued with meaning when they fulfill national, political objectives.

Conclusion

Civilian decision makers now for the first time have some legal and bureaucratic tools to reform the nation's defense system. Authority is invested in

109. These latest figures were provided to me by General Aníbal Laíño, general secretary of the army, interview in Buenos Aires on November 4, 1994.
110. Colonel Villalba, army general staff, interview with author, Buenos Aires, November 4, 1994.
111. Brigadier Major (ret.) Alberto Alegría, interview with author, Buenos Aires, July 12, 1993.
112. Ibid.

the office of the president and his revamped defense ministry to review the state of the nation's security and to propose a collaborative scheme for enhancing its defense readiness. But neither the president nor his ministers have chosen to fully utilize the authority conferred on them. No one in the government wants to step up to the plate to assume command of a reform-minded defense team. The result is a vacuum of power at the political center.

To some degree this state of affairs is a by-product of years of institutional neglect. The defense ministry is still a victim of its ignominious past. Both authoritarian and democratic regimes alike never bequeathed to the ministry the kind of power it deserved. Too much policymaking space was repeatedly reserved for the service commanders, military secretaries, or military-dominated committees and councils. The ministry was finally given a new lease on life in 1983. However, it was not vested with all the administrative authority it needed. Moreover, after decades of inaction it was not easy for the ministry to suddenly flex its newfound muscles. It lacked a kind of institutional memory with which to accumulate knowledge and experiences that would have fostered a more confident policymaking environment. Newly appointed defense officials had no expertise and very little to go on, often having to rely on the advice of defense ministers from abroad.[113] Authority could never be concentrated here because there was a fundamental lack of institutional capacity reinforced by an absence of political will and knowledge.

The armed forces are to blame as well. For too long they grasped tenaciously to defense planning as if it were a subject only they could touch. In placing defense off limits to civilians, the military made it difficult for policymakers to prove themselves capable. As a result, politicians now suffer from a kind of inferiority complex about defense themes. They are too quick to defer to military judgment, which simply increases their dependency on the armed forces they are supposed to lead.

When civilians relinquished leadership, their unused authority first devolved to the EMC. While this advisory agency has drafted some plans for interservice collaboration, it was unable to attract the kind of civilian sponsorship it needed to put these plans into motion. And so authority was transferred again, this time to the armed services, in whose hands the execution of reform policy unofficially then rested. But the Argentine military was still a divided institution, with army, navy, and air force existing largely unto

---

113. Raúl Borrás had conferred more than once with his Spanish counterpart, Narcís Serra, during 1984.

themselves. And so the power that was not utilized by the chief executive, his defense minister, or the EMC was then dispersed across dissimilar military forces, all quite protective of their own institutional interests. This ensured that a coherent, collaborative scheme for transforming the nation's defense system never got implemented. In the absence of any decisive orders from above, each service chose what to do or, more important, what *not* to do about "la cuestión de reforma." The situation is depicted in Figure 6.1.

The irony here is that defense reform is one issue where the military really must rely on the help of the administration. Yet it is precisely here that the executive branch cannot demonstrate the interest or muster the will to seize the authority and autonomy it needs. Without an edict from above, real reform will continue to elude the armed services. As a result, inertia prevails—this despite the devastating crisis in defense preparedness brought on by the Malvinas defeat. This oversized, undernourished, military behemoth lumbers into the twenty-first century, still unprepared to meet the challenges of modern warfare.

Fig. 6.1. Explaining defense reform failure: the role of institutional authority and autonomy

| | Concentration of Authority | |
	High	Low
High Decision-Making Autonomy	A. High Success	B. Moderate Success
Low	C. Moderate Success	D. No Success (defense ref.) 1983–95

CHAPTER 7

Argentina's Neighbors
Institutions and Policy in Uruguay and Chile

When it comes to civil-military affairs, does institutional design matter elsewhere? Do variations in institutional design alter the policy fortunes of politicians and soldiers in other countries? To find out, we turn to two of Argentina's neighbors, Uruguay and Chile. The comparison would seem to be a natural one for three nations that are all members of the same subregion called the Southern Cone. They are linked geographically and historically. Furthermore, they are all highly urbanized, cultured, and literate populations, with well-trained, unionized work forces, medium third-world income levels, professionalized militaries, and democratic traditions broken by particularly repressive tyrannies of the 1970s.

But, as suggested in Chapter 2, the similarities are not as intriguing as are the differences. Uruguay and Chile pose rather difficult hurdles for a thesis about institutional mediation to clear because levels of military influence, during and after the transition to democratic rule, were significantly higher there than in Argentina. Perhaps the armed forces in those countries had sufficient leverage to repeatedly confound civilian efforts to push through objectionable programs. If that were true, it would make variations in issues and institutional arrangements virtually irrelevant, leaving Argentina to stand as a unique case.

Differences in military power can be traced to differences in the passage from authoritarian to democratic rule. These newly restored democracies did not begin on an equal footing. As we have learned, Argentina's recovery followed in the aftermath of an authoritarian collapse that left the military demoralized and in disarray and the new democratic government invigorated. In Uruguay the military was wounded but not vanquished by the popular rejection of its proposed constitution of 1980. That defeat hurled into motion a negotiated transfer of authority to democratic hands, culminating in an agreement between military and civilian representatives at the Naval Club in 1984. The pact was to have served primarily a procedural purpose: to lay down the ground rules governing the transfer of power from military to civilian hands.[1] However, some experts believe the military extracted important substantive concessions out of those talks, while others point to a set of constitutional amendments passed at the last minute by the de facto regime as evidence that the military had preserved security prerogatives well into the new democratic order.[2]

Meanwhile, economic policy accomplishments in Chile contributed to the strength, cohesion, and durability of the Pinochet regime. This allowed the military to dictate the terms of democratic restoration, ensuring that they conform to the 1980 constitution that the regime itself had written.[3] That constitution also called for a plebiscite to be held in 1988 to determine whether Pinochet should stay in office for another eight years or, if not, submit to elections to be held a year later. Unexpectedly, the military lost

1. "Sanguinetti Proposes Amnesty Law for Military," *Foreign Broadcast Information Service—Latin America (FBIS-LAT)*, March 25, 1985, p. K2.

2. Juan Rial argues that the armed forces secured protection of core, institutional interests such as intelligence gathering, education, and socialization. See Juan Rial, *Los militares en tanto partido político sustituto: Frente a la redemocratización*, Serie Documentos de Trabajo 128/86 (Montevideo: Centro Informaciones y Estudios del Uruguay, 1985), p. 65. Also see Juan Rial, *Las fuerzas armadas: ¿Soldados-políticos o garantes de la democracia?* (Montevideo: Centro Informaciones y Estudios del Uruguay, 1986); Luis González, "Uruguay, 1980–81: An Unexpected Opening," *Latin American Research Review* 18 (1983): 63–76; Martin Weinstein, *Uruguay: Democracy at the Crossroads* (Boulder, Colo.: Westview Press, 1988), pp. 74–112; Charles G. Gillespie, "Uruguay's Transition from Collegial Military-Technocratic Rule," in *Transitions from Authoritarian Rule: Latin America*, ed. Guillermo O'Donnell, Philippe C. Schmitter, and Laurence Whitehead (Baltimore: The Johns Hopkins University Press, 1987), pp. 173–95.

3. The success of the economic program—the purest application of free market doctrine in South America—is evidenced by the fact that it has been left virtually intact by the military's democratic successors. Military cohesion has certainly benefited from government performance. In addition, General Pinochet kept his soldiers in line through his adroit manipulation of promotion and retirement regulations. See Genaro Arriagada Herrera, *The Politics of Power: Pinochet*, trans. Nancy Morris (Boston: Unwin Hyman, 1988), pp. 102–69.

both the plebiscite and the elections. This opened up a small bargaining space for the democratic opposition to negotiate changes in law that would help strengthen the new democracy. But Pinochet hung tough, emerging from these talks with most of his constitution unaltered. Thus, it seemed as if the military would retain a decisive advantage in the new democracy.[4]

Whether the system had been constitutionally rigged in advance (Chile) or subsequently negotiated (Uruguay), the fact remains that Argentina's neighbors faced a tougher challenge. Civilians there had to contend with armies that enjoyed more organic unity, professional pride, and political clout. From this a central rival hypothesis emerges: at higher levels of military power the policy impact of institutional mediation diminishes. Procedural along with structural differences across institutional settings fade from view as the military invokes its preference practically wherever and whenever it chooses. Assailed by forces they cannot defend against, and left vulnerable by porous and malleable institutions, politicians run for cover.

As will be shown below, the evidence does not cooperate with the alternative hypothesis. Despite the initial advantages (greater in Chile than in Uruguay) that both military institutions had, features of democratic governance eventually permitted civilian policymakers to carve out their own spheres of influence. In Uruguay we will detail why the military could safeguard its defensive structure against civilian attempts to reform it yet could not protect its budget share from those very same civilians who were determined to enrich other sectors at the military's expense. Chilean President Aylwin, it will be shown, discovered ways of exploiting the authority of his presidency to advance the first part of his human rights program. But completion of his human rights tasks eluded him, as other branches of government got in his way.

Uruguay

Defense Reform

Revamping the nation's defense systems was not high on the list of priorities of the first postauthoritarian, democratic government in Uruguay. Dr. Julio

4. Pamela Constable and Arturo Valenzuela, *Chile Under Pinochet: A Nation of Enemies* (New York: W. W. Norton & Co., 1991), pp. 317–18. Also see Carlos Andrade Geywitz, *Reforma de la constitución política de la República de Chile de 1980* (Santiago, Chile: Editorial Jurídica de Chile, 1991).

Sanguinetti (1985–90) found himself consumed with human rights conflicts from the moment he stepped into office. The problem was not put to rest until April 16, 1989, when by a margin of 57 to 43 percent the Uruguayan electorate chose to uphold a 1986 law that amnestied all military and police offenders.[5] With the coming to power of Luis A. Lacalle, in March 1991, there was time to devote to other military-related matters.

In one of his first acts in office President LaCalle instructed his defense minister, Dr. Mariano R. Brito, to commission a study to define a new defense doctrine. In light of changing world realities and technological advances, the country needed modern concepts that would prepare it for the twenty-first century, according to Brito.[6] In October 1992 LaCalle addressed the issue of military restructuring head-on. With bipolar conflict a thing of the past, and with regional peace now upon us, traditional hypotheses of conflict have been rendered obsolete, he said. The president called for a "rational, rapid, profound, and sincere analysis of the future role for our armed forces."[7] He ordered his minister and the three commanders to his executive office on November 5, where he told them that military warfare doctrines and territorial deployment were outdated: both must adapt to a new geopolitical world.

An executive order was then issued in March 1993 to reappraise the country's system of defense. Calling military restructuring "indispensable," he commissioned each service branch to undertake studies about new hypotheses of conflict, new missions (both external and internal), the development of rapid mobilization forces (both service and joint), the redeployment of bases and troops, and the optimization of resources through the elimination of wasteful, redundant, administrative as well as combative functions.[8]

It is uncertain whether the air force or the navy ever issued their reports. Apparently, the then commander of the army, Lieutenant General Juan C. Rebollo, did respond in writing to the defense ministry in August of that year, just before being unexpectedly relieved of his duties after revelations of an espionage scandal within the army.[9] But the study included absolutely no change in the army's organic structure, and the president ordered his new

5. República Oriental de Uruguay, Ley de Caducidad (Ley 15.848), in *Informática parlamentaria* (Montevideo: Poder Legislativo, November 15, 1995), art. 1, p. 1.

6. *FBIS-LAT*, May 1, 1990, p. 51.

7. *Búsqueda*, November 12, 1992, p. 1.

8. Ibid., April 1, 1993, p. 60.

9. *FBIS-LAT*, August 23, 1993, p. 46. The former defense minister, Dr. Mariano R. Brito, does not have a copy of the army document nor does he know who has. Interview with author, Montevideo, November 22, 1995.

army commander, Daniel Garcia, to begin again.[10] Garcia said he would create an army that was smaller, more mechanized, more agile and rapid, more efficient and professional, with fewer administrative and more combative functions.[11] Evidently, nothing was done. On July 12, 1994, the president made yet another plea for analysis to be completed by year's end. And the new military doctrine Brito had spoken about? The task of writing it was placed in the hands of a military think tank, which by the end of LaCalle's term, still had nothing to show. It seems that when it comes to defense reform, the nation finds itself in a state of perpetual contemplation.

It is clear through interviews with military officials as well as past and present defense ministers and subsecretaries that the repeated calls for reform have gone unanswered.[12] The former commander of the air force from 1990 to 1993 was candid, saying that there was a stream of paper but no action. His successor thought that a report had been written up at LaCalle's request but was left to collect dust.[13] And the then commander in chief of the army, Juan C. Curutchet, when asked whether he would pick up where Daniel Garcia left off, said, "I have not had access to documentation where [the call for] restructuring is made explicit and instrumented."[14]

There is no question but that the opposition to even modest reform runs wide and deep within the armed services, distinguishing it from its Argentine counterpart. Certainly there were and are pockets of resistance to change in Argentina. But as recounted earlier, there were officers predisposed to reform, who awaited orders from above that never came.

Uruguay is somewhat different. Here the institution as a whole is genuinely fearful of change and would rather be left alone. In theory, the decision whether to go forward or not with reform rests with the president in consultation with his defense minister. If they are to propose a revamping of the nation's defense, over and above military objections, they must have information and persuasive arguments at their disposal with which to sustain an

10. The second in command of the army's general staff said that there is no document calling for restructuring. Whatever report was turned over to LaCalle argued for maintaining the current system. Colonel Raúl A. Villar, *subjefe, Estado Mayor del Ejército*, interview with author, Montevideo, November 30, 1995. Also see *Búsqueda*, December 23, 1993, p. 72; September 22, 1994, p. 11.

11. *Búsqueda*, May 19, 1994, p. 11; October 6, 1994, p. 20.

12. The minister of defense, Raúl Iturria, supported the military's position to preserve the status quo. Interview with author, Montevideo, November 30, 1995.

13. Lieutenant General (ret.) Carlos P. Pache, interview with author, November 21, 1995, Montevideo; Lieutenant General (ret.) Raúl V. Sampedro, interview with author, Montevideo, November 22, 1995.

14. *Búsqueda*, March 9, 1995, p. 1. Indeed, I came up empty-handed after requesting a copy of any document regarding reform at army headquarters. Visit to army facility on November 30, 1995.

unpopular position. They would be foolish to blindly compel reforms that the armed forces themselves believed were unwise and potentially harmful. Overhauling a defense system requires a careful elaboration of political and military objectives, identification of security threats, doctrines, and strategic plans to combat those threats, and assessment of current and future capabilities. Defense specialists must obviously be consulted. If the armed forces are reluctant to provide the expertise, then it is left to civilians. But who? On whom will the defense minister depend for alternative points of view? He has no one. A brief look at his ministry explains why.

The Uruguayan ministry of national defense constitutes a form of institutionalized military dominance. In most advanced democracies where the defense ministry is a vital link in the chain of command, civilians are posted at key decision-making points within the agency. But with the exception of the minister and his subsecretary, the governing and administrative arm (called the *Secretaría del Estado*, the State Secretariat) of the Uruguayan defense ministry is completely dominated by armed forces personnel, as shown below. Ninety-nine percent of the employees there have either military or quasi-military status. Civilians with quasi-military status are subject to the rules, regulations, and discipline of the armed forces themselves, but do not wear uniforms or receive military titles and rank.[15]

As can be seen in Table 7.1, most leadership positions are also taken by uniformed personnel. This is not by choice but by law. As first spelled out in the 1974 Organic Law of the Armed Forces (updated in 1995), and subsequently reaffirmed in 1991 under a decree governing the ministry, every tier

Table 7.1.   The militarization of the Uruguayan National Defense Ministry

Personnel status	*Secretaría del Estado*			
	All employees		Leadership positions	
	No.	%	No.	%
Military	564	91.4	53	85.5
Quasi-military	48	7.8	7	11.3
Civilian	5	0.8	2	3.2
Totals	617	100.0	62	100.0

SOURCE: Uruguayan National Defense Ministry, Office of Personnel, November 1995.
NOTE: Figures are for permanent ministerial employees as well as for those on loan from the armed services.

15. See República Oriental del Uruguay, Ley Orgánica de las Fuerzas Armadas (Ley 14.157) (Montevideo: Ministerio de Defensa, October 1995), art. 76, p. 22.

within the administrative hierarchy below that of the subsecretary is to be controlled by a military officer of superior rank (lieutenant colonels, colonels, or navy captains).[16] Even the minister's personal cabinet, which is composed of seven advisors, are all uniformed and nonuniformed military personnel. Conversely, no Uruguayan law obligates any position, including that of the minister himself, to be filled by a civilian.[17] Unlike Argentina, Uruguay lacks an adequate civilian presence within the chain of command.

The ministry is supposed to deal with national defense and security policy.[18] In principle, the minister should be able to rely on his cabinet for policy-relevant information and strategic advice. In practice, however, the cabinet is, as Juan Rial puts it, nothing more than a "small bureaucratic machine" composed of lawyers, public relations officers, and a notary public that takes up routine administrative matters only.[19] In fact, the minister cannot rely on anyone within the ministerial secretariat—be they soldiers or civilians—to provide him with *independent* ideas regarding defense policy. The problem is twofold.

First, the armed forces personnel who control the governing and administrative apparatus of the ministry have a dual dependency.[20] They are not only answerable to the minister, but are also beholden to their military superiors. Obviously, then, they would be enormously reluctant to step out of line by offering up advice that might depart from official army, navy, and air force positions. Therefore, they leave the policy advising to the commanders in chief while attending to more mundane matters.

Second, the ministry is bereft of civilian expertise.[21] Even if the minister could find civilian defense experts (in a country where such specialists are a rare commodity) and then organize them into an internal advisory panel, it would be difficult to see where he would put them.[22] Nowhere in the organizational chart of this state agency is there room for such an advisory

16. Ibid., art. 31, p. 14; also see Decreto 114/991, "Functional Organic Regulations for the Higher Administration of the Defense Ministry," *Diario Oficial*, February 19, 1992, pp. 263–64.

17. Indeed, between November 1987 and March 1990 the minister and his subsecretary were military officers. It just so happens that in recent years those positions have been filled by civilians.

18. República Oriental del Uruguay, Decreto 574/974, in *Ley de ministerios* (Montevideo: Registro Nacional de Leyes, July 1974), art. 5, p. 170.

19. Juan Rial, *Estructura legal de las fuerzas armadas del Uruguay: Un análisis político* (Montevideo: Centro de Informaciones y Estudios del Uruguay/Sociedad de Análisis Político, 1992), p. 80.

20. Ibid., pp. 200–201.

21. Raúl Iturria, Uruguayan Minister of Defense, 1995–present, interview with author, Montevideo, November 30, 1995.

22. Juan Rial speaks of the ignorance of a large portion of the political class on defense matters. See *Estructura legal de las fuerzas armadas del Uruguay*, p. 82.

body. In fact, the subsecretary of defense from 1993 to 1995 tried to assemble precisely such a team to work within the ministry but to no avail.[23]

At the end of 1993 the Center of Higher National Studies (Centro de Altos Estudios Nacionales, CALEN), which offers advanced courses to soldiers and civilians on a wide range of topics, was created and placed under defense ministry auspices. But even this organization cannot serve as an independent think tank for the minister. By decree its director must be an active-duty general who, aside from being responsible for the overall functioning of the school, is also charged with nominating all full-time and part-time faculty members. While there are civilians who offer courses in economics and sociology, all those who teach in the area of military studies are armed services personnel.[24]

In the absence of independent counsel the minister and his subsecretary have nowhere to go for advice but to the "comandantes." They, in turn, are only too happy to oblige. In fact, to date the current Organic Law of the Armed Forces still stipulates that the principal advisor to the president and his defense minister shall be a junta, composed of the three service chiefs. Its powers are important, political, and widespread. The junta is to advise the political leadership on all matters pertaining to the direction and deployment of defense forces, men, and equipment. Among its sundry duties is to write the military doctrine, generate the plans for military deployment, mobilization, and logistics, and assure interforce coordination and instruction.[25]

Many claim that the junta has been disbanded, although no one in the defense ministry or the Congress can seem to find the statute that says so. Unofficially, however, the three military commanders meet regularly with the defense minister to converse on a range of topics.[26] Moreover, no law authorizes the replacement of the junta by a commensurate body, nor is there

23. Rodolfo González, interview with author, Montevideo, November 22, 1995.

24. República Oriental del Uruguay, Decreto 594/993 (Montevideo: Consejo de Ministros, Ministerio de Defensa Nacional, December 30, 1993), art. 5, p. 2; República Oriental del Uruguay, Boletín del Ministerio de Defensa Nacional, no. 9370, "Organización y Funciones del Centro de Altos Estudios Nacionales" (CALEN), Ordenanza 18, art. 11, p. 5, January 5, 1994.

25. República Oriental del Uruguay, Ley Orgánica de las Fuerzas Armadas (Ley 14.157), as amended, October 11, 1995, arts. 15 and 16, pp. 9–10. A ministerial lawyer advised me that while the junta is officially inoperable, its continued insertion into the organic law gives the armed forces the legal right to resurrect it at any moment. Dr. Claudia Zúñiga Barreneche, telephone interview with author, Montevideo, November 16, 1995.

26. What is more, a top-ranking army official acknowledged to me that the junta of comandantes not only exists but meets regularly and often times alone, without the presence of the minister or president, to discuss common concerns (like the budget). Colonel Raúl A. Villar, subdirector of the army general staff, interview with author, Montevideo, November 30, 1995.

anyone in either branch of government who is especially interested in writing such a law. Unlike Argentina, there is no department within the ministry that deals specifically with policy and strategy, nor is there any *policy-oriented* cabinet ministry. Hence no civilian defense specialists can be appointed to them. It would seem that if the junta does not officially exist, there is a serious void that has yet to be filled. And if it does exist—albeit informally— then it owns a monopoly on defense wisdom.

It is not just the minister who is at the mercy of the generals. So too is the president of the republic who is ultimately responsible for the "protection of domestic order, tranquility, and external security."[27] He consults with the military command on a regular basis and in a direct fashion, as they do with him. They are not compelled to go through the defense minister who, according to the constitution, resides *alongside of, not below,* the president in the political-military hierarchy. The military is subordinate to a "superior command" defined as "the president acting with his minister or with his cabinet."[28] Recently retired air force commanders candidly admitted to me that when they were in charge not a week went by when they did not speak or meet privately with the president of the republic at least once.[29]

Neither Uruguayan presidents nor their defense ministers have any defense understanding. Recent defense appointees have had backgrounds in public, administrative law, have held teaching positions at the university, and/or have been interior or finance ministers in past governments.[30] Bereft of expertise themselves, and without the help of supporting civilian staff, the president and his minister seem only too anxious to rely on the military word. Herein lies the fundamental problem for defense planning and reform.

The armed forces would rather preserve the status quo. Their reasons are numerous, often persuasive. Why not leave well enough alone, they say? The current military structure, which deploys units in each of the nineteen national departments (states), has been in place since the turn of the century.[31]

27. *Constitución nacional-actos institucionales* (Montevideo: Librería Editorial la Academía, 1967), art. 168, para. 1, p. 45.
28. Ibid.
29. Lieutenant General (ret.) Carlos P. Pache, interview with author, Montevideo, November 21, 1995; Lieutenant General (ret.) Raúl V. Sampedro, interview with author, Montevideo, November 22, 1995.
30. These career tracks pertain to the following Uruguayan defense ministers: Dr. Mariano R. Brito, March 1990–August 1993; Dr. Daniel Hugo Martins, August 1993–January 1995; and Raúl Iturria, March 1995–present.
31. It dates back to the era of José Battle y Ordoñez (1903–7). According to Juan Rial, Battle's strategy was to keep the military politically neutral and weak by dividing it into increasingly smaller

It has served the nation well, defending its honor, independence, peace, territorial integrity, constitution, and laws, as it is supposed to.[32] Uruguay faces no imminent dangers. The cold war is over, the guerilla movements of the 1970s have been defeated, and the country is at peace with its neighbors. Under these circumstances, why bother tampering with the institution? True, improvements can always be made in defense preparedness. But the army's own intellectual think tank, the Military Institute of Superior Studies (Instituto Militar Estudios Superiores, IMES), is telling it that current deployment must be maintained if the armed forces are to fulfill their broad mandate.[33]

That mandate is not only strategic but economic and social as well. The military, which is an all-volunteer force, is an important national employer. Whenever the rate of unemployment goes up, military centers quickly become filled with young men wishing to be recruited. There are places in the Uruguayan provinces that are entirely dependent upon the military for jobs. A town like Santa Clara de Olimar in the eastern province of Treinta y Tres, with a population of 2,600, would fall off the map were it not for its seventh cavalry regiment.[34] The transfer, consolidation, or closure of bases to serve some strategic objective adversely affects not only soldiers and their dependents but civilians and their families as well. Currently, 5 percent of all those employed in the defense sector are civilians. At a time when the private sector cannot absorb enough labor to keep pace with the demand, would the president himself want to assume the political risk of throwing defense employees back onto the streets in order to close an infantry regiment?

Then there is health maintenance. The armed forces provide health services to one-quarter of a million Uruguayans.[35] Since the Uruguayan armed forces currently number some thirty-two thousand soldiers, that means that 87 percent of those who receive military, medical attention are not active-duty officers at all. They include not only retired officers and military families but the general public as well. The army brings its mobile medical units into

units with no central command while making these units dependent on the ministry of war. See Rial, *Las fuerzas armadas*, p. 12.

32. República Oriental de Uruguay, Ley Orgánica de las Fuerzas Armadas (Ley 14.157), art. 2, p. 7.

33. Speech by General Fernán D. Amado, director of IMES, August 1, 1995, pp. 19–23. Document provided to me by the army general command.

34. A larger town like San Ramón (pop. 7,500) in the province of Canelones is somewhat less militarily dependent but would undoubtedly be hurt economically if its artillery regiment were to be closed or transferred.

35. See *Soldado* 17, no. 136 (June–September 1993): 79; in an interview with the author Lieutenant General (ret.) Carlos P. Pache confirmed a number of at least two hundred forty thousand beneficiaries. Interview with author, Montevideo, November 21, 1995.

rural areas to serve populations that cannot easily reach more distant, public health facilities or that cannot afford private care. If these units were disbanded, some citizens would be placed at risk. Does the president want to assume that political burden as well?

Finally, the military owns and operates many important educational establishments. The only veterinary school in the nation is run by the armed forces. And each year army schools alone rotate some four thousand to four thousand five hundred young men back into civil society with various technical skills they would not have otherwise acquired.[36] Hence, while the president orders his studies, the armed forces confront him with the sobering reality . . . their reality. Former defense minister Mariano Brito readily admitted that "it is one thing to contemplate restructuring on paper, and another to undertake it. In this regard, military advising was very important to us."[37] General Pache agreed, saying "the reality weighed more heavily [on the political leadership] than [did] the studies."[38]

There are undoubtedly alternative points of view. Some for example seriously question whether the armed forces should be engaged so extensively in social-economic functions.[39] It is reminiscent of the developmental roles that national security–minded armies assigned to themselves in the 1960s. It also smacks of the clientelism that flourished during the dictatorship of 1973–85. Back then the armed forces fancied themselves as patrons to their lower-class clients, inducing a dependency within a weakened civil society through the provision of jobs, health, and social services in exchange for compliance with military domination. Unfortunately, the end of the dictatorship did not bring with it the demise of these relations.[40]

But the president has no institutional vehicle at his disposal to equip him with countervailing arguments. And so he and his minister retreat, unwilling and unable to force the issue. With no perceived, short-term political cost to concession, why not let the military have its way? He does, tucking away into some drawer the executive orders and military reports. The paper trail ends where it began . . . on the president's desk.

36. Colonel Raúl A. Villar, interview with author, Montevideo, November 30, 1995.

37. Dr. Mariano R. Brito, interview with author, Montevideo, November 22, 1995.

38. Lieutenant General (ret.) Carlos P. Pache, interview with author, Montevideo, November 21, 1995.

39. Rodolfo González, the former subsecretary of defense, believes the military is mistaken in its notion that it is supposed to perform social functions. This is an excuse to preserve its current structure. It is not clear to me how forcefully González conveyed that view to the armed forces when he was in power. Interview with author, Montevideo, November 22, 1995.

40. Rial, *Las fuerzas armadas*, p. 25.

The Defense Budget

Uruguayan military autonomy is undoubtedly high *on these issues*. Questions of military organization, strategy, doctrine, and even social function are clearly in the hands of the armed forces themselves. But if it were just a matter of military power, we would be hard-pressed to explain why the armed forces have been unable to stop the gradual but steady erosion of their budget since 1985. The military has accepted but not looked kindly upon the political classes' collective decision to eliminate defense as a spending priority. In an effort to trim deficits while redistributing scarce state resources toward education, health, and social welfare, both the Sanguinetti and LaCalle administrations struck the heaviest blows against defense.[41]

Total defense spending in real terms fell by 21.7 percent between 1984 and 1989, and then by 21.8 percent between 1989 and 1993.[42] In 1980 defense's portion represented 18 percent of the federal pie. By 1989 it was down to 11.2 percent, and by 1993 it had shrunk to 9.8 percent, as its funds were redirected to health, housing, and social security.[43] During the democratic period, military salaries declined by 30 percent with respect to average public-sector salaries and 26 percent with regard to consumer prices.[44] Today the highest-ranking general in the armed forces earns just two thousand dollars per month. A major takes home a meager $1,076 monthly.[45]

The democratic governments were determined to reduce the size of the military's all-volunteer force as well, and did so through a strategy of eliminating the number of vacancies that could be filled at mid-level ranks. By 1994 force levels for all three service branches had been brought down by nearly 19 percent. The army was hardest hit. With 21,557 men in 1985, it had already reported a loss of 5,276 junior officers (a 24 percent decline) by 1990.[46] In part, attrition resulted from the inability of some to advance further up in rank as slots were eliminated. But additionally, many officers who

41. This fiscal objective was originally announced on August 31, 1985, in the president's message to Congress. República Oriental de Uruguay, Cámara de Representantes, *Diario de Sesiones* 621 (December 19, 1985): 100.

42. *Búsqueda*, September 22, 1994, p. 29.

43. "A Comparative Analysis of Spending by Ministries, 1986–1994," Office of Planning and Budgeting, Division of Public Sector Planning, The Uruguayan Presidency, November 1995. Also see *Búsqueda*, March 24, 1994, p. 23; September 22, 1994, p. 29.

44. *Búsqueda*, August 3, 1995, p. 1.

45. Ibid., November 9, 1995, p. 9.

46. República Oriental de Uruguay, Ley 16.170, *Diario Oficial*, January 10, 1991, arts. 89, 90, pp. 48–49A.

were dissatisfied with their salaries left to seek more lucrative positions in the private sector.

These cuts were more modest and undertaken more gradually than those in Argentina, in part to avert disequilibria in the labor market. But the losses were substantial nonetheless. The patterns observed in the air force were typical: a depletion of full-time professionals as underpaid officers sought secondary employment, a deterioration in housing conditions, and a reduction of 40 to 50 percent in instructional flight time for pilots in training. In August 1995 an army spokesman declared that salary compensation was the "fundamental issue" for his force.[47] The parallels with Argentina can hardly escape notice. It is not just the loss of budget shares and the negative repercussions on military operations. It is the seeming inability of the military to do much about it. The reasons are largely institutional in nature.

Here, too, the military is left "out of the official loop."[48] Officers certainly can and do meet regularly with the defense minister to discuss their needs. Their commanders also have more direct access to the president than do commanders in Argentina. But when it comes to fiscal matters, the action is in the president's Office of Planning and Budget (Oficina de Planificacíon y Presupvesto, OPP), the Ministry of Economics and Finance, and the Congress. The OPP and the economics ministry prepare the nation's five-year budget, setting the guidelines and establishing the ceilings each ministry must adhere to. After meeting with each of the cabinet officers to discuss their needs and priorities, these two central agencies finalize the budget proposal and deliver it to the president's cabinet for endorsement before it is sent on to the legislature.

From this point on negotiation—*between civilians*—is the name of the game. Differences between the proposals of the president's fiscal planners and the aspirations of Congress and their constituents quickly come to the surface. Several rounds of bargaining occur between congressional leaders of the four major political parties and representatives of the executive branch in order to close the gap. The dynamics are the reverse of those experienced in the United States during the same period: the Uruguayan congressional leaders want more, while the chief executive's financial advisors are urging the president to toe the line. Constitutionally, the Congress can redistribute but not add to the president's budget without imposing additional tax bur-

47. *Búsqueda*, August 3, 1995, p. 1.
48. The budgetary process was recounted by Suely González, assistant director of the national budget, Office of Planning and Budgeting of the Uruguayan Presidency, in an interview with the author in Montevideo on November 30, 1995.

dens.[49] In practice, however, they *propose* nonfinanced increases in the hope that through tough bargaining they can prevail on the chief executive to authorize precisely such changes.[50]

During this process the president has two occasions upon which he can amend his original bill by tagging onto it what is called a *complementary message*. That message may accept some of the increases proposed by the Senate and then the House while vetoing others.[51] Each time, he sends his revised budget back to either chamber for its final consideration. As the vote in either the Senate or House nears, organized pressures intensify. Not a week goes by during the months of November and December when at least one public-sector union is not on strike. Public services are paralyzed as transportation, health, judicial, and educational employees take to the streets. Political parties then exploit these manifestations to leverage budgetary increases for one program or another.[52]

The final Uruguayan budget is a bargained product to be sure. But where are the armed forces in all of this? The deals are struck between members of the political class, not between civilians and soldiers. The armed forces have few entryways into the process. They cannot resort to the pressure tactics deployed by other public-sector employees. Military strikes and protests are forbidden. The military has no legislative lobby nor can it set up liaison offices. In fact, the commanding officers may not even be seen in the legislative palace unless accompanied by the defense minister. On those occasions the minister, who is appearing before the budget committee to defend his program requests, will bring the commanders along—but only to respond to questions that demand their technical expertise.[53]

The military does have one unofficial avenue of influence. It is widely known that senior and junior officers will meet informally, on neutral ground, with legislators from the defense commissions of the Senate and House of Representatives. Whether it be for lunch or over a cup of coffee,

---

49. *Constitución Nacional de la República Oriental del Uruguay*, in *Constitución Nacional—Actos Institucionales* (Montevideo: Editorial La Academia, 1967), art. 85, para. 13, p. 26, and art. 215, p. 61.

50. Suely González, interview with the author, Montevideo, November 30, 1995.

51. This is not an exercise in fiscal recklessness. Having fully expected his original budget to be augmented, the president had already built into it a margin of financial comfort. Diputado Julio Aguiar Carrasco, interview with author, Montevideo, November 20, 1995.

52. See *Búsqueda*, November 30, 1995, p. 1; *El Observador*, November 29, 1995, p. 3.

53. Limitations on military influence peddling within the Congress were cited by the following legislators in interviews with the author: Diputados Julio Aguiar Carrasco and Walter Vener Carboni of the Colorado Party and Senator Walter R. Santoro of the National Party, Montevideo, November 16, 1995. I do not know whether these limits are observed as a matter of custom or of law.

contacts between politicians and soldiers are cordial if not friendly, and occur sporadically. But these meetings also closely observe two fundamental norms. The first is that soldiers may not resort to pressure or veiled threats of any kind. The second is that the politicians may not curry favor with the military representatives in order to bring coercive weight to bear on their colleagues or on the executive branch.[54] These are, by and large, information-gathering exercises: the officers make their pleas, the politicians listen. It is debatable just how much of an advantage the armed forces obtain through these encounters. But if the statistics cited above regarding the decline of military spending are any indication, it would appear that the gains have been negligible.[55]

In short, the Uruguayan civil-military relation has, in some sense, transcended its origins. Uruguayan democracy was conceived through dialogue between politicians and soldiers. Negotiations ending in agreement set the parameters and established the procedural ground rules for the transfer of power to civilian hands. Moreover, many Uruguayans will, in distinguishing themselves from their Southern Cone neighbors, insist that accommodation is much more than a practice among elites; it is a cultural phenomenon. It is a style of problem solving that pervades the society as a whole. Rivals may bicker, but at the end of the day they will discover common ground, so Uruguayans say.[56]

But while all of this should have established a penchant for ongoing, civil-military negotiations, the defining character of the relation had more to do with institutional turf protection than anything else. Where the military believed it had rightful "ownership" of an issue, and where civilian institutions were too weak to mount a challenge, the armed forces would prevail. Policymakers were very reticent to confront the military when they lacked the organizational wherewithal to do so. Conversely, the political class had

---

54. All those members of the congressional defense commissions who were interviewed agreed on this point, despite different party affiliations. Those interviewed were Diputado Brum Canet of the Frente Amplio Party, Diputado Walter Vener Carboni of the Colorado Party, and Senator Walter R. Santoro of the National Party, all spoken to on November 16, 1995.

55. It is more likely that these encounters have been beneficial to the military in terms of dissuading congressmen from considering defense reform bills that would close down military bases in their home districts.

56. This was a strong impression I had based on several formal and informal conversations with Uruguayans from different walks of life. Also, it should be noted that President Julio Sanguinetti defended his amnesty of military human rights offenders on grounds of national and historical exceptionalism. Each country's situation is unique, he argued. What worked in Argentina would not work in Uruguay because the latter state "has its specific conditions." Among those conditions is a penchant for accommodation and forgiveness, he claimed. See FBIS-LAT, June 24, 1985, p. K2.

its own institutional sphere of influence, which the military seemed generally respectful of. Thus if there is a consensual quality to Uruguayan civil-military relations, it can be found not in a bargain but in the phrase *to live and let live.*

Chile

Patricio Aylwin, Chile's president from 1990 to 1994, pursued a human rights strategy of truth and possible justice: to reveal the gravity and extent of the repression under military rule, provide material compensation for the families of the victims, and then to turn over to the judiciary the responsibility for establishing blame.[57] Even before coming to power Aylwin had abandoned the idea that his own government would take military offenders to court. Instead, he would leave that to private citizens and their attorneys, allowing justice to set its own course.[58] State-led efforts to punish the perpetrators would be perceived as a serious challenge to the military institution.[59] In 1978 the dictatorship had written itself an amnesty protecting fellow military and police officers against future reprisals.[60] And Generals Pinochet and Matthei had both issued stern warnings of what would transpire should their men be put on the dock as in Argentina.[61]

Thus, progress on human rights has to be measured against the goals set by the democratic leadership itself in the context of a postauthoritarian order that placed sizable limits on political action. And yet much was done and

57. He also called for the moral rehabilitation of the victims. Rhoda Rabkin, "The Aylwin Government and Tutelary Democracy: A Concept in Search of a Case?" *Journal of Interamerican Studies and World Affairs* 34 (Winter 1992–93): 149.

58. Aylwin said, "It will be the task for the proper courts to judge the particular cases that may exist, so that truth and justice will prevail." See *FBIS-LAT*, March 12, 1990, p. 45.

59. Shortly after assuming office in March 1990 Aylwin said: "We will not call for any trials against the military institution which we consider to be a cornerstone for building the new democratic state." Ibid.

60. In its electoral platform the *Concertación* (which was the center-left electoral coalition behind Aylwin) sought annulment of the amnesty law. But the president realized early on that this could not be achieved. According to José Zalaquett, a member of the committee that drafted the human rights portion of the platform, Aylwin adhered to an unofficial document prepared for him before he assumed office which argued that the amnesty law could not be defeated without raising constitutional questions. While the official platform satisfied the progressive political constituency of *Concertación*, the unofficial document served to guide policy. José Zalaquett, interview with author, Santiago, Chile, July 12, 1995.

61. Pinochet warned that "the day any of my men are touched, the state of law is over." Quoted in Rabkin, "The Aylwin Government and Tutelary Democracy," p. 144.

perhaps more than would have been predicted, leading José Zalaquett, a human rights advisor to the president, to comment that "the most possible has been done in the least time possible."[62] Still, progress was uneven and could be attributed to the fact that institutions did not always cooperate with the administration.

Though Aylwin could use the powers of his own presidency to great advantage, he could not get the Congress or the courts to go along, nor could he circumvent them. The limitations imposed on these two branches of government were the most visible indicators that the institutional design of government, bequeathed to the new democratic leaders by the outgoing military regime, remained largely intact. The component parts of this institutional order formed an interlocking and mutually reinforcing set of restrictions aimed at preventing the next government from undertaking any kind of change that would threaten military interests, such as bringing soldiers to justice for human rights transgressions.[63] None of the *core* features of this system were bargained away in talks held between the armed forces and political party leaders in 1989. And yet, as will be shown, that system was not foolproof, and left open opportunities for the chief executive.

To understand the government's accomplishments, as well as its misfortunes, it is useful to divide the human rights program into two phases. The first, which occurred largely within the executive branch, concerned the official inquest into the worst abuses committed by the dictatorship. That inquest, which culminated with the release of the Rettig Commission Report in March 1991, was an unmitigated success.[64] The second, never brought to fruition, was to facilitate the identification but not punishment of the perpetrators of human rights crimes committed before March 1978.[65] The policy's fate hinged on the cooperation or obstruction of the judicial and legislative branches of government.

---

62. Ibid., p. 150.

63. For a thorough discussion regarding the legal framework that Pinochet established to protect his political order, see Brian Loveman, "¿Misión Cumplida? Civil-Military Relations and the Chilean Political Transition," *Journal of Interamerican Studies and World Affairs* 33 (Fall 1991): 35–74; Felipe Agüero, "Political and Military Elites in the Transition to Democracy: Chile Since the 1988 Plebiscite," paper prepared for the XVI Latin American Studies Association Conference, Washington, D.C., April 4–6, 1991.

64. The government "closed a large chapter" in Chilean history by commissioning and then publicizing the report, according to Felipe Agüero, "Political and Military Elites in the Transition to Democracy," p. 9.

65. The government did favor the punishment and sentencing of security agents who had committed crimes after March 1978, when the amnesty no longer pertained.

Seeking the Truth

It was out of the executive office that the most impressive advances in the human rights program were made. The president took personal charge, drafting the decree that authorized the creation of the Chilean National Commission on Truth and Reconciliation and selecting its members who were well known, respected, and of diverse political viewpoints.[66] The commission had no legal authority to compel testimony from witnesses. Only the moral suasion of its distinguished members and the political force it derived from its association with the Chilean presidency would allow it to elicit cooperation.

The president had to muster all of his considerable influence to defend the commission from its detractors and to contain the fallout from the release of its findings. First of all, Aylwin had assumed some degree of risk in mandating the commission to investigate the plight of the disappeared, since he did so over military objections: an army official met with Raúl Rettig, the commission's president, in an effort to discourage him from moving forward. Moreover, Aylwin had proceeded without the support of the *Renovación Nacional* and the *Unión Demócrata Independiente*—the two leading right-wing parties that could have conferred a broader legitimacy on the commission and preempted any military retaliation. In addition, Aylwin was tempting fate by unleashing a process whose momentum could carry events further than desired. Thus, a final report that implicated the military in human rights abuses could have energized societal calls for justice.[67] Undaunted, the president and his commission proceeded with their tasks.

Less than a year later, on February 8, 1991, the commission had completed its work. The result was impressive: a study in two volumes numbering more than thirteen hundred pages that identified 2,279 deaths and 957 disappearances—mostly at the hands of state security agents who operated between 1973 and 1989. While the report omitted the names of perpetrators, it did send on to the courts incriminating information, enabling some courts to reopen judicial inquiries into human rights infractions.[68] The commission's suggestions that victims be morally rehabilitated and that their survivors

66. Supreme Decree No. 355, "Creation of the Commission on Truth and Reconciliation," April 25, 1990, reprinted in *Report of the Chilean National Commission on Truth and Reconciliation* (Notre Dame: University of Notre Dame Press, 1993), 1: 5–9.

67. David Pion-Berlin, "To Prosecute or to Pardon? Human Rights Decisions in the Latin American Southern Cone," *Human Rights Quarterly* 16 (February 1994): 120.

68. *Report of the Chilean National Commission on Truth and Reconciliation*, 1: xxxii.

receive material compensation were swiftly endorsed by the Congress, which created a national corporation to fulfill those wishes.[69]

The report created quite a stir. While the air force acknowledged responsibility for its misdeeds, the carabineros (Chile's police) navy and army did not. The most scathing criticisms of the commission's findings were delivered by the army. The investigators, they argued, had gone beyond fact-finding to finger-pointing by revealing details that could leave no doubt as to the perpetrators' identities. These "convictions" were unwarranted, unauthorized, and invalid, since the armed forces had used legitimate force in the prosecution of a just war.[70]

The president had to minimize the damage caused by the military response, and he did so. He insisted that the military not articulate its objections publicly but rather through normal institutional channels. All the services complied by registering their complaints within the National Security Council. The NSC served as a forum in which the military was able to make known to the president its opinions regarding actions that in its judgment threatened the institutional order or the nation's security.[71] Aylwin also demanded that these criticisms be the last military words on the subject. Were the services to drag it out, they could easily have created an intolerable climate of animosity and revenge. Here too the military complied with the president's wishes.

The president asserted his authority in one other important respect. He established clear rules of influence with General Pinochet. Aylwin granted Pinochet a meeting on May 28, 1990, at which occasion the army commander had hoped to voice his objections regarding the creation of the Rettig Commission directly to the president rather than going through the defense minister, as the chain of command required. But Aylwin stole the thunder, using the occasion to dress down the aging general. It was not the army's business to question political decisions made by the president or to evade institutional protocol, he advised. Recounting the meeting a year later, Aylwin said: "When I took power, General Pinochet told me, I depend on you; but I will not take orders from the defense minister. I told him, you are

---

69. República de Chile, Ley 19.123, *Diario Oficial*, February 8, 1992, pp. 1–6.

70. *FBIS-LAT*, March 29, 1991, p. 17. The army also said, "Due to its very nature, the legitimate use of force may disrupt the lives of the people or jeopardize their physical safety" (ibid., p. 19). The army point of view was also conveyed to me by General (ret.) Jorge Ballerino, formerly Pinochet's second in command, in an interview in Santiago, Chile, on July 27, 1995.

71. *Constitución política de la República de Chile* (Santiago, Chile: Editorial Jurídica de Chile, 1995), art. 96, p. 78.

wrong; according to your constitution, you respond to me and to the minister of defense; we are your boss and you have to obey us."[72]

Although Pinochet would continue to test the limits of his influence in the new democratic order, in Aylwin he had met his match. The president refused to be intimidated by the general's maneuvers and gradually a new and improved pattern of civil-military interaction emerged. In wielding his presidential powers with Pinochet, Aylwin helped to shield the Rettig Commission from possible military reprisals. In all, the truth-finding phase of the human rights program was quite successful, centered as it was in the executive office, backed by the full force and authority of the president himself.

In Chile the executive branch is dominated by the president. He can issue decrees with the force of law, declare various states of exception whereupon he assumes extraordinary powers to restrict or suspend individual rights and liberties, and name and remove, at his sole discretion, all ministers, undersecretaries, governors, and provincial administrators.[73] With so many key figures within federal and state executive offices operating at the president's pleasure, they are less likely to take exception to his point of view. Decision making is more centralized, since the number of significant, independently minded actors is sharply reduced. This makes it more likely that a uniform set of ideas will emerge from behind closed doors, bearing the unmistakable stamp of presidential preference. These and similar powers were inscribed in the 1925 constitution.[74] Although retained and in some instances amplified by Pinochet, they predate and are not a product of his institutional order; they are part of Chilean democratic history.

Obviously the president must have some commitment to an idea to begin with, and Aylwin certainly did. Chief among the principles he held onto was the notion that the power of states must be limited so that individual freedoms and liberties are not infringed upon. Taking issue with the authoritarian, neoliberal ideology of the Pinochet regime, Aylwin maintained that economic success can never justify the violation of human rights.[75] And in authorizing his commission to begin its investigation into the fate of the dictatorship's victims, he said "only on a foundation of truth will it be possi-

72. *FBIS-LAT*, April 18, 1991, p. 24.

73. See *Constitución política de la República de Chile*, art. 32, nos. 7, 8, and 9, and arts. 39–41, pp. 37–44.

74. See General Secretariat, Organization of American States, *Constitution of the Republic of Chile, 1925* (Washington, D.C.: OAS, 1979), art. 72, nos. 2, 5, 17, pp. 24–25.

75. Aylwin's positions are presented in Patricio Aylwin, *Un desafío colectivo* (Buenos Aires: Planeta, 1988).

ble to meet the fundamental demands of justice and create the necessary conditions for achieving true national reconciliation."[76]

If these convictions provided the motive, then certainly his position as president provided the opportunity. Aylwin's preferences could more easily become priorities because of the institutional environment in which he worked. The executive branch allowed him to concentrate enough authority in his own hands so that his singular views could prevail and become official state policy. Ironically, by preserving the president's powers of decree that enabled the commission to be chartered, the armed forces permitted the president to make policy that was contrary to their own interests.[77] These, then, are the elements that account for Aylwin's initial success.

Establishing Blame

But Aylwin could only do so much himself. He depended on the courts to reopen or initiate cases, to investigate leads based on the evidence provided to them by families, human rights organizations, and the commission itself, and then to establish guilt so that the amnesty could be applied. Should the judiciary not oblige him, it would fall on the Congress to take appropriate measures.

This presented a twofold dilemma for the president. First, both the judicial system and the Congress were products of the military's imposed institutional order. The Supreme Court's members were holdovers from the Pinochet years, whose ideological orientations precluded them from taking human rights cases seriously and whose supervisory, economic, and punitive powers over lower court judges made challenges to the dominant view from below a risky venture.[78] The Congress had been rigged to produce legislative outcomes more favorable to the armed forces by virtue of the fact that nine of the Senate's forty-seven members were appointed by the Pinochet regime

---

76. Aylwin, quoted in *Report of the Chilean National Commission on Truth and Reconciliation*, p. 1.

77. Even more ironic is the fact that the 1980 constitution enhanced the democratic legitimacy of the president by requiring that he be elected directly and by an absolute majority. The 1925 constitution had allowed Congress to decide the victor in those instances where more than two candidates were competing and no one could earn more than half the vote. See *Constitución política de la República de Chile*, art. 26, pp. 34–35.

78. Ibid., art. 79, p. 67.

rather than elected.[79] Meanwhile, the binomial electoral system invented by the Pinochet regime artificially inflated the proportion of contested seats going to the conservative parties. The most popular party (usually one of the parties belonging to *Concertación*) would have to earn a vote double that of its nearest competitor if it were to win both seats within a district. Were it to fall short of this margin, the second seat would automatically go to the party earning at least 33.4 percent of the vote. Traditionally, the political right commands about one-third of the electorate, thus allowing it to win 50 percent of the time under these new rules.

The second problem was, ironically enough, that neither branch could be easily subjected to the president's will under the new democratic order. True, the chief executive enjoyed a certain leverage with Congress, since he could establish with what urgency a particular bill should be introduced, delaying those he did not support, speeding up those he approved of.[80] But although the president influenced legislative priorities, he could not control the outcomes. The president's leverage was further diluted by virtue of the fact that the binomial distribution of seats, along with the designated senators, reduced his ruling coalition's representation. Also, the chief executive could not call for a plebiscite to win popular approval for measures that failed to win passage in the Congress.

The judicial system was especially well insulated from presidential influence by its system of self-regeneration. The Supreme Court designated its own nominees (five of them) for each vacant post, with the president able to choose only from the court-approved list.[81] Nominees had to include the senior justice on the appellate court, while all others had to come from within the ranks of the judicial system itself. Naturally this kind of inbreeding tended to maintain and reproduce legal and ideological sentiments already present in the court system.

The problem with the judicial branch was typified by its highest body, the Supreme Court. The court always enjoyed a *legal* autonomy from the armed forces that was striking. It was not only left untouched by military hands, but

---

79. Of those nine, six were designated by Pinochet and his National Security Council and the other three by the Supreme Court. See ibid., art. 45, p. 46. Their numbers were reduced to eight in November 1990 with the death of Cesar Ruiz Danyau. According to the constitution, his vacancy would not be filled until the eight-year term had expired. See *El Mercurio*, November 22, 1990, p. A1.

80. República de Chile, Ley Orgánica Constitucional del Congreso Nacional (Ley 18.918) (Santiago: Junta de Gobierno, January 26, 1990), art. 26, p. 6.

81. The Chilean Senate meanwhile has no oversight with respect to the Supreme Court.

protected by decree as well.[82] In practice, however, the court was functionally nonautonomous—in fact profoundly servile to the military regime. Its members refused to believe that human rights violations had occurred, and they castigated judges who thought otherwise.[83] The court routinely failed to take standard measures to protect the rights of those who were most vulnerable: the detained. Between 1973 and 1989 there were 8,908 writs of habeas corpus filed on behalf of families by the Church-affiliated *Vicaria de Solidaridad*. Of those only thirty were fully acted upon by the court, and only three of these before 1985.[84]

Among the numerous additional acts of Supreme Court misconduct or omission, the Rettig Commission cited these: the failure to apply the principle of immediacy (forty-eight hours) when acting on habeas corpus petitions, the toleration of arrests without warrants, the acceptance of confessions made under torture, and the refusal either to enforce laws that restricted detention sites or to subject military courts to its oversight.[85] These actions clearly made a mockery of judicial autonomy, as the International Commission of Jurists noted: "It was inconceivable that a judiciary passively administering laws dictated without public consent and which trampled on constitutional guarantees and liberties could be considered truly independent, even if its *formal authority* was respected by the government in power" (emphasis mine).[86]

82. Decree Law No. 1 issued the day of the coup reserved special treatment for the judicial branch. While the Congress had been summarily closed, the decree assured that "powers of the judicial branch remain fully in force" to the extent allowable "in the situation." See *100 primeros decretos leyes dictados por la junta de gobierno de la República de Chile* (Santiago, Chile: Editorial Jurídica de Chile, 1978), p. 7. Although obviously the phrasing left it to the junta to determine how wide a margin of freedom the courts would enjoy in a given context, still the military's respect for judicial independence was exceptional. Seven years later the military's 1980 constitution made judicial autonomy an unequivocal right. As stated by Article 73, "Neither the President of the Republic nor the Congress can ever exercise judicial functions, submit pending cases to a higher court, revise judicial resolutions, or revive suspended trials" (p. 64).

83. According to Article 79 of the Chilean Constitution, the Supreme Court exercises administrative, disciplinary, and economic control over all lower tribunals. In practice this means it can set salaries, control assignments and promotions, and penalize lower court judges for what it believes to be misconduct. Appeals court judge Carlos Cerda Fernández, appointed as a special investigating magistrate (*ministro en visita*), was suspended in 1986 and again in 1991 for refusing to close down an inquiry into the 1976 disappearance of thirteen communist leaders. Carlos Cerda Fernández, interview with author, Santiago, Chile, July 26, 1995.

84. Americas Watch, *Human Rights and the Politics of Agreements: Chile During President Aylwin's First Year* (New York: Americas Watch, 1991), p. 36.

85. *Report of the Chilean National Commission on Truth and Reconciliation*, pp. 114–16.

86. International Commission of Jurists, *Chile: A Time of Reckoning* (Geneva: Centre for the Independence of Judges and Lawyers, 1992), p. 225.

When the democratic transition occurred, the high court's subservience to military interests persisted, creating a number of dilemmas for Aylwin's human rights program. For example, the court ruled in August 1990 that the controversial 1978 amnesty decree, which freed military offenders from criminal wrongdoing, was constitutional.[87] In a letter addressed to the highest court the president implored the magistrates to accept his interpretation of the amnesty, namely, that the law should not prevent a full investigation into the crimes committed before its passage nor prevent disclosure of those responsible. He said: "I would not be at ease in my mind if I did not convey to the honorable Supreme Court that I believe that the amnesty currently in force which the government respects, should not and must not obstruct a judicial investigation that seeks to establish responsibilities in the cases of missing people."[88]

Aylwin's request was consistent with article 413 of the Code of Criminal Procedure, which states: "[D]efinitive halting of procedures cannot be rendered until the investigation that seeks to determine the facts of the case and the identity of the perpetrator has been exhausted."[89] Even one former minister of justice who served the military government asserted that the 1978 law never meant to suggest that courts could apply the amnesty *before* completing their investigations.[90] Telling is the fact that the Supreme Court had been so thoroughly submissive to military will that it had arranged for the premature closure of countless human rights trials, counter to the judgment of Pinochet's own justice minister!

Human rights groups had been filing affidavits in courts for years with little success. The Supreme Court, believing that the 1978 amnesty forbade investigations of any sort, regularly had the cases transferred to military tribunals, where they were abruptly suspended.[91] But the restoration of democratic rule, followed by the release of the Rettig Report and Aylwin's letter, generated a new political climate and a window of opportunity for human rights lawyers and lower court judges. They used this moment, as one attorney put it, "to test the limits of the institutional order."[92]

87. Junta de Gobierno, Decree Law 2191, *Diario Oficial*, April 19, 1978, p. 1.

88. *FBIS-LAT*, March 8, 1991, p. 25.

89. Quoted in the *Report of the Chilean National Commission on Truth and Reconciliation*, p. 125.

90. Ibid.

91. According to the Military Code of Justice, military courts have jurisdiction if crimes are committed by personnel on active duty in any establishment owned or operated by the armed forces or police. Efforts to repeal this provision, thus sending all human rights cases to civilian courts, failed in the Congress. See República de Chile, *Código de justicia militar* (Santiago, Chile: Editorial Jurídica de Chile, 1992), art. 5, no. 3, p. 15.

92. Hector Sálazar, interview with author, Santiago, Chile, July 6, 1995.

An unsolved disappearance, they argued, was a crime in progress. The last thing known about a victim was that he had been detained. After that the subject was never to be heard from again, his whereabouts and his fate unknown. If that was true, the detention was presumed to have continued into the present unless new evidence proved otherwise. The missing person must either be found alive or facts must be unearthed that establish the date and circumstances surrounding his death. Officers suspected of wrongdoing cannot be exonerated unless the time of the victim's death is placed within the period covered by the amnesty, namely September 11, 1973, to March 10, 1978.[93] Only ongoing investigations by the courts could establish these facts.

The Supreme Court never officially ruled against this interpretation of law and did allow some lower court inquests to proceed . . . up to a point. Inquiries into the fate of the disappeared were permissible. But culpability was another matter entirely. Should a civilian magistrate compile enough evidence to place an officer under suspicion or preventive detention, the military courts would rush to the officer's protection, invoke jurisdiction over the case, and then close it.[94] The high court never got in their way and would often facilitate the transfer. This occurred in the fall of 1992 after a rather infamous DINA (Dirección de Inteligencia Nacional) operator stepped forward to offer self-incriminating testimony in a case involving the 1974 disappearance of a student leader named Alfonso Chanfreau Oyarce. The crime was close to being solved when the Supreme Court turned the case over to a military tribunal, thereby provoking impeachment proceedings against three of its magistrates. Charges against one were upheld by the Chilean Senate on January 20, 1993.[95]

Although clearly rattled by the judge's dismissal, the Supreme Court still remained an obstruction to the pursuit of justice. In 1993 alone, it sided with the armed forces some fourteen times in jurisdictional feuds.[96] Even when civilian courts were left alone to do their work, serious problems persisted. Inquiries into the facts surrounding disappearances and criminal wrongdoing were rarely completed. The armed forces simply refused to hand over incriminating information or to allow federal judges to search military premises for

93. The legal argument was related to me in an interview with Hector Sálazar on July 6, 1995, in Santiago, Chile.

94. As a hedge against military usurpation, many lower court magistrates would simply leave the files open or temporarily suspend the proceedings.

95. Human Rights Watch/Americas, "Chile, Unsettled Business: Human Rights in Chile at the Start of the Frei Presidency," Human Rights Watch/Americas 6, no. 6 (May 1994): 7–8.

96. Ibid., p. 3.

evidence.[97] It is little wonder that of 1,116 cases of disappearance, only 155 had been clarified as of July 1995.[98]

Something had to be done to keep the proceedings in the hands of civilians, restrain the power of the Supreme Court, and facilitate the completion of inquests so that the guilty parties could be identified. To advance this human rights agenda, the president attempted three related yet distinct strategies. The first was to legislate changes in the judicial branch itself. The second was to transform the constitution in order to make the Congress a more democratic and representative institution. And the third was to arrange for secret trials in order to secure information regarding the disappeared.

His efforts to transform the judiciary and the constitution brought into sharp relief the dilemma of navigating policies through governmental institutions still burdened by the legacy of military rule. His attempt to hold secret trials reveals how an executive's policy can be thwarted when congressmen—even those of his own coalition—make decisions based on their own institutionally centered self-interest.

In one of his first acts as president, Patricio Aylwin called for sweeping judicial reform before a Magistrates Convention on March 30, 1990. Referring to the "crisis in the administration of justice," he said that no one any more believes that the judiciary acts autonomously (from the armed forces).[99] Its system of self-generation perpetuates promilitary biases in perpetuity, and its concentration of powers at the top stifles judicial independence from below.

A year later the government submitted to Congress a bill that would overhaul the training, assessment, appointment, and promotion of judges, the control over the judicial budget, and the size and composition of the Supreme Court. It created an ombudsman, nominated by the president and charged with safeguarding civil and political rights. But perhaps its most innovative proposal was the creation of a National Council of Justice

97. All human rights lawyers interviewed agreed that the fate of the disappeared will only be known when legislation restores the power of civilian judges to freely search military installations. Pamela Pereira, interview with author, Santiago, Chile, July 11, 1995; Hector Sálazar, interview with author, Santiago, Chile, July 6, 1995.

98. Andrés Dominguez Vial, *Corporación Nacional de Reparación y Reconciliación*, interview with author, Santiago, Chile, July 3, 1995.

99. Independence, he said, "does not reside only in the organic laws or in the subjective belief of judges that they are independent; it demands both but something more: the firm will of the magistrate to discover at all costs the truth and to be just, guarding himself with courage from all forms of influence and pressure, except those of his own judgment and vision regarding the society in its daily occurrences." *El Mercurio*, March 31, 1990, p. C8.

(CNCJ). The council would be composed of fifteen members, including two senators, three representatives of the executive, one member of the Chilean bar, and nine judicial figures. The NCJ would "formulate judicial policy," draft a budget, and nominate judges to the Supreme Court. It would be consulted prior to any bill or constitutional reform that would "regulate the organization and powers of the courts of justice."[100]

The bill ran into immediate opposition from the Supreme Court's conservative allies in Congress, forcing Aylwin to abandon the National Council for a compromise formula. The new proposal would have allowed the high court to select its nominees with the proviso that one-third of its members would be recruited from outside the judiciary and that presidential selections would be ratified by the Senate. Yet even this was too much for the political right which stood together and thus deprived the *Concertación*, of the three-fifths margin it needed for victory.[101] If only one member of either conservative party had broken ranks, it would have been enough to push the judicial reform bill over the top.

The solidarity of the right discouraged the executive branch from pursuing the matter any further. Legally, the president could have resubmitted his bill to the Senate. If it had passed there, it would have become law if when sent back to the chamber of origin, the opposition had failed to muster a two-thirds rejection.[102] Yet the odds of victory in the upper house were slim indeed, where promilitary parties enjoyed a built-in structural advantage. Half the Senate's forty-seven seats were controlled by either elected (33 percent) or designated (17 percent) conservative senators. Even with the twenty-two *Concertación* senators solidly behind him, the president would still have needed to pick up an additional six votes to win—a prospect that was highly unlikely.

The most logical solutions to the human rights problem were often the most elusive. If military tribunals were winning the jurisdictional battles, then why not legally limit their reach? Why not legislate the transfer of cases from military to civilian courts that involved the commission of crimes against humanity by armed forces personnel? Although such a measure was

100. *FBIS-LAT*, May 1, 1991, p. 32.
101. *Concertación* controlled 70 out of the 120 seats in the lower house. For judicial reforms of this sort requiring constitutional change a three-fifths majority was needed, meaning seventy-two votes. Aylwin's coalition held together and picked up one additional vote from the independent left-wing MIDA (*Movimiento de Izquierda Democrática Allendista*) Party. Still, the measure failed by one vote, when a second member of MIDA refused to show up for the balloting.
102. *Ercilla*, September 26, 1990, pp. E16–E17.

originally contemplated in 1990 by Justice Minister Francisco Cumplido, it was quickly abandoned. The minister reasoned that in order to win conservative concessions on other reforms aimed at restoring individual rights and guarantees, reducing penalties for crimes, and granting presidential pardon for political prisoners currently detained by military authorities, the more controversial effort to strip military courts of their authority over military suspects would have to be sacrificed.[103] It was. And still the remaining legislation that did pass, that came to be known as the *"Leyes Cumplidos,"* accomplished considerably less than had been hoped for mainly because right-wing, promilitary, congressional resistance to more profound change was so formidable.

The institution of Congress, as bequeathed to Chilean society by the outgoing dictatorship, consistently spoiled presidential efforts to transform provisions of the constitution and its organic laws—changes that would have directly or indirectly facilitated passage of his human rights program. Each year, beginning in 1990, the Aylwin administration introduced a package of constitutional amendments; each year it went down to defeat either in committee or in full session. The proposals would have eliminated the non-elected senators after completion of their terms in 1997, shifted from the binomial to a proportional electoral system, empowered the president to remove his military commanders in chief, and provided a civilian advantage within the National Security Council by making the president of the House of Deputies a voting member.[104]

Two features of the system conspired against the president. The first was the heretofore-mentioned electoral system that had assigned a disproportionately large share of the congressional seats to the conservative parties. And the second was the supermajorities needed for passage of constitutional revisions that would fundamentally alter the institutional order. A three-fifths vote of both chambers was required for changes in the electoral system or for termination of the designated senators, while two-thirds was the threshold to diminish the power and autonomy of the armed forces or the National Security Council.[105] Aylwin's forces occupied 58 percent of the seats of the lower house and only 47 percent in the Senate, meaning that cooperation with elements from the political right was essential for victory. Such cooperation was never secured. A spokesman for the *Renovación Nacio-*

103. International Commission of Jurists, *Chile: A Time of Reckoning*, pp. 163–81.
104. *Hoy*, April 1–7, 1991, pp. 14–16.
105. *Constitución Política de la República de Chile*, art. 116, p. 86.

nal Party typified the sentiments of the opposition when he said "we will not favor . . . a process that rejects the foundations of the prevailing institutional order."[106]

Aylwin knew that it was in the self-interest of the political right to hold onto features of the institutional design that afforded them numerical advantages in the Congress while aiding their military allies. However, he also reasoned that his own coalition would reap electoral gains by repeatedly offering up legislative proposals that however unfeasible would nonetheless fulfill campaign promises. He also surmised that the right would eventually pay a heavy price at the voting booth for too closely associating itself with institutional vestiges of an authoritarian past.[107] Indeed, conservative forces did suffer badly in the municipal elections of June 1992, followed by their defeat in the presidential election of 1993.

The president's final bid to secure partial justice took place toward the end of his term, following on the heels of an unusual and disturbing movement of troops that took place around army headquarters in downtown Santiago on May 28, 1993. Soldiers wearing camouflage, combat fatigues, and berets called *boinas* encircled the building while others steered tanks through crowded streets. Inside army headquarters Pinochet was meeting with his top commanders. The "boinazo," as it was called, startled the nation and caught the government off guard.[108] While the causes of the incident were numerous, ongoing human rights investigations by the courts that could have potentially implicated dozens of active-duty officers in human rights crimes figured prominently.[109]

The president worked out a formula to both accelerate the judicial process and provide confidentiality to those officers willing to disclose what they knew about the human rights crimes. Fifteen special investigatory judges would be assigned to the Federal Court of Appeals to handle just these cases, thus making the Supreme Court's workload more manageable. Witnesses and defendants would divulge evidence in secrecy; court officials or attorneys who violated rules of confidentiality would be subject to punishment.[110] The

---

106. *El Mercurio*, April 24, 1991, p. 1.

107. *Hoy*, no. 802, November 30–December 6, 1992, p. 19.

108. "La Semana de los Enriques," *Hoy*, no. 829 (June 7–13, 1993), pp. 10–13.

109. Officers were being subpoenaed as witnesses, which was especially traumatic for them not only because they could eventually be placed under suspicion or arrest but also because of the publicity generated by their appearances. Human rights groups along with the press were there in court to expose them to public shaming for their alleged wrongdoing.

110. Ministro de Justicia, "Proposición de Mensaje y Proyecto de Ley" (Santiago, Chile: Ministerio de Justicia, July 30, 1993).

president presented the proposal, dubbed the *Ley Aylwin*, to the nation on August 4, 1993, and delivered his bill to the Chamber of Deputies the next day.

Aylwin's encounter with the legislature would prove to be frustrating, pointing up quite persuasively how the self-interest of congressional politicians can place them on a collision course with the president. On August 17 the House of Deputies approved the *Ley Aylwin* only in part. By a vote of fifty-seven to thirty-eight, it rejected a key article that would have allowed military testimony to be delivered confidentially. Stripped of its secrecy provision, the president's legislative initiative was rendered useless. What had happened?[111]

Surprisingly, members of Aylwin's own *Concertación* coalition, and the Socialist Party in particular, defected. They argued that the special trials amounted to a form of impunity. Without a public airing of the proceedings, the full events surrounding the deaths of political prisoners and the identities of the perpetrators would never be known, while offending officers would testify in private and then be exonerated.[112] The families of the disappeared would never discover the truth. The socialists were joined in opposition by nearly all members of the conservative *Renovación Nacional* (RN) and *Union Demócrata Independiente* (UDI) parties. Having lost to the *Concertación* in the municipal elections the year before, the political right was now a committed adversary and in no mood for compromise. Moreover, right-wing opposition was clearly opportunistic and disingenuous, since conservative legislators had signaled their approval of the bill when it was first announced and since its secrecy provisions were precisely what they had been angling for. But this was also a moment to embarrass the administration and they chose to exploit it.

Aylwin sent his proposal onto the Senate. But there he would have to please an opportunistic right who controlled the Senate, while having to

111. A full account of the unfolding deliberations in the Congress can be found in *El Mercurio*, August 22, 1993, pp. D1, D14.
112. The Socialist Party arguments were not generated in a societal vacuum. They reflected the views of human rights groups who had been working feverishly behind the scenes to generate congressional resistance to the measure. In particular, lawyers associated with these groups and who themselves were Socialist Party militants planted doubts in the minds of party reps about both the feasibility and the morality of the measure. The bill, they said, would not only fail to achieve its objectives but would reflect poorly upon the party that had always stood in defense of victims of the dictatorship. See *La Segunda*, August 24, 1993, p. 14. A hunger strike to protest the bill, staged by women of victimized families, was timed to coincide with these deliberations and seemed to give greater urgency to a reconsideration. See *El Mercurio*, August 22, 1993, p. D14.

simultaneously please the intransigent left within his own coalition. The president attempted just that, but it was an impossible mission. And so on September 2 he withdrew the measure. *Ley Aylwin* was dead.[113]

In defeating this measure, congressmen were looking out for their own careers. Left-leaning members of Aylwin's own coalition were nervous about how charges of impunity would sit with their constituents were they to endorse the secret trials. Right-wing congressmen meanwhile believed their electoral interests would be best served by handing the president a major defeat that would hopefully weaken the Christian Democratic Party's standings in the polls as the December congressional elections drew nearer.

El Mercurio noted wryly that "the view these days is that perhaps the greatest error of the President was to look for a legislative solution."[114] Perhaps. The Congress had been more of a hindrance than a help to Aylwin when it came to advancing the second phase of his human rights agenda. But what alternatives were open to him? It is not clear that he could have single-handedly cajoled the judiciary to hold special trials. This initiative, along with the other elements of Aylwin's program, could not be fully managed from the executive office. Authority was dispersed across several decision-making centers: the Supreme Court, the military tribunals, and the legislative branch were all "players," and uncooperative ones at that. While President Aylwin ably exploited the authority of his own office to investigate human rights abuses, he could go no further so long as other branches of government stood in his way.

Congressional obstruction can be traced to two causes. The first is that by virtue of its design, the Congress was still protective of certain military interests. The president could not overcome the built-in structural advantages that rightist forces enjoyed and that were bequeathed to them by the outgoing dictatorship. In this respect the congressional institution lacked sufficient sovereignty, since it still operated within the confines of the larger institutional order left by Pinochet.

The second resides in the fact that while the Congress retained vestiges from an authoritarian past, it also embodied elements of a new, reinvigorated democracy. Aside from the designated senators, all other legislators from either end of the political spectrum had been voted in, and thus each had to calculate the electoral impact of every decision they made if they were to retain their seats in the next election. Calculations based on voter appeal

---

113. *La Segunda*, September 2, 1991, pp. 11–12.
114. *El Mercurio*, August 22, 1993, p. D14.

might very well drive a policy wedge between a congressman and a president who by law cannot be immediately reelected.[115] This is precisely what occured in August 1993 as legislative representatives from Aylwin's own coalition abandoned him to further their own ambitions, confirming Barbara Geddes's observation that "within modern democratic regimes, particular institutions . . . determine what kinds of behavior are most likely to contribute to career advancement."[116] Chilean congressmen occupied a different institutional niche and faced a set of different job requirements than did the president. Hence on this occasion (not always) their policy preferences and those of Patricio Aylwin diverged.

Conclusion

The evidence presented in this chapter dispels the notion that the institutional mediation of civil-military relations observed in Argentina was unique. Political life may not have been identically organized in each of the three countries, but organization played an undeniably important role in each instance. By intervening between politicians and soldiers, institutions created a mix of constraints and opportunities for both sides. The more powerful armies in Uruguay and Chile could not block initiatives or extract concessions from civilians at will. They had to put up with certain features of democratic governance that denied them or limited their policy entrée and thus provided civilian decision makers with some measure of autonomy.

In Uruguay the budget-making process was not as centralized as it was in Argentina. Nonetheless, it was very much an autonomous, civilianized operation that offered the military only limited access. Even in Chile, where the rules of the game had been rigged by the outgoing dictator, the democratic leadership still found room for maneuver. When it came to human rights inquiries, General Pinochet and his colleagues discovered in Aylwin's presidency a source of unexpected, concentrated, democratic authority resistant to military intimidation. As Rhonda Rabkin stated: "The military's careful arrangements failed to prevent the work of the Rettig Commission

---

115. *Constitución Política de la República de Chile*, art. 25, p. 34.
116. Barbara Geddes, *Politician's Dilemma: Building State Capacity in Latin America* (Berkeley and Los Angeles: University of California Press, 1994), p. 12.

and subsequent investigations by the courts, nor an emotional presidential apology, nor official acts of reparation."[117]

The Chilean case demonstrates that the terms of transition from authoritarian to democratic rule do not cast the civil-military balance of power in stone. Although the military there managed the transfer of authority to democratic hands largely on its own, devising rules of behavior for future regimes, it could not foresee all the consequences of its action . . . and inaction. As it turned out, it left in place certain presidential powers that Patricio Aylwin could exploit in furthering the cause of human rights. This is why it is important to treat institutional arrangements as independent forces in their own right and not as mere artifacts of political actors.

By the same token, institutions did not always cooperate with civilians. In Uruguay, like Argentina, the defense ministry constituted a source of institutional frailty for a democratic leader who entertained notions about transforming his nation's defense system. President LaCalle soon found out how difficult it would be to overcome military resistance to defense reform without a ministry situated in the chain of command and staffed by civilians well trained in the field of defense. By contrast, the Argentine defense ministry was in the chain of command and had been sufficiently civilianized. But inadequate preparation on defense issues, rapid personnel turnover, and an absence of presidential leadership translated into a lack of ministerial competence, continuity, and resolve. This in turn prevented the agency from utilizing the legal authority vested in it. And Chilean institutions such as the Congress and the judiciary, both of which had military fingerprints all over them, posed numerous obstacles for civilians trying to advance their human rights agenda.

Even so, vulnerability to military influence was not the only problem encountered by policymakers. We found in the Chilean case as we did with Argentina that the normal division of powers within a democratic state can pose hurdles for policy clearance when authority is dispersed across branches of government. The president's policy wishes may diverge from those of justices or legislators since each of these political actors occupy different institutional roles and thus defines his or her interests differently as well. In Argentina federal judges interfered with the second phase of Alfonsín's human rights program because they subscribed to standard judicial procedures. In Chile congressmen denied Aylwin a last-minute human rights victory because their first priority was to get reelected.

---

117. Rabkin, "The Aylwin Government and Tutelary Democracy," p. 151.

If one is keeping score, Southern Cone politicians in general did not gain any appreciable ground over the armed forces with respect to contested policy: they won a few and lost a few. This comparative analysis might suggest to some that there is not much to cheer about. If civilians cannot compile a record of consistent superiority, then have they not failed to advance the goal of civilian control? Such a conclusion would be inadvisable. While on substantive grounds the record is mixed, on procedural grounds it is quite good. The evidence points to a practice, especially on the part of the armed forces, of repeated adherence to institutional conventions, even where such conventions may deprive them of valued influence and prerogatives. In the concluding chapter we discuss just what contribution this compliance may make to the cause of civilian control and democratic consolidation.

CHAPTER 8

Conclusion

Political power cannot automatically translate preferences into policy; it must work its will through governing institutions. Compelling evidence has been presented in the Argentine, Uruguayan, and Chilean cases to show that policy gains or setbacks have less to do with the measurable exertion of influence and more to do with the organized context through which that influence is either expressed or suppressed. Military pressures are only as effective as institutions allow them to be. Where institutions are porous, where their structures, norms, or rules of procedure open up avenues of ingress, then the armed forces can make their views felt. Where institutions are impregnable, then policymakers can more easily fend off military advances.

Yet autonomy from the armed forces is not enough. Unless executive decision makers can concentrate enough authority in their own hands, they run the risk of losing control over the shape and ultimate fate of their programs, not to armies, but to other civilian, governmental actors. If the formulation and implementation of all military-related policies could be assigned to the executive branch only, then we might expect outcomes to bear the indelible stamp of presidential preference. But where military policy is apportioned to other branches of government as well, and thus exposed to their rules of behavior, then the president's insignia may very well fade from view. As some of the cases have revealed, military issues were indeed taken up by different institutional actors, each leaving its own unique imprint on the final policy product.

Nowhere was this more apparent than in the realm of human rights. The Argentine judiciary took up its assigned tasks with a dedication, passion, and independence that pleased activists but surprised and ultimately frustrated the president in his later bid to limit prosecutorial action. It is not that the courts went out of their way to pursue justice; they didn't have to. They simply fulfilled their duties, guided as they were by the traditional norms of judicial behavior. So long as he upheld the principle of separation of powers, Alfonsín could not coerce the justices to deliver verdicts pleasing to him. As control over the human rights agenda slipped from his grasp, so too did his ability to contain unrest within the military rank and file. For months his more conservative advisors had been urging him to propose legislation to reduce to a handful the number of offenders that would be brought to trial. The rebellion of April 1987, which was the logical consequence of a policy already in trouble, merely hastened that decision.

The Argentine judiciary demonstrated not only independence from the president but autonomy from the armed forces as well. The same could not be said for the Uruguayan defense ministry. Legally dominated by uniformed personnel, it served as the perfect institutional vehicle with which to stymie civilian-led efforts to reform the defense system. The armed forces stood their ground while the democratic leadership, lacking the organizational means to assert its will, conceded. Yet even in the more civilianized defense ministry of Argentina, historical legacies of an institution consigned to obscurity confounded reform efforts. A habit of organizational idleness that had developed due to decades of neglect was difficult to quickly overcome. One defense minister after the next seemed incapable of spearheading change. Accordingly, the armed services were left to their own devices. But confronted with difficult, often painful choices, each service preferred to do less or nothing at all.

Of course civilians had their victories too. As discussed, the initial stages of the human rights program in both Argentina and Chile were hugely successful, even though each was conceived and executed over and above military objections. In both instances chief executives enjoyed substantial control over the commissions that were designed to discover the truth about past terror. In Argentina the president also profited from an early affinity (that would later disappear) between his punitive ambitions and those of the courts. And in the realm of budgetary politics, civilians revealed a strong

hand as well. Institutionally removed as they were from direct military influence, insulated from potential detractors within government, and unflinching in their adherence to economic criteria, fiscal officers in Argentina
prepared budgets that were often displeasing to the armed services. The
power over the purse was concentrated in their hands alone. One ministry
had in its possession the sole authority to set the expenditure limits that
would reverse a near decade-long pattern of military gluttony. The armed
forces protested through official channels but usually to no avail.

Politicians and soldiers traded policy victories and defeats on the same
general field of play. The action may have shifted from one corner of the
field to another, and the score may have changed now and then, but the
outer boundaries of the game remained fixed. The victors were elated, yet
their gains were not calamitous for the other side. The losers were disgruntled
but returned for another game and another season. The contest was not an
all-or-nothing proposition because certain norms were beyond contention:
neither the military's place in the chain of command, nor the authority of
elected officials, nor the viability of the democratic regime was up for grabs.
But neither in question was the military's right to try to influence policies
that affected its professional interests. With a few exceptional moments,
these terms of play were held to remarkably well.

This adherence is what could be described as a victory of democratic process over prospects.[1] Well-defined procedures were generally respected, even
though they did not ensure substantive gains. Nothing about the arrangements of a democratic state can assure the armed forces or any other political
or social group that policy outcomes will be to their consistent advantage.
They all submit to rules of engagement that are binding yet not always beneficial. Furthermore, democracy creates a more level playing field. Hitherto
oppressed and disenfranchised groups can now more meaningfully contest
the armed forces for shares of public and private resources. They enjoy an

---

1. Democracy is often thought of in procedural and institutional terms, a trend that actually
began with Joseph Schumpeter. Eschewing classical doctrine based on the sources or goals of democratic behavior that were awfully difficult to identify (such as the "will of the people" or the "common good"), Schumpeter first suggested the logical alternative: institutional terminology that
focused on the "democratic method" for selecting leaders and reaching political decisions. See Joseph A. Schumpeter, *Capitalism, Socialism, and Democracy* (New York: Harper & Row Publishers,
1950), p. 269. Since his time Robert Dahl has led the charge, conceiving of democracy as a set of
institutional guarantees that maximize participation and competition. See Robert Dahl, *Polyarchy:
Participation and Opposition* (New Haven: Yale University Press, 1971), pp. 1–16. The majority of
contemporary democratic theorists accept the essential Dahlian framework, either adding or subtracting to it.

access to political institutions that was previously denied under autocratic rule. As influential as they may still be, the armed forces must now compete with other groups for scarce federal resources and political attention. The results of that competition are not completely indeterminate since institutional biases make it more probable that some groups will advance their interests at the expense of others.[2] Still, under democratic auspices no actor's welfare can be assured. As Przeworski argues: "Democracy means that all groups must subject their interests to uncertainty. It is this very act of alienation of control over outcomes of conflicts that constitutes the decisive step toward democracy."[3]

Uncertainty should be particularly unnerving to a military organization that has recently enjoyed the spoils of power. Having held office with nearly unchallenged supremacy, having had unrestrained access to state resources, and having held within its grasp the power to decree that which it desired, it would be understandably difficult for the military to accommodate to the more unpredictable conditions of a constitutional regime. Perhaps more than any other political actor the armed forces stand to lose a decisive edge once they relinquish their hold on the state, turn power over to elected officials, and submit themselves to the terms of democratic life. But despite its somber recognition that it will no longer accomplish all it sets out to achieve, the military seems willing to adhere to the very procedures that constrain its reach.

Why it does so is a question that was partially addressed in Chapter 2. In the current international, regional, and domestic context, there are few if any viable alternatives to the democratic option. Any plot to subvert the democracy will have undesirable consequences for those joined to the conspiracy. Thus, the armed forces calculate that the costs to defection from the competitive system are still appreciably greater than the costs to cooperation.

At a more specific policy level the military realizes that the influence "game" is not consistently rigged to anyone's disadvantage, especially its own. While in agreeing to abide by the new rules the military does relinquish some power, it is also comforted by the fact that its losses are neither insufferable nor irretrievable. The armed forces can only lose so much. Scholars concur that the transition sets an irreducible minimum: the institutional existence of the military cannot be forsaken; its professional survival must

---

2. Adam Przeworski, "Some Problems in the Study of the Transition to Democracy," in *Transitions from Authoritarian Rule: Comparative Perspectives*, ed. Guillermo O'Donnell, Philippe C. Schmitter, and Laurence Whitehead (Baltimore: The Johns Hopkins University Press, 1986), p. 58.

3. Ibid.

be guaranteed.[4] Moreover, short of any full-scale lethal attack on the profes-sion the military can absorb policy defeats so long as it believes that what it loses in one institutional context it may recoup in another. The flip side to this is the civilian government's own erratic policy record, prevailing over the armed forces on certain occasions while losing to them on others. While we might wish that democratic leaders triumph over the armed forces each and every time a policy is in dispute, their occasional failure to do so may serve up yet another inducement for military collaboration.

The Benefits of Military Compliance

The armed forces' observance of legal norms is a welcome change, one that should have a clear payoff for democratic society. The mere fact that they consent to work within organizational confines is helpful since doing so places reasonable constraints on their political behavior. Systems that are institutionalized exact a price on social and political forces for their partici-pation in politics. That price, says Samuel Huntington, involves "limitations on the resources that may be employed in politics, the procedures through which power may be acquired, and the attitudes that power wielders may hold."[5] In a nation where political contenders too often brandished the sword and not the pen, the mere absence of coercion is itself noteworthy. Democracy is the great beneficiary of this newfound restraint.

A resort to violent means, if not checked, eventually debases the very institutions a democracy needs to survive. Sometimes it takes only a minority of offenders to cause systemwide damage. Even if the majority of citizens are law-abiding, they may lose confidence in democratic processes once these fall prey to relentless attacks by a handful of armed and well-organized saboteurs. Alternatively, the repeated use of legal channels by the military and other power contenders heightens the public perception that these institutional forums matter. The more utility attributed to them, the more credible and legitimate they become, thus solidifying the organizational base of the demo-cratic system.

---

4. Guillermo O'Donnell and Philippe C. Schmitter, *Transitions from Authoritarian Rule: Tentative Conclusions About Uncertain Democracies* (Baltimore: The Johns Hopkins University Press, 1986), pp. 67–69.
5. Samuel Huntington, *Political Order in Changing Societies* (New Haven: Yale University Press, 1968), p. 83.

Democracy clears a most difficult hurdle when armies decide to voice their preferences and displeasures up through the institutional hierarchy and not around it. After all, if those political actors theoretically *most* capable of evading or overturning the democratic order now decide (for whatever reason) to live within it, then why not everyone? It is the military that must summon the greatest levels of restraint since not only has it suffered losses but is more than anyone else capable of forcefully reversing those losses (only assuming it receives sufficient societal support). Certainly, if the military could resist the lure of praetorianism, then others should be able to do likewise.

But even when others cannot forgo the temptation to act outside the legal limits, their efforts may end up being spoiled nonetheless. Civilian opponents to the regime who were hoping to win via the coup what they could not win democratically soon discover to their dismay that the armed forces are not prepared to collaborate. When the military practice political restraint, they deny to these citizens the very conduit they need to push the antidemocratic conspiracy along. When this channel of influence dries up, it may prompt erstwhile civilian defectors to either retreat from politics altogether or to more positively renew their efforts to win change at the ballot box. The electoral mainstreaming of rightist, formerly pro-coup political parties is one indicator of this kind of change. Thus, military respect for institutional protocol could indirectly invigorate the competitive process.

Military Compliance and Civilian Control

The military's observance of legal norms, not to mention its reluctance to subvert the constitutional order, have obvious benefits to a nation struggling to rebuild a democracy. But coup avoidance is not the same as civilian control. The armed forces may refrain from provocative actions designed to upset the legal framework and yet not fully accept their subordinate status. For example, they could make their compliance contingent on civilian performance. How elected leaders manage the economy, react to social unrest, and conduct foreign policy would be subjected to military scrutiny. As self-proclaimed trustees of the national interest, the armed forces might inappropriately voice political objections once leaders falter in their execution of policy, as they inevitably will do. This will lead the military to overstep the limits to its institutional sphere of influence, collide with government's efforts to expand its own authority, and ignore the principle that it is for civilian leaders alone to decide the permissible areas of military responsibility.

The military could enlarge its political role not only by pronouncing disfavor with policy and policymakers but by acting on its displeasures as well. Claiming it has a responsibility and capacity to right the policy wrongs, it slowly but steadily assumes authority within the state. Nudging civilian officeholders aside, it then exploits its new positions to advance its own agenda, which, if left unchecked, could pose serious problems. As Huntington states: "In a democratic country, the military may undermine civilian control and acquire great political power through the legitimate processes and institutions of democratic government and politics."[6] Taking its actions to an extreme, the armed forces may so penetrate official chambers as to turn a once democratized state into a militarized one.[7] On a much smaller scale this is what happened to the Uruguayan defense ministry.

While a comprehensive military takeover of state functions is unlikely in the current political context, it is mentioned to stress the point that military adherence to institutional norms is a necessary but insufficient ingredient for civilian control. Control is a demanding term that connotes much more than a legal adherence, however habitual that adherence may be. It goes beyond restrictions on military means, ends, and prerogatives to the issue of values. In the final analysis compliance must be not only ritualized but internalized.[8] Civilian control depends on conviction—the notion that a professional soldier submits to a higher, political authority. That he executes but does not question either policy or those who made it must represent a principle, an article of faith. The soldier must wear his submission as a badge of merit and distance himself from those who do not. Only with that level of commitment would a democratic society be permanently inoculated against military subversion.

6. Samuel Huntington, *The Soldier and the State: The Theory and Politics of Civil-Military Relations* (Cambridge, Mass.: Harvard University Press, 1957), p. 82.

7. J. Samuel Fitch, "Military Role Beliefs in Latin American Democracies: Context, Ideology, and Doctrine in Argentina and Ecuador," paper prepared for delivery at the 1995 meeting of the Latin American Studies Association, Washington, D.C., September 28–30, 1995, p. 4. Too often in Third World settings, civilian leaders have acquiesced to such incursions in order to pacify the military while holding onto the formal trappings of power. In a perverse kind of way this still constitutes an institutionalized situation, since influence is exerted from within the state while power is expressed through the possession of roles. But this condition renders government democratic in name only. Once civilians relinquish a sufficient number of key administrative and political positions to soldiers, what remains is a democratic veneer that at its very best thinly cloaks a nondemocratic core.

8. S. E. Finer, *The Man on Horseback: The Role of the Military in Politics*, 2d ed., revised and updated (Boulder, Colo.: Westview Press, 1988), pp. 24–26.

This is a tall order for any Third World military organization to fill. But the advantage to imposing exacting criteria for civilian supremacy is that it guards against premature declarations of achievement. It is a scholarly hedge against an untimely pronouncement that the armed forces have finally renounced all rights to political intervention when they may not have. Patterns of cooperative military behavior could conceal underlying attitudes of resentment toward elected officials or toward the system as a whole, which could spill over into acts of defiance. As military rebellions in the once stable democracy of Venezuela made all too clear, habits of compliance with civilian rule can be forgotten under the right political and economic conditions. Custom is not enough. In the longer term, restraint must become a virtue. For now, in Argentina, it is not; it is simply a rational adaptation to a new political environment. For this reason the full realization of civilian control—if it is to be achieved at all—must await a profound value reorientation among soldiers, to occur sometime in the future.

Democratic Consolidation and Civilian Control

Because civilian control is a lengthy process that takes time to complete, it is bound to lag well behind democratization itself.[9] As a system becomes more democratic, it consolidates. To consolidate is to congeal; hitherto fragile components of a political system merge into a more solidified whole. Unfortunately, the parts to a system seldom congeal at the same rate, causing democratization to advance unevenly.[10] Democracies must crawl before they can walk, and walk before they can run. Obviously, the easier tasks are often accomplished first, while more difficult challenges are met afterward. For example, once voter registration lists are compiled and electoral commissions selected, then elections can be called even before all democratic rights have been restored and political parties have been fully institutionalized. Legislative assemblies of one form or another can be convened and in some in-

9. As Felipe Agüero has said, "Civilian supremacy is unlikely to be asserted in one blow." It is, according to him, a lengthy series of decisions involving some civil-military negotiations that help define the final limits to military influence. See his *Soldiers, Civilians, and Democracy: Post-Franco Spain in Comparative Perspective* (Baltimore: The Johns Hopkins University Press, 1995), p. 20.

10. This conforms with Schmitter's notion that some "partial regimes" (i.e., electoral, pressure, clientelist) that represent networks of exchanges, each with its own organizational rules and principles, can consolidate before others. See Philippe C. Schmitter, "The Consolidation of Political Democracy in Southern Europe," unpublished manuscript, Stanford University, 1987, pp. 54–65.

stances must be convened before important constitutional revisions are to be made.

The sequence with which these and other moves are made will no doubt vary from case to case; democracies do not follow any standard script.[11] But because civilian supremacy is so difficult a step, it is one that will normally be completed later, not earlier. In fact, it is best thought of as a destination, not a gateway. When democracy has "arrived," when it is finally congealed, it can count among its victories the achievement of civilian control. As Laurence Whitehead notes, "A thoroughly consolidated democracy is one [in] which the military establishment fully accepts its subordination to legally constituted civil power."[12] It is desirable and in fact necessary to include among the traits assigned to a completely consolidated democratic state, military submission to civilian will.[13] What is ill-advised is to consider civilian control as a precondition for democratic consolidation. If military loyalty to civilian authority was the litmus test for democratic advancement, no Latin American country could, in a reasonable amount of time, progress. Placing civilian control at the front end of the process imposes an unfair burden of proof on societies that are otherwise making concerted headway in their democratic rebuilding efforts.

In reality, democracy in Latin America has already taken significant strides forward, belying the thesis that civilian supremacy must precede or accompany it. The latest democratic wave, which washed ashore in 1979, has swept along with it every country in the region except for Cuba. None of these new democracies has reverted back to authoritarian rule.[14] Many, such as Argentina, Peru, Uruguay, Ecuador, Brazil, and Bolivia, have already passed the "two turnover test" for consolidation, where the baton is handed peacefully from one elected government to another and then another.[15] More voters have participated in these elections than ever before. Anti-in-

11. Philippe C. Schmitter, "Transitology: The Science or the Art of Democratization?" in *The Consolidation of Democracy in Latin America*, ed. Joseph S. Tulchin (Boulder, Colo.: Lynne Rienner Publishers, 1995), pp. 18–19.

12. Laurence Whitehead, "The Consolidation of Fragile Democracies: A Discussion with Illustrations," in *Democracy in the Americas: Stopping the Pendulum*, ed. Robert A. Pastor (New York: Holmes & Meier, 1989), p. 81.

13. Terry Lynn Karl, "Dilemmas of Democratization in Latin America," in *Comparative Political Dynamics: Global Research Perspectives*, ed. Dankwart A. Rustow and Kenneth Paul Erickson (New York: HarperCollins Publishers, 1991), p. 165.

14. Karen Remmer, "The Process of Democratization in Latin America," *Studies in Comparative International Development* 27 (Winter 1992–93): 4–5.

15. Samuel Huntington, *The Third Wave: Democratization in the Late Twentieth Century* (Norman: University of Oklahoma Press, 1991), pp. 266–67.

cumbent movements are alive and well, but citizens take out their anger and frustration about current leaders at the ballot box, not at military headquarters. And the public's embrace of democratic institutions, processes, and the regime itself appears to have remained steady, despite demoralizing economic downturns. In all, "the legacy of the 1980's," writes Karen Remmer, "was thus a set of competitive regimes that was larger, more durable, more inclusionary, and more consensually based than any in the past."[16] That legacy is now the reality of the 1990s.

The military's greater adherence to institutional conventions has, for reasons given, indirectly helped to sustain this new democratic wave. And while a foundation for civilian supremacy has also been laid, the edifice of supremacy is yet to be fully erected. Conceivably, democratization itself could eventually lend a hand in the construction. Public support for and participation in democratic practices could inspire a more profound, lasting military submission to the will of elected authorities. After all, soldiers are also citizens and voters; despite their insular training and socialization, they can never completely divorce themselves from the society they come from. Public sentiments have a way of creeping into the military mindset. Should the perception within the general electorate that democratic institutions, procedures, and governments are legitimate become widespread, firmly rooted, and self-sustaining, it could readily disperse to military society. If soldiers are then persuaded that elected governments are rightfully constituted, they may come to believe that subordination to their political superiors is an obligation, not a preference.

All of this is quite speculative, and Keynes has forewarned us about the long term. For now, what we know with some certainty is that at least in Argentina, and perhaps throughout the Southern Cone, soldiers are generally respectful of the rules of the game, even if they have not as yet sworn allegiance to them. The governing institutions that embody those rules cannot be shunted; for better or worse they are in the way. They mediate the politician's quest for policy fulfillment. And they stand between the soldier's desires and achievements. They calm his anger, channel his demands, and routinize his influence. He has not forsworn and probably never will forswear his political role. But democracy is no worse off so long as he continues to move through the corridors of power.

---

16. Remmer, "The Process of Democratization in Latin America," p. 7.

Selected Bibliography

Books and Articles

Abraham, Henry J. *The Judicial Process*. 5th ed. New York: Oxford University Press, 1986.

Abrahamsson, Bengt. *Military Professionalization and Political Power*. Beverly Hills: Sage Publications, 1972.

Agüero, Felipe. "Political and Military Elites in the Transition to Democracy: Chile Since the 1988 Plebiscite." Paper presented at the XVI Latin American Studies Association Conference, Washington, D.C., April 4–6, 1991.

———. "The Military and the Limits to Democratization in South America." In *Issues in Democratic Consolidation: The New South American Democracies in Comparative Perspective*, edited by Scott Mainwaring, Guillermo O'Donnell, and J. Samuel Valenzuela, 153–98. Notre Dame: University of Notre Dame Press, 1992.

———. *Soldiers, Civilians, and Democracy: Post-Franco Spain in Comparative Perspective*. Baltimore: The Johns Hopkins University Press, 1995.

American Association of Jurists. *Juicios a los militares: Argentina*. Buenos Aires: Asociación Americana de Juristas, 1988.

Americas Watch. *Truth and Partial Justice in Argentina*. New York: Americas Watch, 1987.

———. *Human Rights and the Politics of Agreements: Chile During President Aylwin's First Year*. New York: Americas Watch, 1991.

Ames, Barry. *Political Survival: Politicians and Public Policy in Latin America*. Berkeley and Los Angeles: University of California Press, 1987.

Amnesty International. *Argentina: The Military Juntas and Human Rights*. London: Amnesty International Publications, 1987.

Anderson, Charles. "Toward a Theory of Latin American Politics." In *Politics and Social Change in Latin America: Still a Distinct Tradition?* edited by Howard J. Wiarda, 309–26. Boulder, Colo.: Westview Press, 1992.

Angel Scenna, Miguel. *Los militares*. Buenos Aires: Editorial de Belgrano, 1980.

Argentine National Commission on the Disappeared. *Nunca Más: The Report of the Argentine National Commission on the Disappeared*. New York: Farrar, Straus & Giroux, 1986.

Arias, Omar Breglia, and Omar R. Gauna. *Código penal y leyes complementarias*. 2d ed. Buenos Aires: Editorial Astrea, 1993.

Arriagada, Genaro H. *El pensamiento político de los militares*. Santiago, Chile: Centro de Investigaciones Socioeconómicas, 1981.

———. *The Politics of Power: Pinochet*. Translated by Nancy Morris. Boston: Unwin Hyman, 1988.

Arrow, Kenneth J. *Social Choice and Individual Values*. New Haven: Yale University Press, 1951.

Aylwin, Patricio. *Un desafío colectivo*. Buenos Aires: Planeta, 1988.

Brinzoni, Colonel Ricardo. "Military Restructuring: When More Is Done Than What Is Said." *Agora, Centro de Estudios Internacionales* (April 1993): 1–5.

Brysk, Alison. *The Politics of Human Rights in Argentina: Protest, Change, and Democratization*. Stanford: Stanford University Press, 1994.

Calvert, Susan, and Peter Calvert. *Argentina: Political Culture and Instability*. Pittsburgh: University of Pittsburgh Press, 1989.

Calvo, Roberto. "The Church and the Doctrine of National Security." *Journal of Interamerican Studies and World Affairs* 21 (February 1979): 69–87.

Camarasa, Jorge, Rubén Felice, and Daniel González. *El juicio: Proceso al horror*. Buenos Aires: Sudamericana/Planeta, 1985.

Campos, German Bidart. *The Argentine Supreme Court: The Court of Constitutional Guarantees*. Buenos Aires: Allende and Brea, 1982.

Canitrot, Adolfo. "Discipline as the Central Objective of Economic Policy: An Essay on the Economic Programme of the Argentine Government Since 1976." *World Development* 8 (1980): 913–28.

Caporaso, James A., ed. *The Elusive State: International and Comparative Perspectives*. Newbury Park: Sage Publications, 1989.

Carranza, Mario Esteban. "The Role of Military Expenditure in the Development Process: The Argentina Case, 1946–1980." *Nordic Journal of Latin American Studies* 12 (1983): 115–66.

Carrío, Alejandro D. *The Criminal Justice System of Argentina: An Overview for American Readers*. Baton Rouge: Paul M. Hebert Law Center, 1989.

Carrío, Genaro. *El caso Timmerman: Materiales para el estudio de un "Habeas Corpus."* Buenos Aires: Editorial Universitaria de Buenos Aires, 1987.

Catterberg, Edgardo. *Los Argentinos frente a la política: Cultura política y opinión pública en la transición Argentina a la democracia*. Buenos Aires: Planeta, 1989.

Cavarozzi, Marcelo, and María Grossi. "Argentine Parties Under Alfonsín: From Democratic Reinvention to Political Decline and Hyperinflation." In *The New Argentine Democracy: The Search for a Successful Formula*, edited by Edward C. Epstein, 173–202. New York: Praeger Publishers, 1992.

Centro de Estudios Legales y Sociales. *692: Responsables del terrorismo de estado*. Buenos Aires: Centro de Estudios Legales y Sociales, 1986.

Chalmers, Douglas. "The Politicized State in Latin America." In *Authoritarianism and Corporatism in Latin America*, edited by James M. Malloy, 23–95. Pittsburgh: University of Pittsburgh Press, 1977.

Collier, Ruth Berins, and David Collier. *Shaping the Political Arena: Critical Junctures, the Labor Movement, and Regime Dynamics in Latin America*. Princeton: Princeton University Press, 1991.

Comisión Nacional Sobre la Desaparición de Personas. *Nunca Más: The Report of the Argentine National Commission on the Disappeared*. New York: Farrar, Straus & Giroux, 1986.

Constable, Pamela, and Arturo Valenzuela. *Chile Under Pinochet: A Nation of Enemies.* New York: W. W. Norton & Co., 1991.

Crawford, Kathryn Lee. "Due Obedience and the Rights of Victims: Argentina's Transition to Democracy." *Human Rights Quarterly* 12 (1990): 17–52.

Dahl, Enrique, and Alejandro M. Garro. "Argentina: National Appeals Court (Criminal Division) Judgment on Human Rights Violations by Former Military Leaders: An Introductory Note." *International Legal Materials* 26 (January–May 1987): 317–406.

Dahl, Robert. *Polyarchy: Participation and Opposition.* New Haven: Yale University Press, 1971.

Danopoulos, Constantine. "From Military to Civilian Rule in Contemporary Greece." *Armed Forces and Society* 10 (1984): 229–50.

Diamint, Rut. "Gasto militar y ajuste económico en Argentina." In *Gasto militar en América Latina: Procesos de decisiones y actores claves,* edited by Francisco Rojas Aravena, 139–81. Santiago, Chile: Centro Internacional para el Desarrollo Económico, 1994.

Donadio, Lic. Marcela R. *El papel del Estado Mayor Conjunto de las fuerzas armadas en el sistema de defensa nacional.* Buenos Aires: Centro de Estudios para el Proyecto Nacional (CEPNA), 1993.

Dye, Thomas R. *Understanding Public Policy.* 6th ed. Englewood Cliffs, N.J.: Prentice-Hall, 1987.

Eckstein, Harry, and Ted R. Gurr. *Patterns of Authority: A Structural Basis for Political Inquiry.* New York: John Wiley & Sons, 1975.

El libro del diario del juicio. Buenos Aires: Editorial Perfil, 1985.

Elster, Jon. *Ulysses and the Sirens: Studies in Rationality and Irrationality.* Cambridge: Cambridge University Press, 1979.

English, Adrian J. *Armed Forces of Latin America: Their Histories, Development, Present Strength, and Military Potential.* London and New York: Jane's Publishing, 1984.

Epstein, Edward C. "Labor-State Conflict in the New Argentine Democracy: Parties, Union Factions, and Power Maximizing." In *The New Argentine Democracy: The Search for a Successful Formula,* edited by Edward C. Epstein, 124–56. Westport: Praeger Publishers, 1992.

———. *The New Argentine Democracy: The Search for a Successful Formula.* Westport: Praeger Publishers, 1992.

FAMUS (Familiares y Amigos de los Muertos por la Subversión). *Operación independencia.* Buenos Aires: FAMUS, 1988.

Ferrer, Aldo. "The Argentine Economy, 1976–1979." *Journal of Interamerican Studies and World Affairs* 22 (May 1980): 131–61.

Finer, S. E. *The Man on Horseback: The Role of the Military in Politics,* 2d ed., revised and updated. Boulder, Colo.: Westview Press, 1988.

Fitch, J. Samuel. "Military Role Beliefs in Latin American Democracies: Context, Ideology, and Doctrine in Argentina and Ecuador." Paper prepared for delivery at the 1995 meeting of the Latin American Studies Association, Washington, D.C., September 28–30, 1995.

Fontana, Andrés. "Fuerzas armadas, partidos políticos, y transición a la democracia en Argentina, 1981–1982." Kellogg Institute Working Paper No. 28, July 1984, 1–38.

———. "Political Decision Making by a Military Corporation: Argentina, 1976–83." Ph.D. diss., University of Texas at Austin, 1987.

———. "La política militar del gobierno constitucional Argentino." Centro de Estudios de Estado y Sociedad *CEDES* (July 1987): 1–44.

Fraga, Rosendo. *La cuestión militar: 1987–89.* Buenos Aires: Editorial Centro de Estudios Union para la Nueva Mayoría, 1989.

Franko, Patrice. "De Facto Demilitarization: Budget-Driven Downsizing in Latin America." *Journal of Interamerican Studies and World Affairs* (Spring 1994): 37–73.

Freedman, Lawrence, and Virginia Gamba-Stonehouse. *Signals of War: The Falklands Conflict of 1982.* Princeton: Princeton University Press, 1991.

Gabrielli, Adolfo R. *La Corte Suprema de Justicia y la opinión pública, 1976–1983.* Buenos Aires: Abeledo-Perrot, 1986.

Garro, Alejandro M., and Henry Dahl. "Legal Accountability for Human Rights Violations in Argentina: One Step Forward and Two Steps Backward." *Human Rights Law Journal* 8, nos. 2–4 (1987): 283–345.

Geddes, Barbara. *Politician's Dilemma: Building State Capacity in Latin America.* Berkeley and Los Angeles: University of California Press, 1994.

Geywitz, Carlos Andrade. *Reforma de la constitución política de la República de Chile de 1980.* Santiago, Chile: Editorial Jurídica de Chile, 1991.

Gibson, Edward L. "Democracy and the New Electoral Right in Argentina." *Journal of Interamerican Studies and World Affairs* 32 (Fall 1990): 177–228.

Gillespie, Charles G. "Uruguay's Transition from Collegial Military-Technocratic Rule." In *Transitions from Authoritarian Rule: Latin America,* edited by Guillermo O'Donnell, Philippe C. Schmitter, and Laurence Whitehead, 173–95. Baltimore: The Johns Hopkins University Press, 1987.

Gillespie, Richard. *Soldiers of Perón: Argentina's Montoneros.* London: Clarendon Press, 1982.

González, Luis. "Uruguay, 1980–81: An Unexpected Opening." *Latin American Research Review* 18 (1983): 63–76.

Goodman, Louis W., Johanna S. R. Mendelson, and Juan Rial, eds. *The Military and Democracy: The Future of Civil-Military Relations in Latin America.* Lexington, Mass.: Lexington Books, 1990.

Groisman, Enrique I. *La Corte Suprema de Justicia durante la dictadura (1976–1983).* Documento 89. Buenos Aires: Centro de Investigaciones Sociales Sobre el Estado y la Administración, 1987.

Hall, Peter. *Governing the Economy: The Politics of State Intervention in Britain and France.* New York: Oxford University Press, 1986.

Hobkirk, Michael D. *The Politics of Defense Budgeting: A Study of Organization and Resource Allocation in the United Kingdom and the United States.* London: Macmillan Publishing Co., 1984.

Human Rights Watch/Americas. "Chile, Unsettled Business: Human Rights in Chile at the Start of the Frei Presidency." *Human Rights Watch/Americas* 6, no. 6 (May 1994): 1–35.

Hunter, Wendy. "Back to the Barracks? The Military in Post-Authoritarian Brazil." Ph.D. diss., University of California, Berkeley, 1992.

———. "Politicians Against Soldiers: Contesting the Military in Postauthoritarian Brazil." *Comparative Politics* 27 (July 1995): 425–43.

———. *Eroding Military Influence in Brazil: Politicians Against Soldiers.* Chapel Hill: University of North Carolina Press, 1997.

Huntington, Samuel. *The Soldier and the State: The Theory and Politics of Civil-Military Relations.* Cambridge, Mass.: Harvard University Press, 1957.

———. *Political Order in Changing Societies.* New Haven: Yale University Press, 1968.

———. *The Third Wave: Democratization in the Late Twentieth Century.* Norman: University of Oklahoma Press, 1991.

Igounet, Dr. Oscar, and Dr. Oscar Igounet (hijo). *Código de Justicia Militar.* Buenos Aires: Librería de Jurista, 1985.

Ikenberry, James G. "Conclusion: An Institutional Approach to American Foreign Economic Policy." *International Organization* 42 (Winter 1988): 219–43.

Immergut, Ellen M. "The Rules of the Game: The Logic of Health Policy-Making in France, Switzerland, and Sweden." In *Structuring Politics: Institutionalism in Comparative Analysis,* edited by Sven Steinmo, Kathleen Thelen, and Frank Longstreth, 57–89. Cambridge: Cambridge University Press, 1992.

International Commission of Jurists. *Chile: A Time of Reckoning.* Geneva: Centre for the Independence of Judges and Lawyers, 1992.

Johnson, John. *The Military and Society in Latin America.* Stanford: Stanford University Press, 1964.

Karl, Terry Lynn. "Dilemmas of Democratization in Latin America." In *Comparative Political Dynamics: Global Research Perspectives,* edited by Dankwart A. Rustow and Kenneth Paul Erickson, 163–91. New York: HarperCollins Publishers, 1991.

Keegan, John. *World Armies.* 2d ed. London: Macmillan Publishers, 1983.

Kemp, Kenneth W., and Charles Hudlin. "Civil Supremacy over the Military: Its Nature and Limits." *Armed Forces and Society* 19 (Fall 1992): 7–26.

Klare, Michael T., and Cynthia Arnson. *Supplying Repression: U.S. Support for Authoritarian Regimes Abroad.* Washington, D.C.: Institute for Policy Studies, 1987.

Knight, Jack. *Institutions and Social Conflict.* Cambridge: Cambridge University Press, 1992.

Kohn, Richard. "Out of Control: The Crisis in Civil-Military Relations." *The National Interest* 35 (Spring 1994): 3–17.

Korb, Lawrence. "The Budget Process in the Department of Defense, 1947–1977: The Strengths and Weaknesses of Three Systems." *Public Administration Review* (July–August 1977): 334–46.

Krasner, Stephen D. "U.S. Commercial and Monetary Policy: Unravelling the Paradox of External Strength and Internal Weakness." *International Organization* 31 (August 1977): 635–71.

Lewis, Paul H. *The Crisis of Argentine Capitalism.* Chapel Hill: University of North Carolina Press, 1990.

Lieuwen, Edwin. *Armies and Politics in Latin America.* New York: Frederick A. Praeger, 1960.

Linz, Juan, and Alfred Stepan. *The Breakdown of Democratic Regimes: Crisis, Breakdown, and Reequilibration.* Baltimore: The Johns Hopkins University Press, 1978.

Little, Walter. "Civil-Military Relations in Contemporary Argentina." *Government and Opposition* 19 (Spring 1984): 207–24.

López, Ernesto. *Seguridad nacional y sedición militar.* Buenos Aires: Legasa, 1987.

———. *El último levantamiento.* Buenos Aires: Editorial Legasa, 1988.

———. "La reducción del gasto militar en Argentina: Algunas implicaciones económica y políticas." Seminario sobre proliferación de armamentos y medidas de fomento de confianzo y la seguridad en América Latina, asunción del Paraguay, January 18–20, 1993.

———. *Ni la ceniza ni la gloria: Actores, sistema político, y cuestión militar en los años de Alfonsín*. Buenos Aires: Universidad Nacional de Quilmes, 1994.

López, Ernesto, and David Pion-Berlin. *Democracia y cuestión militar*. Buenos Aires: Universidad Nacional de Quilmes, 1996.

Loveman, Brian. "¿Misión Cumplida? Civil-Military Relations and the Chilean Political Transition." *Journal of Interamerican Studies and World Affairs* 33 (Fall 1991): 35–74.

Loveman, Brian, and Thomas M. Davies Jr., eds. *The Politics of Antipolitics: The Military in Latin America*. 2d ed. Lincoln: University of Nebraska Press, 1989.

Lowenthal, Abraham F., and J. Samuel Fitch, eds. *Armies and Politics in Latin America*. Revised edition. New York: Holmes and Meier, 1986.

Mainwaring, Scott. "Transitions to Democracy and Democratic Consolidation: Theoretical and Comparative Issues." In *Issues in Democratic Consolidation: The New South American Democracies in Comparative Perspective*, edited by Scott Mainwaring, Guillermo O'Donnell, and J. Samuel Valenzuela, 294–341. Notre Dame: University of Notre Dame Press, 1992.

Malamud-Goti, Jaime. "Transitional Governments in the Breach: Why Punish State Criminals?" *Human Rights Quarterly* 12 (1990): 1–16.

Malloy, James M., ed. *Authoritarianism and Corporatism in Latin America*. Pittsburgh: University of Pittsburgh Press, 1984.

March, James G., and Johan P. Olsen. "The New Institutionalism: Organizational Factors in Political Life." *The American Political Science Review* 78 (September 1984): 734–49.

Masterson, Daniel M. *Militarism and Politics in Latin America: Peru from Sánchez Cerro to Sendero Luminoso*. New York: Greenwood Press, 1991.

McGuire, James W. "Union Political Tactics and Democratic Consolidation in Alfonsín's Argentina, 1983–1989." *Latin American Research Review* 27, no. 1 (1992): 37–74.

McKelvey, Richard D., and Peter C. Ordeshook. "An Experimental Study of the Effects of Procedural Rules on Committee Behavior." *Journal of Politics* 46 (1984): 182–205.

Migdal, Joel S. *Strong Societies and Weak States: State-Society Relations and State Capabilities in the Third World*. Princeton: Princeton University Press, 1988.

Milenky, Edward S. "Argentina." In *Security Policies of Developing Countries*, edited by Edward A. Kolodziej and Robert E. Harkavy, 27–51. Lexington, Mass.: Lexington Books, 1982.

Monroe, Kristen Renwick, ed. *The Economic Approach to Politics: A Critical Assessment of the Theory of Rational Action*. New York: HarperCollins Publishers, 1991.

Nino, Carlos S. "The Duty to Punish Past Abuses of Human Rights Put into Context: The Case of Argentina." *Yale Law Journal* 100, no. 8 (June 1991): 2619–40.

Norden, Deborah L., *Military Rebellion in Argentina: Between Coups and Consolidation*. Omaha: University of Nebraska Press, 1996.

Nordlinger, Eric. *Soldiers in Politics: Military Coups and Governments*. Englewood Cliffs, N.J.: Prentice-Hall, 1977.

———. *On the Autonomy of the Democratic State*. Cambridge, Mass.: Harvard University Press, 1981.

Nun, José. "The Middle Class Military Coup Revisited." In *Armies and Politics in Latin America*, edited by Abraham F. Lowenthal and J. Samuel Fitch, 59–95. New York: Holmes & Meier, 1986.

Nunn, Frederick M. *Yesterday's Soldiers: European Military Professionalism in South America, 1890–1945*. Lincoln: University of Nebraska Press, 1983.

———. *The Time of the Generals: Latin American Professional Militarism in World Perspective*. Lincoln: University of Nebraska Press, 1992.

O'Donnell, Guillermo. "State and Alliances in Argentina, 1956–1976." *Journal of Development Studies* 15 (October 1978): 3–33.

———. *Modernization and Bureaucratic-Authoritarianism: Studies in South American Politics*. Berkeley: Institute of International Studies, 1979.

———. *Bureaucratic-Authoritarianism: Argentina, 1966–1973, in Comparative Perspective*. Berkeley and Los Angeles: University of California Press, 1988.

O'Donnell, Guillermo, and Philippe C. Schmitter. *Transitions from Authoritarian Rule: Tentative Conclusions About Uncertain Democracies*. Baltimore: The Johns Hopkins University Press, 1986.

Osiel, Mark. "The Making of Human Rights Policy in Argentina: The Impact of Ideas and Interests on a Legal Conflict." *Journal of Latin American Studies* 18 (1986): 135–80.

Peralta-Ramos, Monica. *The Political Economy of Argentina: Power and Class Since 1930*. Boulder, Colo.: Westview Press, 1992.

Perlmutter, Amos, and Valerie Plave Bennett, eds. *The Political Influence of the Military: A Comparative Reader*. New Haven: Yale University Press, 1980.

Philip, George. *The Military in South American Politics*. London: Croom Helm, 1985.

Pion-Berlin, David. "The Fall of Military Rule in Argentina: 1976–1983." *Journal of Interamerican Studies and World Affairs* 27 (Summer 1985): 55–76.

———. *The Ideology of State Terror: Economic Doctrine and Political Repression in Argentina and Peru*. Boulder, Colo.: Lynne Rienner Publishers, 1989.

———. "Between Confrontation and Accommodation: Military and Government Policy in Democratic Argentina." *Journal of Latin American Studies* 23 (October 1991): 543–71.

———. "Military Autonomy and Emerging Democracies in South America." *Comparative Politics* 25 (October 1992): 83–102.

———. "To Prosecute or to Pardon? Human Rights Decisions in the Latin American Southern Cone." *Human Rights Quarterly* 16 (February 1994): 105–30.

Pion-Berlin, David, and Ernesto López. "A House Divided: Crisis, Cleavage, and Conflict in the Argentine Army." In *The New Argentine Democracy: The Search for a Successful Formula*, edited by Edward C. Epstein, 69–73. Westport: Praeger Publishers, 1992.

Pion-Berlin, David, and George Lopez. "Of Victims and Executioners: Argentine State Terror, 1975–79." *International Studies Quarterly* 35 (March 1991): 63–86.

Potash, Robert. *The Army and Politics in Argentina, 1928–1945: Yrigoyen to Perón*. Stanford: Stanford University Press, 1969.

———. *The Army and Politics in Argentina, 1945–1962: Perón to Frondizi*. Stanford: Stanford University Press, 1980.

Przeworski, Adam. "Some Problems in the Study of the Transition to Democracy." In *Transitions from Authoritarian Rule: Comparative Perspectives*, edited by Guillermo O'Donnell, Philippe C. Schmitter, and Laurence Whitehead, 47–63. Baltimore: The Johns Hopkins University Press, 1986.

Rabkin, Rhoda. "The Aylwin Government and Tutelary Democracy: A Concept in Search of a Case?" *Journal of Interamerican Studies and World Affairs* 34 (Winter 1992–93): 119–94.

Ranis, Peter. *Argentine Workers: Peronism and Contemporary Class Consciousness.* Pittsburgh: University of Pittsburgh Press, 1992.

Rattenbach Commission. *Informe Rattenbach: El drama de Malvinas.* Buenos Aires: Ediciones Espartaco, 1988.

Remmer, Karen. "Redemocratization and the Impact of Authoritarian Rule in Latin America." *Comparative Politics* 17 (April 1985): 253–75.

———. *Military Rule in Latin America.* Boston: Unwin Hyman, 1989.

———. "The Process of Democratization in Latin America." *Studies in Comparative International Development* 27 (Winter 1992–93): 3–24.

República de Chile. *Código de justicia militar.* Santiago, Chile: Editorial Jurídica de Chile, 1992.

———. *Constitución política de la República de Chile.* Santiago, Chile: Editorial Jurídica de Chile, 1995.

Rial, Juan. *Los militares en tanto partido político sustituto: Frente a la redemocratización.* Serie Documentos de Trabajo 128/86. Montevideo: Centro Informaciones y Estudios del Uruguay (CIESU), 1985.

———. *Las fuerzas armadas: ¿Soldados-políticos o garantes de la democracia?* Montevideo: Centro Informaciones y Estudios del Uruguay (CIESU), 1986.

———. "The Armed Forces and Democracy: The Interests of Latin American Military Corporations in Sustaining Democratic Regimes." In *The Military and Democracy: The Future of Civil-Military Relations in Latin America,* edited by Louis W. Goodman, Johanna Mendelson, and Juan Rial, 277–80. Lexington, Mass.: Lexington Books, 1990.

———. *Estructura legal de las fuerzas armadas del Uruguay: Un análisis político.* Montevideo: Centro de Informaciones y Estudios del Uruguay/Sociedad de Análisis Político, 1992.

Ricci, María Susana, and J. Samuel Fitch. "Ending Military Regimes in Argentina: 1966–73 and 1976–83." In *The Military and Democracy: The Future of Civil-Military Relations in Latin America,* edited by Louis W. Goodman, Johanna Mendelson, and Juan Rial, 55–74. Lexington, Mass.: Lexington Books, 1990.

Rock, David. *Argentina 1516–1987: From Spanish Colonization to Alfonsín.* Berkeley and Los Angeles: University of California Press, 1987.

Rouquié, Alain. *Poder militar y sociedad política en la Argentina.* Vol. 1. Buenos Aires: Emecé Editores, 1981.

———. *Poder militar y sociedad política en la Argentina.* Vol. 2. Buenos Aires: Emecé Editores, 1982.

———. *The Military and the State in Latin America.* Berkeley and Los Angeles: University of California Press, 1987.

Rustow, Dakwart A. "Transitions to Democracy." *Comparative Politics* 2 (April 1970): 337–63.

Sancinetti, Marcelo A. *Derechos humanos en la Argentina post-dictatorial.* Buenos Aires: Lerner Editores Asociados, 1988.

Sarkesian, Sam. *Beyond the Battlefield: The New Military Professionalism.* New York: Pergamon Press, 1981.

Schmitter, Philippe C. "Transitology: The Science or the Art of Democratization?" In *The Consolidation of Democracy in Latin America,* edited by Joseph S. Tulchin, 11–41. Boulder, Colo.: Lynne Rienner Publishers, 1995.

Schumpeter, Joseph A. *Capitalism, Socialism, and Democracy.* New York: Harper & Row Publishers, 1950.

Schvarzer, Jorge. *Martínez de Hoz: La lógica política de la política económica.* Centro de Investigaciones Sociales Sobre el Estado y la Administración (CISEA), Ensayos y Tesis 4. Buenos Aires: CISEA, 1983.

Sikkink, Kathryn. *Ideas and Institutions: Developmentalism in Brazil and Argentina.* Ithaca, N.Y.: Cornell University Press, 1991.

Simon, Herbert A. "A Behavioral Model of Rational Choice." *Quarterly Journal of Economics* 69 (1955): 99–118.

Skocpol, Theda. "Bringing the State Back In: Strategies of Analysis in Current Research." In *Bringing the State Back In,* edited by Peter Evans, Dietrich Rueschmeyer, and Theda Skocpol, 3–37. Cambridge: Cambridge University Press, 1985.

———, ed. *Vision and Method in Historical Sociology.* Cambridge: Cambridge University Press, 1984.

Smith, Peter H. *Argentina and the Failure of Democracy: Conflict Among Political Elites, 1904–1955.* Madison: University of Wisconsin Press, 1974.

Smith, William C. *Authoritarianism and the Crisis of the Argentine Political Economy.* Stanford: Stanford University Press, 1989.

———. "Hyperinflation, Macroeconomic Instability, and Neoliberal Restructuring in Democratic Argentina." In *The New Argentine Democracy: The Search for a Successful Formula,* edited by Edward C. Epstein, 20–60. Westport: Praeger Publishers, 1992.

Snow, Peter G., and Luigi Manzetti. *Political Forces in Argentina.* 3d ed. Westport: Praeger Publishers, 1993.

Steinmo, Sven, Kathleen Thelen, and Frank Longstreth, eds. *Structuring Politics: Historical Institutionalism in Comparative Analysis.* Cambridge: Cambridge University Press, 1992.

Stepan, Alfred. "State Power and Civil Society in the Southern Cone of Latin America." In *Bringing the State Back In,* edited by Peter Evans, Dietrich Rueschmeyer, and Theda Skocpol, 317–43. Cambridge: Cambridge University Press, 1985.

———. *Rethinking Military Politics: Brazil and the Southern Cone.* Princeton: Princeton University Press, 1988.

Tapia Váldez, Jorge A. *El terrorismo del estado: La doctrina de la seguridad nacional en el Cono Sur.* Mexico City: Editorial Nueva Imagen, 1980.

Tokman, Victor E. "Global Monetarism and Destruction of Industry." *CEPAL Review* 23 (August 1984): 107–21.

Truman, David B. *The Governmental Process: Political Interests and Public Opinion.* New York: Alfred A. Knopf, 1960.

Turner, Frederick. "The Aftermath of Defeat in Argentina." *Current History* 2 (1983): 58–61, 85–87.

Unión Cívica Radical (UCR). *Platform electoral nacional de la Union Cívica Radical, 1983.* Buenos Aires: UCR, 1983.

Varas, Augusto, ed. *Democracy Under Siege: New Military Power in Latin America.* New York: Greenwood Press, 1989.

Verbitsky, Horacio. *Civiles y militares: Memoria secreta de la transición.* Buenos Aires: Editorial Contrapunto, 1987.

Waisman, Carlos H. *Reversal of Development in Argentina: Postwar Counterrevolutionary Policies and Their Structural Consequences.* Princeton: Princeton University Press, 1987.

Waldmann, Peter, and Ernesto Váldez, eds. *El poder militar en la Argentina: 1976–1981*. Buenos Aires: Editorial Galerna, 1983.

Weinstein, Martin. *Uruguay: Democracy at the Crossroads*. Boulder, Colo.: Westview Press, 1988.

Welch, Claude E., Jr. *Civilian Control of the Military: Theories and Cases from Developing Countries*. Albany: State University of New York Press, 1976.

————. *No Farewell to Arms: Military Disengagement from Politics in Africa and Latin America*. Boulder, Colo.: Westview Press, 1987.

Wesson, Robert, ed. *New Military Politics in Latin America*. New York: Praeger Publishers, 1982.

————. *The Latin American Military Institution*. New York: Praeger Publishers, 1986.

Whitehead, Laurence. "The Consolidation of Fragile Democracies: A Discussion with Illustrations." In *Democracy in the Americas: Stopping the Pendulum*, edited by Robert A. Pastor, 76–95. New York: Holmes & Meier, 1989.

Wildavsky, Aaron. *Budgeting: A Comparative Theory of Budgetary Processes*. Boston: Little, Brown and Co., 1975.

Wildavsky, Aaron, and Jeffrey L. Pressman. *Policy Implementation*. Berkeley and Los Angeles: University of California Press, 1984.

Wixler, Lt. Keith E. "Argentina's Geopolitics and Her Revolutionary Diesel-Electric Submarines." *Naval War College Review* 42 (Winter 1989): 86–107.

World Bank. *Argentina: From Insolvency to Growth*. Washington, D.C.: World Bank, 1993.

Wynia, Gary. *Argentina in the Postwar Era: Economic Policymaking in a Divided Society*. Albuquerque: University of New Mexico Press, 1972.

Zagorski, Paul W. *Democracy vs. National Security: Civil-Military Relations in Latin America*. Boulder, Colo.: Lynne Rienner Publishers, 1992.

Interviewees

(A Partial List)

Argentina

Alegría, Brig. Maj. Alberto (Ret.)
Alfonsín, Dr. Raúl R.
Antonio Remetin, Gen. Mario (Ret.)
Auel, Gen. Heriberto (Ret.)
Beltrán, Dr. Virgilio
Berhongaray, Antonio (Dip.)
Bisciotti, Victorio O. (Dip.)
Brinzoni, Col. Ricardo
Costa, Juan Carlos
Cruces, Lt. Col. Néstor J. (Ret.)
Cucchiara, Emilio
D'Alessio, Andrés José
Deambrosio, Carlos
de la Torre, Enrique J.

De'Orué, Julio Alberto
Diamint, Rut
Entelman, Ricardo
Etchechoury, Dr. Guillermo Federico
Fernández Torres, Gen. Julio (Ret.)
Ferreira Pinho, Juan
Giadone, Dante
Giavarini, Dr. Adalberto Rodríguez
Horton, Cap. José Maria
Hugo Storani, Conrado (Dip.)
Jaunarena, Dr. José Horacio (Dip.)
Laíño, Gen. Aníbal
Lavedra, Ricardo R. Gil
Manuel Ugarte, José
Mignone, Emilio
Nino, Carlos
Osses, Almirante Emilio
Patiño Mayer, Hernán
Reyser, Contraalmirante Horacio F.
Stafforini, Eduardo M.
Steyerthal, Navy Cap. Leonardo Arnoldo

Tello, Angel
Toma, Miguel Angel (Dip.)
Torzillo, Dr. José Alberto
de Vergara, Col. Evergisto
Villalba, Col.
Zabala, Lt. Gen. Carlos María

Raúl Ferreira, Juan
Sampedro, Lt. Gen. Raúl V. (Ret.)
Santoro, Walter R. (Sen.)
Sosa, Col. Julio M.
Trabal, Col. Ramón
Vener Carboni, Walter (Dip.)
Villar, Col. Raúl A.

Chile

Ballerino, Gen. Jorge (Ret.)
Bitar, Sergio (Sen.)
Castillo, Jaime
Cerda Fernández, Carlos
Cumplido Cereceda, Francisco
Daza Valenzuela, Pedro
Domínguez Vial, Andrés
García, Gonzalo
Gutiérrez, Hugo
Letelier del Solar, Fabiola
Margarita Morel Gumucio, Isabel
Pereira, Pamela
Rojas Saavedra, Dr. Patricio
Sálazar, Hector
Sánchez Edwards, Marcos
Viera-Gallos, José Antonio (Dip.)
Zalaquett, José

Uruguay

Aguiar, Julio (Dip.)
Barreneche, Dr. Claudia Zúñiga
Bonino, Daoiz Librán (Sen.)
Brito, Dr. Mariano R.
Canet, Brum (Dip.)
Carrasco, Julio Aguiar (Dip.)
Casaravilla, Juan Young
Fernández Parés, Navy Cap. Juan José
   (Ret.)
Gadea, Navy Col. Bernabé
González, Rodolfo
González, Suely
Iturria, Raúl
Lazbal Burgos, Navy Cap. Eduardo
Licandro, Gen. Víctor M. (Ret.)
Martins, Dr. Daniel Hugo
Pache, Lt. Gen. Carlos P. (Ret.)

Newspapers

Argentina

Ambito Financiero
Clarín
Clarín Edición Internacional
La Nación
La Nación Edición Internacional
Página Doce
La Prensa
La Razón
Review of the River Plate

Chile

Ercilla
Hoy
El Mercurio
La Segunda

Uruguay

Búsqueda
El Observador

International

El Financiero Internacional de México
Latin American Monitor
*Latin American Regional Report: Southern
   Cone*
Latin America Weekly Report
New York Times

Index

Abrahamsson, Bengt, 15 n. 8
Agosti, Brig. Osvaldo, 83
Agüero, Felipe, 220 n. 9
airforce, 172, 172 n. 100, 173
Alfonsín, Raúl R.
    and the civil-military balance of power, 76–77, 101–2
    and Congress, 103
    and due obedience law, 99–101
    human rights advisors, 80, 80 n.
    human rights policy of, 75–77, 93–94, 96; formulation of, 77–80, 79 n. 8; long-term impact of, 104–6
    and judiciary, 92–94, 96, 102
    limiting military power, 116, 121; by reducing military spending, 121
    and defense reform 142, 149, 152, 152 n. 34
    and the Ministry of Defense, 158
    apprehension about defense reform, 166
    and punto final, 97–99
    views about military, 80–81
Alfonsín Government, 92–95, 95 n. 64, 149–50
Alsogaray, Gen. Alvaro, 66, 72
Ames, Barry, 115
amnesty law, Chilean, 194, 202
Andrés Perrotta, Rafael, 59
Argentine civil-military relations. See civil-military relations
Argentine institutions. See institutions
Argentine military. See military
Argentine National Commission on the Disappeared (CONADEP), 58–59, 78–79, 82, 90–91 n. 46
armed forces. See military
army
    in Chile, 197

counterinsurgency operations, 145
    headquarters of, 154
    self-reform, 171, 175
    in Uruguay, 182–83
arms industry, 143–44
Asamblea Permanente de Derechos Humanos, 90
Astiz, Lt. Alfredo, 82, 95
Auel, Gen. Heriberto, 165–66
Australia, 114, Table 5.2
authority, decision-making
    concentration of, 4–5, 36–37, 39, 139, 213
    dispersion of, 102–5, 176–77, 209, 211, 214
    and human rights policy, 214
    and institutional design, 36, 39
    and policy outcomes, 39–40, 104–5, 139, 177, 198–99, 210–11
autonomy, decision-making
    and budgeting, 137
    functional, 37–38
    and leadership, 38–39
    levels of 4, 38–39, 139, 177
    of military, 33–34, 34 n. 69, 190
    and policy outcomes, 39–40, 102–3, 105, 137–39
    types of, 4, 37–38
Avenida Leandro Alem, 154
Aylwin, Patricio
    decision-making authority over military, 197–98
    defense of Rettig Commission, 198
    human rights policy of, 194–210, 194 nn. 58–60; first phase, 196–99; and institutions, 204; risks of, 196; strategy of, 204; second phase, 199–210; secret trials, 207–8, 208 n. 112, 209; success of, 198–99
    interpretation of amnesty law, 202
    principles of, 198

Bahia Blanca, 152
Balbín, Ricardo, 51, 70
Battle y Ordoñez, José, 187–88 n. 31
Beagle Islands, 112, 170 n. 90
Bennett, Valerie, 13
Berhongaray, Antonio, 126
Bignone, Gen. Reynaldo, 62, 91 n. 47, 158 n. 51
boinazo, 207
Bolivia, 221
Borrás, Raúl, 80–81, 81 n. 14, 82, 92–93, 99,
    142 n. 1, 149, 162, Table 6.1, 165, 174 n.
    108, 176 n. 113
Brazil, 114–15, Table 5.2, 221
Brinzoni, Col. Ricardo Guillermo, 171
Brito, Mariano R., 182, 182 n. 9, 183, 187 n. 30,
    189
budgeting, defense
    and chain of command, 138
    civilian influence over, 127–37, 215
    and concentration of authority, 137–40,
        214–15
    Congressional role in, 133–36
    cost appraisal, 131–32
    and defense reform, 140, 153, 154
    and government cabinet, 129
    and institutions, 127–28, 136–37
    military influence over, 108–9, 109 n. 6, 113,
        113 n. 13, 128–30, 139
    military spending requests, 131
    prioritization of, 132
    to reduce military power, 116
    rules of, 130, 138–39
    in Uruguay, 191–93; civilian influence over,
        191; negotiation over, 192; military influ-
        ence over, 192–93
Buenos Aires, 142 n. 2, 145
Burns, James M., 38

Cáceres, Col. Gustavo (r), 151 n. 30
Camilión, Oscar, 162, Table 6.1
Campo de Mayo, 71–72, 100
Camps, Ramón, 90, 91 n. 47
Canada, 114, Table 5.2
Canale, Brig. Hector N., 94
Canelones, Province of (Uruguay) 188 n. 34
Canitrot, Adolfo, 111
carabineros, 197
carapintadas, 71, 73, 101 n. 85, 103, 168
Caridi, Gen. Dante, 99 n. 79

Carranza, Roque, 23, 91, 93 n. 59, 150, 162,
    Table 6.1
Casa Rosada, 154
case selection. *See* methodology
Castro, Fidel, 143
Cavallo, Domingo, 123–26
Centro de Altos Estudios Nacionales (CALEN),
    186
Centro de Estudios Legales y Sociales (CELS), 90,
    90 n. 45, 91, 91 n. 49
CGT. *See Confederación General de Trabajadores*
chain of command, 137–38, 197–98
Chalmers, Douglas, 128–29
Chamorro, Adm. Rubén, 82
Chanfreau, Oyarce Alfonso, 203
Chile
    binomial electoral system, 200, 206
    compared to Uruguay and Argentina, 42–44,
        179
    Congress: blocking of judicial reform, 205,
        205 n. 101, 206; military influence over,
        199; opposition to trials, 208–9
    constitutional reform, 206–7
    designated senators, 199–200, 200 n. 79
    human rights, 194–210
    judiciary: autonomy of, 200–201, 201nn.
        82–83; criticisms of, 201; lack of reform,
        206; impeachment of judge, 203; military
        influence over, 199, 201–2; supreme court,
        200–204
    military budget, 115
    military courts, 205
    military size, 114, Table 5.2
    presidency, 198–99
    political right, 205
    separation of powers, 200, 211
    transition to civilian rule, 43, 180–81
Chilean National Commission on Truth and
    Reconciliation. *See* Rettig Commission
civil-military relations
    and Argentine democracy, 46
    balance of power in, 3–4, 6–7, 13–14, 30,
        108–9
    and democratic institutions, 1–3, 5, 7–8
    in equilibrium, 13–19
    and law, 20
    institutional mediation of, 21, 31–32, 34–41
    normalization of, 19–20, 19 n. 20, 74
    and policy, 20
    and the state, 9, 45
    in Uruguay, 193–94

civilian control, 1 n., 9, 15, 16, 19 n. 19
and democratic consolidation, 220–21, 220
n. 9
subjective, 155–56
civilian empowerment, 39, 160. *See also* autonomy
civilian supremacy. *See* civilian control
civilians. *See* politicians
Clausewitz, Carl von, 27
Clinton, Bill, 8n
Colombia, 114
Comandante del Teatro de Operaciones Atlántico del Sur (CTOAS), 146–47
Comité Militar (COMIL), 146–147, 157, 163
Comodor Rivadavia, 147
Concertación, 194 n. 60, 200, 205, 205 n. 101, 208
Confederación General de Trabajadores (CGT), 55, 67–69, 72
Confederación Rurales Argentina, 57
Congress
in Chile: congressional self interest, 209–11; opposition to trials, 208–9
committee on budgeting and finance, 135
human rights legislation, 103
limited budgetary power of, 133, 134, 134 n. 78, 136
military influence in, 136, 136 n. 82
in Uruguay, 191–93
Consejo Nacional de Seguridad (CONASE), 157, 157 n. 46, 163
conservative elites, 65–66
Córdoba, 98, 123, 145
Corrientes, Province of, 147
counterinsurgency, 144–45. *See also* military courts. *See* judiciary
Crespo, Brig. Gen. Ernesto, 118, 147
Cumplido, Francisco, 206
Curutchet, Gen. Juan C., 183

D'Alessio, Andrés, 86, 96
Dahl, Robert, 215 n. 1
defense establishment, 169
defense law, 6, 155, 158, 166
defense minister, 158, 161–62, 168, 186–87
defense reform, 7, 40
absence of 141, 152–53, 165–69
and budget cuts, 153
indicators of, 148
and institutions, 35, 41

and national defense, 151
obstacles to, 142
planning of, 165
and presidential role, 142, 164–70, 173, 175, 177
superficiality of, 152
and unified action, 148
in Uruguay: military opposition to, 183, 187–89; presidential role in, 183–84; presidential weakness and, 189
democratic breakdown, 52–53
democratic consolidation, 220–21
democratic institutions, 3, 222. *See also* institutions
democratic process, 215, 215 n. 1
democratic state, 3. *See also* institutions
Department of Defense (DOD), 135, 138
DINA (Dirección de Inteligencia Nacional), 203
Dirección General de Fabricaciones Militares (DGFM), 143
Dirty War, 58, 61, 71, 78, 79, 82, 84, 90, 93, 97–98, 102 n. 88, 105, 109 n. 5, 110, 144
dominant classes, 56–58
due obedience, law of, 99–101, 100 n. 81, 101 n. 85
due obedience, principle of, 78–79, 85, 86, 88, 94–95, 100 n. 83, 102, 102 n. 88

economic policy, 120–21, 123–25
Ecuador, 221
Edificio Libertador, 154
Ejército Revolucionario del Pueblo (ERP), 144, 145
El Cronista Comercial (Buenos Aires), 59
El Mercurio (Santiago), 209
EMC. *See Estado Mayor Conjunto*
EMC Policy and Strategy Department. See *Estado Mayor Conjunto*
Escuela Mecánica de la Armada (ESMA), 99
Estado Mayor Conjunto (EMC), 98, 126, 128, 132, 152, 155, 163–65, 164 n. 71, 167–69, 169 n. 85, 174, 176–77
Etchechoury, Guillermo, 130

Federal Court of Appeals. *See* judiciary
Fernández Torres, Gen. Julio, 119–20, 165
Finer, S. E., 14–15, 34 n. 69
Fitch, J. Samuel, 17–18
Frondizi, Arturo, 51–52, 52 n. 20, 156–57

Galtieri, Gen. Leopoldo, 61–62, 147–48
Garcia, Gen Daniel, 183
Geddes, Barbara, 210
Gibson, Edward, 66
Gil Lavedra, Ricardo R., 86
González, Antonio Erman, 162, Table 6.1, 167, 170
González, Rodolfo, 189 n. 39
governmental agencies. See institutions
guerrillas, 142, 144–45

Hagelin, Dagmar, 82, 95
human rights
    policy, 7, 9, 40; and the balance of power, 76, 101–2; in Chile, 194; and Congress, 75, 103; formulation of, 77–80, 194
    trials, 80–83; benefits of, 105–6; and military judiciary, 80–82; prolongation of, 84, 91–94, 97; in Chile, 207–8, 208 n. 112
    policy outcome, 102, 104–5; and authority, 102–5, 214; and autonomy, 102–3, 105, 214; in Chile, 195, 214; and institutional design, 104–5
human rights groups
    in Chile, 202–3
    and judicial procedure, 90–91, 90 n. 45
    repression against, 90, 90 n. 45
    tactics of, 91, 91 n. 49
human rights violations. See state terror
Hunter, Wendy, 33 n. 66
hypotheses of conflict, 165–66, 182

Illia, Arturo, 50–51, 52, 157
institutional protocol, 8
institutional theory, 22, 24–25
institutions, 3–4, 7–8
    and authority, 36–37
    and budgeting, 137
    and civil-military balance of power, 35
    and decision-making autonomy, 37–39, 213
    defense, 154–64, 184–87, 189
    and defining self-interest, 209–10
    design of, 3, 34–41, 195
    interest group influence over, 32
    and issues, 41, 41 n. 82
    legitimacy of, 217
    mediating influence of, 21, 34–41, 222
    military influence over, 7, 31, 101, 213
    and military rebellion, 103
    military respect for, 212, 215–17, 222

and policy outcomes, 21, 35, 39, 41, 104, 181, 195, 206–7, 209
    procedural dimensions of, 5, 215–17, 222
    relative strength of, 2, 31
Instituto Militar de Estudios Superiores (IMES), 188
interest group theory, 27–29, 29 n. 48
interest groups, 27, 30, 57
Inzaurralde, María Amelia, 95
item thirty. See judiciary
Iturria, Raúl, 183 n. 12, 187 n. 30

Jaunarena, Horacio, 92, 93 n. 59, 94–96, 99, 101 n. 87, 162, Table 6.1
Johnson, Lyndon, 8 n. 7
Joint Chiefs of Staff (Argentina). See Estado Mayor Conjunto
Joint Chiefs of Staff (United States), 138
judiciary
    analysis of state terror, 84–86
    autonomy of, 10, 85, 86–88, 86 n. 32, 96–97, 102, 214
    caseload of, 91, 91 n. 47
    conviction of junta members, 83, 83 n. 19
    and human rights trials, 82–84
    institutional interests of, 211
    jurisdiction of, 96
    procedures of, 88–92; compulsory prosecution, 89–90; and human rights groups, 90–91; and military defendants, 92; and prolongation of trials, 91–92; rights of plaintiffs, 89–90
    reform efforts in Chile, 204–6
    rulings of, 84–85
Junta Militar. See junta, military
junta, military, 54–55, 61–62, 82–83, 87, 93, 98, 147, 163
junta, military (Uruguay), 186–87, 186 n. 25
Justo, Gen. Agustín P., 65

Keynes, John Maynard, 222
Knight, Jack, 20 n. 21
Krasner, Stephen D., 24

La Nación (Buenos Aires), 96
La Opinión (Buenos Aires), 59
LaCalle, Luis A., 182–83, 183 n. 10, 190, 211
Lambruschini, Adm. Armando, 83
Las Madres del Plaza del Mayo, 90
Lavelle, Gen John D., 8 n. 7
leadership, 38, 169

legal system, Argentine, 88–90, 89 n. 40. See also judiciary
legality principle, 90
Ley Aylwin, 208–9
Ley de Desacato, 51
Leyes Cumplidos, 206
Libro Blanco (White Book), 167–69
Lieuwen, Edwin, 26
Lombardo, Vice Adm., 147
López, Ernesto, 141
López, German, 93 n. 59, 94, 162, Table 6.1
López Rega, José, 52
Lucero, Gen. Franklin, 156
Luder, Italo, 109, 109 n. 5, 162, Table 6.1

MacArthur, Gen. Douglas, 8 n. 7
MacDonnell Douglas, 135
Mainwaring, Scott, 19 n. 19
Malamud-Goti, Jaime, 78 n. 7, 80, 80 n. 10
Malvinas War, 31 n. 56, 142–43, 145–48, 146 n. 13, 147 n. 18, 174
Manzetti, Luigi, 69
March, James, 22
Martínez de Hoz, José, 56–57, 57 n. 40, 110, 112–13
Martins, Daniel Hugo, 187 n. 30
Massera, Adm. Emilio, 83
Matthei, Gen. Fernando, 194
McNamara, Robert, 138 n. 85
Menem, Carlos
    curbing of government spending, 123
    and defense reform, 142, 150, 167
    economics as priority, 123, 127
    economic policy of, 123–24
    and military spending, 125–26
    pardoning of military rebels, 108
    relations with defense minister, 133, 168
    relations with economics minister, 125, 133
    relations with EMC, 168
Menéndez, Gen. Luciano Benjamin, 91 n. 47, 95, 147
methodology, 41–44, 44 n. 88
Mexico, 114, Table 5.2
middle class, the, 46–47, 50
Mignone, Emilio, 91 n. 49
military
    arms industry, 143–44
    arms procurement by, 146 n. 13
    autonomy of, 33–34, 34 n. 69
    contingent compliance, 218–19

counterinsurgency operations of, 144–45
educational control, 161
expanding its influence, 219, 219 n. 7
expertise, 161, 176
intelligence gathering, 146
interservice coordination, 146–47, 155
lack of joint military action, 173–74
modernization of, 143, 144 n. 7
and national defense, 151
performance in war, 146–48
planning, 131
professional self-image of, 144–45
professionalism of, 146
reduced autonomy of, 158
repression by, 150
resistance to change, 148–49
respect for institutions, 215, 218–19; and civilian control, 218–19
self-reform, 170–75; in army, 170–71; budgets and, 171; limits of, 170, 174, 174 n. 108, 175; and national defense plan, 173
service chiefs' power, 159–60
size of, 114, 150, 151, 151 n. 30
subordination, 16, 16, n. 11, 219–20
military, Chilean, 144, 194, 197, 203. See also Chile
military, Uruguayan
    autonomy of, 190
    bases, 188
    counterinsurgency operations, 144
    as educator, 189
    as employer, 188
    force structure, 187–88, 187–88 n. 31
    as health service provider, 188–89
    influence with Congress, 192–93, 193 n. 55
    influence with defense ministry, 184
    opposition to reform, 187–89
    roles, criticism of, 189, 189 n. 39
    size reduction, 190
    spending cuts, 190–91
Military Academy, 156
military autonomy, 32–34
military budget, 6–7, 35, 40–41. See also budgeting, defense
military-centric approaches, 25–27
military contestation, 7
    over budget cuts, 121–22, 122 n. 40, 125–26
    in Chile, 43, 197
    in Uruguay, 43
Military Code of Justice, 78–81

military coup, 2
and Argentina, 45
avoidance of, 218
and budgets, 115
and civilian control, 218
conditions for, 16–17
labor support for, 67
and national security doctrines, 17–18
of 1930, 49
opposition to, 16–18, 74
societal support for, 49–50, 52
versus rebellions, 73
military crisis, 59–63
military influence. See also military
and budgeting process, 129
and budgets, 109, 115
in Chile, 43–44, 44 n. 88
in Congress, 136, 136 n. 82
and coups, 115
and dispersion of authority, 37
limited by trials, 105–6
limits to, 14, 14 n. 5, 15, 74, 109; in Uruguay, 191
and Hipólito Yrigoyen, 48
informal nature of, 192–93
and institutional design, 35, 44, 181, 213
Southern Cone comparisons, 179–81
in Uruguay, 43–44, 44 n. 88
military insubordination, 8, 8 n.7
military interests. See military, military influence
Military Joint Staff. See Estado Mayor Conjunto
military judiciary, 81–82, 91, 91 n. 47, 95. See also judiciary
military policy. See policy
military professionalism, 15, 48, 146. See also military
military rebellion 7, 47–48
in Argentina, 47
in Chile, 207
and Hipólito Yrigoyen, 48
and the Radical Party, 47
and the Sáenz Peña Law, 47
Semana Santa, 71–73; causes of, 71, 99; consequences of, 100, 109, 109 n. 6; and decline of rebels, 73; pardon of rebels, 108; and presidential weakness, 72–73; public opposition to, 71–73
in Venezuela, 220
military reform. See defense reform

military regime, 5. See also Proceso de Reorganización Nacional
military spending. See also budgeting, defense
and arms procurement, 113
and borrowing, 113
budget share, 115, 117
country comparisons, 117
decline in, 109, 117–18, 121, 126; army, 121; impact on service, 121; military opposition to, 118, 121; reason for, 121, 126
and economic performance, 112
and fiscal deficits, 111
and institutions, 109
and prior budgets, 116
motives to reduce, 109–10, 118
during the Proceso, 110–12
requests for funds, 132
in Uruguay, 190–91
Military Supreme Council. See military judiciary
Ministry of Defense (MOD), 108, 154–63
budgeting and reform, 153
building, 154–55
bureacratic expansion of, 159, 159 n. 56
in chain of command, 158
and defense budgeting, 108, 137
and EMC, 164
lack of expertise, 160–61, 169
and military spending, 119–20, 132
and national security, 157
neglect of, 155–58
origins of, 155
personnel turnover within, 162, 167
and presidential leadership, 169
relations with military, 118–19
in Uruguay, 184–87, 211
weakness of, 159–60, 162–63, 214
Ministry of Economics (MOE), 107
autonomy of, 120
budgetary powers of, 127–29, 132–33, 137, 139
and military spending, 120–21
and ministers, 120–21, 123–26
and national budgeting office, 127
during the Proceso, 112
and secretary of finance, 127
in Uruguay, 191
Misiones (province of), 150
Montoneros, 59, 145
Movimiento de Izquierda Democrática Allendista, 205 n. 101

Movimiento Popular Neuquino, 79
Mozarelli, Vice Adm. Antonio, 126

national budgeting office. *See* Ministry of Economics
National Council of Justice (NCJ), 204–5
national defense, 151, 159, 163, 182–83. *See also* defense reform
National Security Council (NSC), 197, 206
national security doctrines (NSD), 17–18, 102 n. 88, 157, 166–67
navy, 58–59, 172
Nino, Carlos, 77 n. 4, 80, 85, 101, 104
Nordlinger, Eric, 40, 115
NSD. *See* national security doctrines

O'Donnell, Guillermo, 50 n. 15
obediencia debida. See due obedience
Office of Management and Budget (OMB), 134, 138
Office of the Secretary of Defense (OSD), 135, 138
Oficina de Planificación y Presupuesto (OPP), 191
oligarchy, the, 4, 47
Olsen, Johan P., 22
Onganía, Gen. Juan Carlos, 81, 87, 157
Operation Independence, 144
organized labor, 50, 54, 67–69. *Also see* Peronism
Osses, Adm. Emilio, 126, 167–68

Pache, Gen. Carlos P., 189
pardon, 108
Patagonia, 119, 150
Perlmutter, Amos, 13
Perón, Evita, 156
Perón, Isabel, 52, 54, 157
Perón, Juan, 50–51, 67, 70, 155–56
Peronism, 50–52, 54, 66–67, 70, 87, 93, 103, 105, 144, 154, 167. *See also* Menem
Peronist Party, The, 51
Peru, 115, 142 n. 2, 221
Pianta, Gen. Ricardo, 120
Pinochet, Augusto, 11, 43 n. 87, 115, 144, 180–81, 180 n. 3, 194, 194 n. 61, 197–98, 200, 202, 207, 209–10
Plan de Lucha, 67
Plan Europa, 143, 143 n. 6
planning, programming, and budgeting system (PPBS), 138 n. 85
political parties, 69–71

political repression. *See* state terror
politicians
  compliance with institutions, 215
  impact of institutions on, 7–8, 21, 36–41, 210–11, 213–15
  and issues, 8
  lack of political support, 52
  lack of defense expertise, 161, 176
  mishandling of military, 51–52
  policy influence, 7
policy
  budgets, 6
  and civil-military relations, 20
  civilian success, 6
  clearance of, 36–37 nn. 73–74
  defense law, 6
  formulation of, 77–80
  implementation of, 22–24
  military, 6
  military contestation of, 4
  outcomes, 21; and judicial autonomy, 102–3; and institutions, 213. *See also* autonomy, authority
  and power, 2
policymakers, 129, 137, 139, 213. *See also* politicians, policy
Port Stanley, 147, 147 n. 18
Powell, Gen. Colin, 8 n. 7
presidency, 4 n. 4, 196, 198–99
Proceso de Reorganización Nacional, 58 n. 41, 65, 73–74, 150
  and civil-military relations, 45–46
  collapse of, 6, 43, 76, 101
  and conservative elites, 65
  and democratic recovery, 53
  and fiscal deficits, 110, 111
  harm to capitalist interests, 55–56
  harm to civilians, 9, 54–59; economic costs, 54–56; human costs, 54
  harm to military, 9, 59–63
  and human rights, 77, 90, 93–95, 98, 105
  and judiciary, 87
  and military spending, 109, 112–13, 116
  and organized labor, 67, 67 n. 72
  policy failures of, 5
  use of repression, 58–59
Przeworski, Adam, 21, 216
public opinion, 63–71
Punto Final, 93, 93 n. 57, 97–99, 103

querellante, 89

Rabkin, Rhonda, 210
Radical Party, The (UCR), 66, 81, 126
  and Congress, 93, 103, 166
  and Ministry of Defense, 118–19
  exclusion of, 65
  government of Arturo Illia, 50–51
  government of Raúl Alfonsín, 64, 67, 104,
    108; and budgeting, 127, 129, 139, 154;
    and defense reform, 149–50, 152 n. 34; and
    labor, 67–68; policy toward army, 121
  and military rebellion, 47–48
  platform of, 76, 117 n. 24
  principles of, 80–81, 116
  relations with Peronist Party, 121
Ranis, Peter, 67, 68
rational choice theory, 22–25
Rattenbach Commission, 148, 170, 174
Rebollo, Lt. Gen. Juan C., 182
Reforma Ricchieri, 142–43
regime, 3
Remmer, Karen, 222
Renovación Nacional, 196, 206–7
Rettig, Raúl, 196
Rettig Commission, 195, 196–99, 201–2, 210
Revolución Argentina (1966–73), 65
Revolución Libertadora (1955–58), 87, 156
Reyser, Rear Adm. Horacio F., 172
Rial, Juan, 32 n. 65, 180 n. 2, 185, 185 n. 22
Ricci, María Susana, 17
Rico, Lt. Col. Aldo, 71–72, 73
Ríos Ereñú, Gen., 71, 150
Rodríguez Giovanini, Adalberto, 138 n. 85
Romero, Humberto, 109, 109 n. 5, 162, Table
    6.1, 167–68, 170
Rosario, 98, 145
Rouquié, Alain, 27 n. 42, 46
rules of the game, 215. See also institutions, pro-
    cedural dimensions of

Sábato, Ernesto, 90 n. 46
Sáenz Peña, Roque, 47
San Martín, Gen., 142 n. 2
San Ramón (Uruguay), 188 n. 34
Sanguinetti, Julio, 181–82, 190, 193 n. 56
Santa Clara de Olimar (Uruguay), 188
Santa Rosa (Argentina), 170 n. 90
Sapag, Elias, 79, 86 n. 32
Schumpeter, Joseph, 215 n. 1
secretariat of finance. See Ministry of Economics
Secretary of Defense (SECDEF), 138

Seineldín, Col. Mohamed Alí, 168
Semana Santa, 62, 71–73, 99, 109 n. 6
Skocpol, Theda, 32
Snow, Peter, 69
Socialist Party (Chile), 208, 208 n. 112
Sociedad Rural Argentina, 57
Sosa Molina, Gen., 156
Sourrouille, Juan, 109 n. 6, 120–21
Southern Cone, 42, 179–81
state, the, 30–32, 31 n. 57, 74. See also institu-
    tions
state terror, 53, 58–61, 84–85, 90
  in Chile, 196, 201, 203
Steyerthal, Cap. (navy) Leonardo, 172
Strassera, Julio, 82–83, 83 n. 19, 87
Superior War School, 156
Suaréz Mason, Gen. Carlos, 91 n. 47

Timmerman, Jacobo, 59
transitions to civilian rule
  in Argentina, 43, 180
  in Chile, 43, 180–81
  and institutional arrangements, 211
  and pacts, 104
  terms of, 6
  in Uruguay, 43, 180
  via collapse, 7
Treinta y Tres, Province of (Uruguay) 188
Troccoli, Antonio, 80
Truman, David, 29, 29 n. 48
Truman, Harry S., 8 n. 7
Tucumán, Province of 144–45
Tupamaros, 144

Ubaldini, Saúl, 68, 69, 72, 72 n. 94
UCD. See Unión del Centro Democrático
UCR. See Radical Party, The
uncertainty, 21, 216
Unión Cívica Radical. See Radical Party, The
Unión del Centro Democrático (UCD), 66, 72
Unión Demócrata Independiente, 196
Unión Industrial Argentina, 57
United States
  arms exports to Latin America, 143
  defense budgeting procedures, 133–35; civil-
    military interaction, 138; military influence
    over, 135
  judicial procedures, 88–89
  opposition to military coups, 16
Uriburu, Gen. José, 49

Uruguay
army, 183
budgeting in, 190–93
chain of command in, 187
compared to Chile and Argentina, 179
Congress, 191–92
defense ministry; cabinet of, 185; lack of civilian expertise in, 185, 187; military influence in, 184–87, 214
and defense reform failure, 181–89
economics ministry of, 191
junta, 186, 186 nn. 25–26
Organic Law of the Armed Forces, 186
president, 187, 192. *See also* LaCalle, Luis
transition to civilian rule, 180

Venezuela, 114, Table 5.2
Vicaria de Solidaridad, 201
Videla, Gen. Jorge, 54, 83
Viola, Gen. Roberto, 83

Waldner, Gen. Teodoro, 98
Welch, Claude E., Jr., 14–15
Whitehead, Laurence, 221
Wildavsky, Aaron, 107, 116

Yrigoyen, Hipólito, 47–49, 51, 65

Zagorski, Paul, 31 n. 65
Zalaquett, José, 194 n. 60, 195